The Notebooks for

The Idiot

Fyodor Dostoevsky

Edited and with an Introduction by
Edward Wasiolek

Translated by Katharine Strelsky

The University of Chicago Press
CHICAGO & LONDON

International Standard Book Number: 0–226–15961–2
(clothbound)

Library of Congress Catalog Card Number: 67–25513

The translation is based upon the Russian edition of
Dostoevsky's notebooks: *Iz arkhiva F. M. Dostoevskogo:*
"Idiot," Neizdannye materialy, edited by N. N. Sakulin
and N. F. Belchikov (Moscow & Leningrad, 1931)

The University of Chicago Press, Chicago 60637
The University of Chicago Press, Ltd., London

Contents

Illustrations

The illustrations included in this edition of Dostoevsky's *Notebooks for "The Idiot"* are facsimiles of original pages of the notebooks.

Introduction

I

Of all the novels, *The Idiot* came hardest for Dostoevsky. It was written abroad—in Geneva, Vevey, Milan, Florence—in cold flats, poverty, sickness, personal tragedy, homesickness, despair, and in hope. Threatened by creditors with imprisonment, and suffering from bad health, Dostoevsky left Russia in April, 1867, in hope of repairing both health and fortune abroad; but he found, as always, what he was running away from: the epileptic fits became more frequent and the poverty sharper. Dostoevsky and his new wife Anna Grigorievna subsisted on advances, loans, and pawn tickets, in countries he found spiritually dead and among people he detested. "Oh, Sonetchka!" he wrote to his niece, "If you only knew how hard it is to be a writer, to carry this burden! I know for sure that if I had two or three secure years for this novel, as Turgenev, Goncharov, and Tolstoy have, I would write a work that they would talk about for a hundred years! I'm not at all bragging. You know me well enough to know that I don't talk idly. The idea I have is so good and so pregnant with meaning that I worship it. And yet what will come of it? I know beforehand. I'll work on it for eight or nine months, and I'll make a mess of it. Two or three years are needed for something of this kind." But he did write a work that has lasted for a hundred years and will last a hundred more. He wrote it between fits of gambling and fits of epilepsy, when there was no money and very little hope. He wrote it because the novel itself was the hope, the redeeming act, the atonement for the crushing guilt he felt for his self-destructive passions.

Dostoevsky and his young wife were no sooner in Europe—in Dresden and Baden-Baden—than Dostoevsky was passionately trying to wrest fortune from the gaming tables, as he had tried futilely to do two years before during a trip to Europe. His unmurmuring and uncomplaining wife patiently recorded for posterity the abjections

1

to which Dostoevsky subjected her, and himself as well. When there was no money Dostoevsky conducted a systematic depredation of their household goods and personal effects. Anna Grigorievna had already sold most of what she owned—as well as liquidated her dowry—to make the European trip possible. Now Dostoevsky demanded her clothes, kitchen utensils, earrings, even her wedding ring, and gave her in return—but not in mockery—his tears and his endless avowals of guilt. The fits of passion were always followed by fits of repentance in which Dostoevsky would weep audibly, kiss his wife's feet, hands, breasts. The novel would then appear as the answer to everything. After losing in November, 1867, at Saxon-les-Bains (a few months after beginning *The Idiot*), he wrote to his wife: "Only the novel now, only the novel will save us, if you only knew how I was counting on it. Be sure that I will make it come off and earn your respect. I will never, never play again. I was in the same fix in 1865. I couldn't have been in a worse situation then, but my work got me out of it. I take up my work with hope and love, and you will see the results in two years." He repeated this drama many times, but in 1871 he wrote to his wife, inevitably after a crushing loss: "The foul fantasy which has tortured me for ten years has disappeared. For ten years (or rather since the death of my brother, when I was suddenly crushed with debts), I have been dreaming of making a killing. I dreamed seriously, passionately. Now all that is finished! I'm going to think about the things I have to do now, and not spend whole nights thinking of gambling, as I have been doing." He was never to gamble again.

Despite the attractions of its gaming tables and museums—he saw Claude Lorrain's *Acis and Galatea* in Dresden and Hans Holbein's *Christ in the Tomb* in Basle—Dostoevsky could not abide Germans or Germany. He expressed this aversion to things German in a bristling attack on the hopeless inferiority of Germans to the common people of Russia in a brief meeting with Turgenev in the summer of 1867 in Baden. The exchange was polite and cold enough to keep the two men unreconciled until the occasion of Dostoevsky's triumphant Pushkin speech in 1880, a short time before his death.

Settled in Switzerland, the spiritual quagmire of Germany behind him, Dostoevsky did not—predictably—find things any different or any better. The Swiss climate was intolerable, the Swiss themselves petty and dirty, the Russian emigrants incomprehensible, and the scenery panoramic and trivial. He wrote to Maykov in June, 1868: "The scene from Lake Geneva is, of course, magnificent; from Vevey it is better than from Montreux and Chillon. But outside of that panorama (and to be sure a few places where one can walk, which are not to be had in Geneva), the rest is really disgusting; one has to pay too dearly for the panorama alone." And to his niece: "Geneva on the banks of Lake Geneva. The lake is fantastic, the shoreline picturesque, but Geneva itself is boring beyond belief. This is the ancient Protestant city, and furthermore filled with drunks." Life abroad, he wrote her, was worse than exile to Siberia. He was too far away, and he was not a Turgenev or a Gogol who could see Russia better for the distance. He had to breathe Russian air. To a friend he wrote: "I grow dull here, small, foreign to Russia. There's no Russian air here, no people. I can't understand the Russian emigrants here at all. It's mad." And Geneva was full of Russian emigrants.

Herzen, Bakunin, Ogarev, and many other distinguished Russian intellectuals had settled in Geneva, but this was cheerless comfort for Dostoevsky, who looked with disapprobation at Russian emigrants and expressed more than once an inability to understand how any Russian could voluntarily live in Europe. Geneva in 1867 was also a center for radical and progressive activity, a phenomenon that Dostoevsky followed closely with some foreboding and much disgust. He listened to the speeches of Bakunin and others at the meetings of the International Peace Congress and recorded in his letters dismay at the recommendations of the congress for the abolition of monarchies, Christianity, and capital. The rhetoric was familiar—his involvement in the Petrashevsky circle twenty years before came to mind—and only fire and the sword had been added to false ideas.

Devoured by a passion for gambling and then by guilt, humiliated by poverty, driven by deadlines, choking on foreign air, alarmed and disgusted by political currents, forced to move restlessly from apartment to apartment with a pregnant wife, and forced to bear the shock of the death of his three-month-old daughter—these comprise Dostoevsky's physical and spiritual environment during the eighteen months *The Idiot* was in the making. Dostoevsky had a hard time settling down to it, a harder time finding his way toward the first part, and an impossible time writing the second part. The third and fourth parts came more easily, but only a little more easily. He did not begin to work seriously on *The Idiot* until after settling in Geneva, in August of 1867. He wrote Maykov in the middle of August from Geneva: "I've done practically nothing up to this point, and it is only now that I've really sat down to work on it seriously." Dostoevsky was optimistic and spoke of finishing it in six months.

From August to December, 1867, Dostoevsky seemed to be looking for his novel more than writing it. He went through at least eight plans and many variations of each plan. Less than a month before submitting the first part to his publisher, he destroyed much that he had written and virtually began writing the novel again. He wrote to his niece at the beginning of January, 1868: "And so just before sending my novel off to the editor, I began all over. What I had written ceased to please me (and if you stop liking it, you can't do it right). I destroyed much that I've written. Three weeks ago (December 18 according to the New Style), I started a new novel and worked day and night on it. I wrote the first part in 23 days and I've just sent it off. I'll finish the second, which I'm starting today, in a month. (I've worked that way all my life.)" The first and second parts that Dostoevsky refers to here compose the first part of the published version of the novel.

The burst of inspiration did not hold. After completing a magnificent first part—and Dostoevsky knew it was magnificent—he had no idea how to continue the novel. Nastasia Filipovna had gone off with Rogozhin, and Myshkin had followed after. The action of the first part is self-contained, and the second part begins like a new novel, consisting largely of exposition. Dostoevsky was not able to deliver the second part, as he had hoped, in time for the March issue of *The Russian Messenger;* he was able to eke out only two chapters for the April issue, three more for the May issue, and three more for June; and he completed the second part only for the July issue. The rest of the novel went a bit more quickly, but Dostoevsky was not able to send off the conclusion until January, 1869, almost a year and a half after he started it.

The creative history of most of Dostoevsky's major works can be traced back to some "key" idea and some intense emotional need. Dostoevsky broke off the publication of *The Diary of a Writer* because *The Brothers Karamazov* was burning to be written; *The Possessed* began as a heated political pamphlet, a passionate revenge on his own youthful political mistakes; the idea for *Crime and Punishment* arose with astonishing completeness when he himself suffered the humiliation of virtual incarceration in a German boarding house; *Notes from the Underground* was fed by rage at Chernyshevsky's *What Is To Be Done?* No burning conviction, no special rage, no clear idea moved him to begin *The Idiot*. The International Peace Congress, his quarrel with Turgenev, his alarm before the shameless immorality of socialist movements—the things that were touching him most immediately in Switzerland in the fall of 1867—had not yet sunk deeply enough to touch *The Idiot* significantly. They found expression a few years later in *The Possessed*.

The intention of creating a positively good man was not there at the beginning. It did not come until after Dostoevsky had been through at least six plans, and as late as a month before he submitted the first part of the novel to the publisher. In January, 1868, he wrote to Maykov: "For a long time an idea has tortured me, but I was afraid of writing a novel about this idea because it is too difficult and I'm not up to it. But the thought is very tempting and I love it. This idea is to depict the wholly beautiful man. There's nothing more difficult to do, especially in our age." Dostoevsky did not begin with a beautiful Myshkin. He began with an impoverished gentry family, with vengeful heroines, a proud, demonic, and contradictory Idiot, and with much vagueness and uncertainty. He began, most of all, with the Umetsky case on his mind.

The name Olga Umetskaia appears in the very first plan, and we

have Dostoevsky's wife's word that he was very interested in the
process of the trial, which took place from September 15 to 17, 1867.
The facts were essentially these: the parents had shamelessly neglected
twin boys and two daughters; they had kept them in a half-
starved condition, beaten them, neglected their education and church
duties, and oppressed them with heavy work. The younger daughter,
Lipochka, was completely deaf up to the age of seven; the two boys
could hardly speak a word at the age of six; and Olga Umetskaia's
body—the treatment of her was the issue in the case—was covered with
bruises at the time of the trial—her finger had also been broken by her
mother. She had attempted to burn down the buildings of her father's
estate several times, as well as the house itself. Obviously torn by con-
flicting feelings, she had on several occasions set fire to the house and
then awakened everyone. Olga Umetskaia was charged with setting
fires to buildings, and the father and mother were charged with mis-
treating a child. Olga was acquitted, the father was condemned for
neglecting the religious duties of the child, and the mother was condemned to six months in prison for beating her.

Dostoevsky liked to point to actual happenings in the world that
confirmed his "fantastic" creative world, and the Umetsky case was
as fantastic as anything he had written about. The case surely provided grounds for the notebook of horrors that Ivan kept, although
by the time Dostoevsky had come to write *The Brothers Karamazov,*
he had accumulated further confirmations in life of what he could
imagine. The Umetsky case seemed to be a fairly clear illustration of
monstrous environment creating monstrous actions and relationships.
In burning down her parents' house, Olga Umetskaia was obviously
paying back her parents for what they had done to her, and her threat
on several occasions to throw herself into the fire was both a desperate
act and a desperate appeal. One can point to a number of motifs that
Dostoevsky took from the facts of the trial and used over and over
again in the notes: setting fire to buildings, the breaking of a finger,
running away from home, the hating mother, the victimized childhood, and the vengeful repaying of hurts, real or imaginary. Dostoevsky attempted to explain the vengefulness by environmental

causes. The Idiot burns with vengeance because he has been hated by his mother, or had too little beauty in his childhood; Mignon, a minor character, lives to avenge herself on her childhood; and the "heroine" is eaten by destructive rage, which in different ways comes from her past.

The environmental causes are vague, and Dostoevsky seemed unable or was unwilling to refine them. Increasingly, he moved in the notes to the causeless vengeful act, as indeed the actions of Nastasia Filipovna in the novel in their fury, illogicality, self-destructiveness, pass far beyond any sense of logical proportion to the original hurt she had suffered in her childhood at the hands of Totsky. What finally fascinated Dostoevsky was the outraged heart itself, desperate and sick, burning on uncaused hate and turned on itself. The Umetsky case finally could not be grafted; it remained what those real-life happenings always were for Dostoevsky: confirming instances of his imaginative world. Life did not offer up explanations—only the instances which Dostoevsky's creative mind had already imagined. The meaning of the gestures—of an Olga Umetskaia punishing her parents by threatening to throw herself into a fire, and of a Nastasia Filipovna punishing those who have hurt her by seeking Rogozhin's knife—have to be sought in the creative crevices of Dostoevsky's imagination. Art must illuminate reality, but when Dostoevsky began *The Idiot,* his lamp was dim and his path exasperatingly difficult to find. The difficulties tell us much about the way he worked, much about *The Idiot,* and much about the creative process in general. The notes for *The Idiot* are a record of a search for what Dostoevsky knew he had to find.

II

The creative world of the notes for *The Idiot* is unstable, fluctuating, insubstantial, fluid. The relationships between characters fluctuate from plan to plan: sisters are and are not sisters, nephews become sons, fathers become uncles. The Idiot is sometimes the son of the Uncle, sometimes the nephew, sometimes the foster son, sometimes illegitimate, and sometimes legitimate; acts are committed and die abortively in the next plan, or even a few lines later; people hang themselves but then perhaps don't hang themselves; the same people die by hanging, poisoning, broken hearts, and drowning. It is not always clear who is who, where they come from, and where they are going. Characters appear and disappear, crowd on the periphery, nudge their way into the author's consciousness for a time and then melt away; some appear without names and personalities, take on flesh, and then waste away. Some persist to the very threshold of publication and immortality, only to find no place in the final conception.

In the early notes for *The Idiot* we are apparently at that point of creativity when an author's brain teems with "many worlds," voices fill the chambers of his mind, and "possible" people jostle for his attention. The creative process of *The Idiot* was more one of exasperation than of inspiration. The plans show us too eloquently that Dostoevsky did not "know" what he wanted to express. He had no over-all conception of the plot; he had, rather, actions, situations, gestures, plots, all too many and all begging for the center of attention. The notebooks show us an author in search of his subject, feeling his way in bewilderment. What he wanted to say lay buried, I am certain, in his sensibility, instinct, feel of things; otherwise, there would have been no norm by which to measure. But this norm is not conscious and is made conscious only painfully and slowly.

The same was not true of the notes for *Crime and Punishment*. In a very real sense—as Dostoevsky's famous letter to his editor Katkov shows—he had his subject from the very beginning. He knew what he was going to write about; the center was firm and the structure clear. He was going to write about a young student who murders a useless old moneylender to do good for himself, for his family, and for society. And this is what he writes about in the finished version of *Crime and Punishment*. In both notes and novel the test fails and the need for punishment takes the student to confession and redemption. There is only one Raskolnikov in the notebooks, but there are many Idiots. The notes for *Crime and Punishment* do not show us Dostoevsky looking for his subject, but looking for the best way of expressing it. They do not show us Dostoevsky looking for Raskolnikov or for Raskolnikov's act, but looking for the motives for the act. The process of creation from original conception to finished version was one of refinement of motive, craft, and structure.

Croce's theory that the "intuition" or "image" (that is, the total work) is complete in the soul of the poet before it is externalized in technique and language seems extravagant in the face of notes of this kind. These notes seem to point to the very opposite: that it was by way of technique, by way of those endless experiments with characters and situations, that Dostoevsky found his subject. The intuition that was first externalized in the notes seems disjointed, halting, provisional, and remote from the intuition that found final expression. *The Idiot* for Dostoevsky lay at the end of arduous and painful and exasperating technical experimentation; it seems to be the result of experimentation, not the cause. To be sure, in one sense technique is always the consequence of what is first in the soul; technique obviously does not cause creativity. But it is just as clear that technique can help to clarify what is potential but unformed in the soul. Each seems to act upon the other in a reciprocal way—technique helping to make clear what is in the soul and the soul helping to guide technique.

We cannot go to *The Idiot* with theories of the organic fitness of every part, of the necessity of every positioning, every image, every sound. Such "close reading" has become cant today, and I venture that at least in intention it constitutes our chief literary pedagogical procedure. Structure, I hazard, is never as exquisite as our current theories would have it, at least not in this novel. We are considering here a great novel and a great novelist, and the notes show convincingly not only that Dostoevsky was trying out many routes, but that more than one route could have taken him to the same destination. Something is necessary in the novel, but not everything, and some things are more necessary than others. Ipolit and Lebedev, for example, were almost afterthoughts of Dostoevsky, not to speak of dozens of characters who do not even appear in the notes. They are, to be sure, magnificent afterthoughts, but others are not afterthoughts:

they are at the center of the creative process and nothing can dislodge them nor can Dostoevsky forget them.

What is it, specifically, that persists throughout all the sifting, sorting, winnowing; what is it that Dostoevsky holds on to in the teeming world of shifting, flickering, failing possibilities? What is it that he cannot give up and that will not give him up? The situation that persists throughout all the plans and into the final version of the novel is that of a young woman who flies from one suitor to another, compelled to attract and reject, hating and loving, punishing and seeking punishment. In the first plan, this young woman, "the heroine," is described in the following way: "She is extraordinarily proud, she rides roughshod over all the conventions, and *therefore* the worst extravagances of the Idiot neither shock nor outrage her (once he almost killed her, another time, he broke her hands). But once such moments are over, she flees in aversion. These moments arise partly out of her terribly abnormal and incongruous position in the family. In general, she is unquestionably of an original, frivolous, capricious, *provocative* and poetic nature, superior to her environment." The heroine of the first plan is already in essential gesture the Nastasia Filipovna of the final version: pursued by General Epanchin, Gania, Rogozhin, Totsky, and the Idiot, and attracting and rejecting throughout the novel both Rogozhin and the Idiot.

Dostoevsky will change almost everything, but he will not change this situation. Characters will be born, die, and will be reborn; they will take on flesh and waste away; the Idiot will be reborn; and the heroine herself will take on different names and different relationships. But throughout all the plans and throughout the notes and into the final version we will have a proud, vengeful, sometimes hysterical woman, fatally compelled to provoke and reject love, to punish and to be punished.

Dostoevsky is sure of the gestures, even when he is unsure of what they mean. He senses what is right before he knows what it means. We don't know in the first plan, or, frankly, in subsequent plans, why the heroine acts as she does: why she attracts and rejects, punishes others and herself, why she is proud, vengeful, hysterical.

Dostoevsky seizes the situation, but not the motives. Not that he doesn't try to understand the motives! Again and again he alludes to something in her past, some rejection by a cousin and by others, some ambivalence of social situation. In the first six plans she has no mother and father, and when she is given a father in the seventh plan, in Umetsky, he is a monster. In this same plan Dostoevsky tries to account more fully for Nastia's (to be identified with the earlier heroine and with Nastasia Filipovna of the final version) motives in the following way: "The Idiot was in the province of Saratov. When Nastia's seducer abandoned her, he took her in, she gave birth, and he took over the child *et cetera*. In her anguish and rage at having been deserted, she inveighed against *him* and jeered at him, but afterwards she threw herself at his feet, and in the end she fell in love with him, he offered his hand, and she *ran away* ('I'm furious, I won't ask pardon, I am defiled')." Nastia here punishes herself, "I am defiled," and others, "jeered at him," because she has been seduced and abandoned. But the explanation explains by complicating. We can understand why, having been abandoned, she should want to abandon, but we do not know why she should jeer at her savior and worship him at the same time, and why she, as victim, should see herself as defiled. Dostoevsky himself senses that what he has outlined holds more meaning than he can seize at the moment, for he says: "*Absolutely has to be worked out:* He assented and believed as she did, so that he ridiculed himself, as if he were as distorted as she made him out to be. She is stunned by his *simplicity and humility*."

Dostoevsky's vision precedes his understanding: it is not the idea that—in some abstract way—creates the situation, but the situation that creates the ideas. The paradoxical gestures of the heroine are explained by the paradoxical gestures of Nastia. The new situation bristles with ambiguities, and these ambiguities are never fully worked out, not even in the final version—not because of some failing on the part of Dostoevsky, but because the situation holds more meaning than the discursive intellect can make explicit. A Nastia seduced and abandoned, defiled and self-defiling, jeering and worshiping the Idiot is, of course, close to Nastasia Filipovna of the final ver-

sion, defiled and abandoned by Totsky, spiritually "saved" by Myshkin, and worshiping and fleeing from the Idiot.

Something of the same kind of process can be seen in the fate of the
Idiot in these notes. But unlike the heroine-Nastia-Umetskaia-Ustinia
nature, his character changes drastically from beginning to end. The
Idiot we find in the final version is almost totally different from the
Idiot we find in the first six plans: cruel, proud, vengeful, hating, and
struggling with a double nature. Rogozhin and Gania more accurate-
ly represent this early Idiot than does Prince Myshkin. The following
description of the Idiot, taken from the first plan, is characteristic:
"*The Idiot's* passions are violent, he has a burning need of love, a
boundless pride, and out of pride he means to dominate himself, conquer himself. He takes delight in humiliation. Those who do not
know him make fun of him; those who do know him begin to fear
him." In the seventh plan he becomes compassionate, forgiving,
humble; he helps the fallen Nastia and astounds her with his humility and simplicity; and he is surrounded by children. He becomes the
Idiot of the final version. In the ninth section of these notes, "Notes
on Part II of the Novel," we have this view of the Idiot: "N.B. His
way of looking at the world: he forgives everything, sees reasons for
everything, does not recognize that any sin is unforgivable."

The change in the Idiot's character is abrupt, extreme, intriguing,
and puzzling. It comes barely a month before Dostoevsky submitted
the first part of the novel to his publisher. But one must keep in
mind, in considering this change, that Dostoevsky held out the possibility of some drastic change, of some movement to redemption in
the Idiot's character from the very beginning. Thus, in the very first
plan we find the following: "N.B. *The Idiot's basic character*. Domination of himself out of pride (not morality) and rabid self-license in
everything. As yet, however, self-license is but a dream, whereas at
the moment he has only convulsive impulses. Consequently, he could
turn into a monster, but love saves him. He becomes imbued with the
most profound compassion and he forgives faults in others. (This had
already become evident when he forgave the father. *The father's
death.*) In compensation he progressively develops a high moral sense,
and performs a heroic action." In the second plan Dostoevsky speaks

of the Idiot's "spontaneous thirst for life" which "impels him eventually *to reflection and to a new path in life.*" And in plan three a prankish and intriguing Idiot is brought to renunciation of his slanders, intrigues, and covetousness. The possibility of some kind of regeneration—usually as redemptive love—is persistent throughout every plan.

Dostoevsky looks for his "beautiful" Idiot from the very first plan and in the seventh he finds him. The Idiot of the first six plans is a "double" character. Dostoevsky makes this explicit in plan five when he talks of "The Dualism of a deep nature," of an Idiot who feels contempt for others and for himself, hate and love for the same people, a desire to make others suffer and himself to suffer on the cross for them. It is clear, I think, that Dostoevsky hoped to wrench the good Idiot from this dual nature, as he had nudged Raskolnikov into God's camp. From the very beginning he has the Idiot perform good actions, which are somehow corrupted by his pride. In the first plan the Idiot loves the heroine, who hurts him; he gives up money that the uncle gives him; he protects his father when he is falsely accused of theft: the acts are virtuous, but they are corrupted because they serve a voluptuous feeling of self-satisfaction. Dostoevsky looks at the Idiot's evil as a distortion of some fundamental drive for life. In the fourth plan he says, *"The chief idea of the novel:* how much strength, how much passion, in contemporary youth, yet they are unbelievers. Boundless idealism together with boundless sensuality." Something in his nature—Dostoevsky calls it the "tongue in the mirror"—corrupts his good impulses, changes the love into hate, the sacrifice for others to the sacrifice of others, the drive to self-worth to the drive for self-will. Dostoevsky apparently planned to take the Idiot from "revenge and self-love" to "lofty love and regeneration" by these stages:

In the beginning:
1) Revenge and self-love (a *causeless* revenge, he himself sees this, and that it is *characteristic* of him).
Then:
2) Frenzied and merciless passion.
3) Lofty love and regeneration.

The deadline approaches, and the Idiot's character obstinately refuses to give itself to Dostoevsky. One must imagine an exasperated Dostoevsky trying the Idiot out again and again in the same situations, moving him from one household to another, from dark to prankish evil and back again; taking him through the motions of hate-love for the heroine and hate-love for a wife and then hate-love for both; trying to wrench from the Idiot's unyielding and corrupting character some redeemed Idiot, and yet stayed by his sensitivity and fidelity to probabilities. As late as the sixth plan Dostoevsky does not know what or who he is. The mystery has deepened: *"Enigmas. Who is he? A terrible scoundrel or a mysterious ideal?"* And then following immediately, a shaft of inspiration: *"He is a Prince."* And, "Prince *Yurodivyi.* (He is with children.)"

In the seventh plan he is the Myshkin of the pure heart; he feels compassion without hatred, love without cruelty, sacrifice without pride. The tongue in the mirror is gone: before this the Idiot had been generous, self-sacrificial, loving, but the generosity had been followed by selfishness, the sacrifice by the sacrifice of others, the love by hatred, and the thirst for life by the hate for life. The shadow of corruption that had fallen athwart each of his impulses lightens; the double disappears. Dostoevsky was not able to wrest his beautiful Idiot from the ambiguities, ambivalences, and dualism of the Idiot's character, and gradually he seemed to become aware that he *could* not. The world would not grant him his beautiful Idiot, so he gave the world the beautiful Idiot, not without trepidation at placing innocence in the world's maelstrom of greed and hate, but also not without some hope.

Some have not wanted a beautiful Idiot and have insisted upon thrusting him back into the darkness from which he emerged. According to Murray Krieger, for example, Prince Myshkin drives Nastasia Filipovna into the arms of Rogozhin and death, and Aglaia into the arms of a Polish Catholic and a fate worse than death: "As for Aglaia herself, Myshkin has destroyed her, has converted her childlike idealism into fraudulent and decadent romanticism, and has brought her incipient demonism into the open."[1] Myshkin suffers from a "psychosis of humility" and gives to all those about him a moral burden greater than they can carry and 'under which they crack. In short, according to Krieger, Myshkin does not bring light but darkness, not help but destruction; he does not still the outrages of the world, but generates them; he is not a bright angel, but a dark emissary. Mr. Krieger has not been alone in putting forth such views. Ronald Hingley is another who holds such a view of the character of Prince Myshkin.[2]

Is there anything to this view? We can grant that the Idiot is ineffectual, that the world he leaves is no better and perhaps worse, that by his nature he places a moral burden upon those about him. We can grant all this and still have our beautiful Idiot. By giving the world an "innocent" Myshkin, Dostoevsky did not give it an abstraction. He knew that innocence and humility were explosive forces. Myshkin was not meant to quiet the world, but to threaten it. He could offer forgiveness, but could not move the heart of the other to accept it. He could offer the world love, but he could not transform it. He could take upon himself the pain of the world, even if he could not still the rage that inflicted it. It is only a hopelessly pragmatic and schematic mind, weighing moral worth by some statistic of help and harm, that would read the tally sheet of results as the measure of Myshkin's worth. This is not Dostoevsky's mind. If we were to measure Christ by pragmatic results, he too might appear to be an emissary of darkness rather than of light. Myshkin is a good Prince. The notes tell us he is good, the letters tell us he is good, and the novel tells us he is good. I dwell on this point because the early notes for *The Idiot*—where the Idiot is pictured as a double character—may tempt us to read those ambivalences into the final version of the

---

[1] "Dostoevsky's 'Idiot': The Curse of Saintliness," from *The Tragic Vision* (New York: Holt, Rinehart and Winston, 1960), pp. 209–27.

[2] See *The Undiscovered Dostoevsky* (London: Hamish Hamilton, 1962), pp. 112–13: "The view which will be put forward here is that Myshkin is a comic figure. As for the suggestion sometimes made that he represents a serious ethical ideal, this is perhaps the richest piece of comedy about him."

novel. I think this would be a mistake. The cruel, cynical, hating, vengeful qualities of the Idiot in the early plans of the novel were given to the world, and more specifically to Rogozhin, Gania, Lebedev, and to others. In the early plans it was the Idiot against himself; in the novel it is the world against the Idiot.

The notes tell us that Dostoevsky persistently wanted a redeemed Idiot, and when he could not wrench him from the ambivalences of the world, he created him. They tell us that he gave the Idiot's threats to kill the heroine to Rogozhin, his pettiness and vengefulness to Gania, his prankish intrigues to Lebedev. And they tell us that Radomsky—on whose words Krieger's whole thesis rests—is not the moral norm of the novel against which Myshkin is to be judged. Radomsky has one of those glib, rational, pragmatic, balance-sheet minds that Dostoevsky held in loathing. If the irony with which he is treated in the novel is not apparent, the notes, where he is called Velmonchek, make it so: "Velmonchek—a brilliant character, flippant, skeptical, *a genuine aristocrat,* devoid of any *ideal* (not the kind of man we like, and this is what distinguishes him from the Prince). An odd mixture of cunning, subtlety, calculation, mockery, vanity. He kills himself out of vanity." The notes make it clear—and the novel does too, but perhaps a bit more subtly—that he is no Dostoevskian ideal, but a character without any kind of ideal, a prey to vanity, aimlessness, and the endless games of a reason ruled by itself.

In the notes to the second part of the novel, Velmonchek-Radomsky is pictured as someone who doesn't know what he is or what he wants: he doesn't understand Aglaia, or Lebedev's daughter, or the Prince, or himself. Only his vanity and his swaggering are constant: he falls in love with Lebedev's daughter "out of perversity" and "out of braggadocio"; he doesn't know whether or not he loves Aglaia, whether or not he should shoot himself, whether or not the Prince is absurd. Dostoevsky makes it clear that Velmonchek-Radomsky does not understand the Prince. He underestimates the Prince's perception: "Velmonchek sees that the Prince does not understand that Aglaia loves him (but the Prince does understand this)." And as a "skeptic and unbeliever" he "laughs incessantly at the Prince and makes fun of him." He is the embodiment of that rudderless reason, buoyed by nothing but itself and seeking no port but its own. Dostoevsky speaks of him as "eternal and continual mockery of an artful and supercilious sort" and as sinking "lower and lower" in vanity. Referring to him as one of a type, Dostoevsky says: "It's not so much that they are vapid but rather that they have no sense of nationality, they have only a feeble attachment to the soil, that's why they are so flighty."

I have dwelled perhaps unduly long on a minor character and a single interpretation, but both tell us something about the pitfalls of Dostoevsky criticism and the part that notes of this kind can play in avoiding those pitfalls. There is always in criticism the temptation—even from the best of motives—to impose one's views on an author. I am at a loss to understand how one can take Radomsky and his brittle, pragmatic, uncommitted, rational tallies as Dostoevsky's, but if the point must be argued, the notes in their explicitness do so. If Myshkin's moral quality is to be measured and a shadow cast over his nature, someone other than Radomsky will have to cast it.

The notes are a schema of Dostoevsky's creative intentions, and as such often make clear and sharp what may be veiled and disputable in the novel. Dostoevsky, for example, may have expressed in heavily veiled and strongly oblique fashion something of his horror of incestuous relationships in the hurt that Nastasia Filipovna suffers at the hands of Totsky. In the seventh plan and in part in other places Dostoevsky pursues rather openly the theme of violation of a daughter by a father, and throughout the notes the violation of a ward by the head of a household. He also experimented with the attitudes of horror, indifference, and even cynicism on the part of the perpetrator. In the novel itself, Nastasia Filipovna is violated by Totsky, who assumes the fatherly function of bringing up and educating the girl and who betrays the trust by systematic and indifferent depredation. The father-child relationship may have its symbolic social analogue in Totsky's aristocratic position. Totsky is not only a corrupt "father," but he is also a corrupt representative of those who violated the trust they had been given.

I am well aware that the novel itself is the final test of Dostoevsky's intention, that the first conception may be warped and distorted by the contexts and tensions of the novel's body, so that the notes and the novel do not stand in direct correspondence. Such disjunctions in themselves are fascinating, and the value of notes such as these in showing them up is great. More frequently, however, the relationship of notes to novel is one of progressive refinement and exposure to the contingency of the world of what was first conceived in relatively abstract terms. The notes tell us, for example, what is evident in the novel: that Gania's role was never fixed and that he is structurally something of a failure in the novel. When the first part of the novel had already been published, Dostoevsky was still asking himself what he was supposed to do with Gania. The notes tell us that Myshkin's outburst against Roman Catholicism late in the novel was probably a late addition by Dostoevsky; Myshkin voices no anti-Catholic sentiments in the notes, even though there are some hints in the notes that the gathering of aristocrats at which the outburst occurs was already on his mind. Ipolit has sometimes been interpreted by critics—with more justification than Radomsky—as some kind of ideal, but the notes make it clear that Dostoevsky saw his suicide as an act of vanity. Commenting on Ipolit's attempted suicide, Dostoevsky says: "There is pride in helplessness," and the Prince himself says in the notes: "No, he won't kill himself now, having missed out on it, for it would make no impression on those people, so now he won't kill himself." The notes also tell us that Dostoevsky hungered for some bearer of Christian humility in the novel, that he planned for a redeemed Idiot from the very beginning, and that he conceived of the beautiful Idiot as he conceived of him in his letters—without taint.

Most of all, the notes tell us that the desperate conditions Dostoevsky complained of, the pressure of money and time, did not prevent him from agonizing over every detail in the novel. He wanted a good novel—he rummaged through plan after plan to find it—and when he could not find it, he destroyed what he had written and started over again. He faced deadline after deadline, but when he could not meet the deadline and his own exacting sense of what was right, he gave up the deadline. *The Idiot* has its faults: it is structurally untidy; it has inconsistent characters; it fails to translate some of Dostoevsky's political passion into aesthetic impassion; and it does not always make the most of its materials. For example: both Gania and Aglaia beg for structural elaboration as analogues to Rogozhin and Nastasia Filipovna, but Dostoevsky never passed beyond hint and fragment. But in the face of characters like Nastasia Filipovna, Prince Myshkin, Lebedev, Madame Epanchin, Ipolit, and scenes such as the burning of the hundred thousand rubles, Ipolit's attempted suicide, and the meeting between Nastasia Filipovna and Aglaia, one is embarrassed to ask for structural tidiness.

The Idiot is one of the world's great novels, and between the great man who created it and the great novel lie the notebooks.

III

This manuscript is a translation of the Soviet edition of the notebooks for *The Idiot,* edited by P. N. Sakulin and N. F. Belchikov, published in 1931. The text of the Soviet edition has been followed, except for these alterations: the original pagination of the notebooks has not been reproduced, nor has the division of the material into three notebooks (Notebooks 3, 10, and 11), since neither served any useful purpose. The Soviet editors divided the text of the notebooks into twelve sections: eight plans, an intermediate plan, and notes for the second, third, and fourth parts. I have divided the text into ten sections: the first and second plans have been combined into one plan for substantive reasons which are explained in the introductory chapter to the first section; the intermediate plan has become the eighth plan; and notes for the third and fourth parts have been combined into one section. I have also added an introductory commentary to each of the sections.

In the preparation of this volume, these editorial devices have been adopted: crossed-out material is crossed out in the text, and marginal and interlineal material (whether additions, variants, or authorial commentary) has been placed in the text between brackets.

20 *Note on Preparation of the Translation*

As editor I have supervised the preparation of the translation and have written both the introduction and the ten interchapters. Mrs. Strelsky translated the text and compiled the footnotes. We have co-operated, by much consultation, to prepare a manuscript that we hope will do honor to Dostoevsky, the novel, and the notebooks.

EDWARD WASIOLEK

Translator's Note

The task of translating the private working notes of a great novelist like Dostoevsky swings one between joy and despair. The elation springs from the many insights as to meanings contained in the published version of the novel, and sometimes—rarely—from the sense of having hit upon a happy equivalent. On the other hand, there is a certain residue of insoluble and frustrating obscurity. We have attempted by and large to produce a readable English translation without unjustified guesswork.

In the Russian original the first half-dozen pages are almost unparagraphed. These long passages have been broken up. For the rest, the paragraphing and indentation have been preserved. In the Russian text the spelling of names, the punctuation, and the capitalization are highly irregular. Such stylistic matters have been largely regularized; but a minimum number of such peculiarities have been kept, for it would be misleading to offer the reader a stylistically polished text. The unfinished aspects convey something of the pressure and haste under which Dostoevsky continually worked.

The italics are all Dostoevsky's own. Foreign words not italicized are reproduced as found, sometimes with accents missing. The antecedents of pronouns are frequently missing; the tenses of verbs are often uncertain. All parentheses are Dostoevsky's. The angle brackets represent interpolations by the translator. When many successive periods are found, they are his; three or four periods indicate an ellipsis, or omitted matter.

The nineteenth-century Russian calendar (Old Style) was twelve days behind that of Europe. Dostoevsky sometimes indicated this by writing "4/12 October"; at other times, since he was living abroad, he adopted the European style. Otherwise, dates are written according to day, month, and year, as "28 January 1909." In the twentieth century the difference in dates is not twelve but thirteen days.

The following pages, in short, attempt to convey to the reader the most transparent expression of Dostoevsky's thoughts while struggling with the creative process—given his idiosyncrasies—with the least possible interference from the translator. His use of special words (such as "idiotism") has been preserved. The footnotes are confined to factual material, and the interpretation of the notebooks has been left entirely to the editor.

I should like particularly to record my extensive indebtedness to two consultants, Professor Catherine Pastuhova and Mrs. Maria Manley. They have been extraordinarily generous with their assistance. Whatever errors may be found are my own responsibility.

KATHARINE STRELSKY

The First Plan

The first notes for *The Idiot* are uncertain, complex, and remote from the final version of the novel. They are not easy to understand. The reader is likely to be impressed on first reading with a bewildering diversity of actions, characters, and relationships. Dostoevsky seems to have started with certain situations, dramatic nodes, without having a clear idea of how different situations relate to one another, or why his people act as they do. He has no over-all conception of the action, but seems to be trying out various combinations, connections, and relationships.

Most of the material has to do with "economic situations" and "love relationships," and, as in the novel itself, Dostoevsky has difficulty finding a bridge between the two. The principal situation seems to be the following: an impoverished gentry family finds itself in St. Petersburg in straitened circumstances, which it tries to brave through. The father goes abroad for a while, where he is pursued by debts; when he returns, he maintains appearances for a while and then degenerates. The family is supported by the Idiot, who is hated by his mother; the elder son, the handsome youth, who is adored by his mother, is looking for a position. The daughter Masha gives piano lessons, and her fiancé, an officer and moneylender, helps out the family with a small subsidy. These sources are insufficient, and the mother turns for help to the uncle. The uncle, whom Dostoevsky calls the chief character of the novel, is a widower and moneylender. He is proud, vain, suspicious. His childhood, which is only alluded to, was apparently difficult. He was abandoned on the streets of St. Petersburg, but managed by privation and will to make a million and a half rubles. In the novel itself, Ptitsyn made his money in a similar way; Ipolit regrets that he had not been cast on the sidewalks of St. Petersburg hungry, badly clothed, and penniless; and Gania himself has similar ambitions. One may call this the Rothschild motive, and it provides one of the core situations of *The Raw Youth*.

The love relations have to do principally with the Idiot, Mignon, and the heroine. Mignon is a foster daughter in the family of impoverished gentry. She is the daughter of a landowner, and she had been mistreated in childhood. She is similarly mistreated in this family, where she is treated worse than a house servant. Mignon suffers and has visions. When the Idiot is falsely accused of stealing money and is chased from the house, she roams St. Petersburg with him for three days, telling him about her dreams of gold and her desire to be a woman of the streets.

Dostoevsky explores four possibilities of arranging the romantic situation, punctuating the versions with phrases like *"or else," "or perhaps like this," "or like this (definitely)."* In all of them the heroine, in a proud, passionate, and spiteful way, seems intent on playing one suitor off against another. In different versions and in different ways she manages to make the handsome youth, the uncle, the Idiot, and the uncle's son fall in love with her. Her commitment to any man seems provisional, even playful, and is almost always motivated by spite or revenge. This matrix situation anticipates what we have in the final version, when in the first part Gania, Rogozhin, General Epanchin, Totsky, and the Prince are suitors for Nastasia Filipovna's hand. Like Nastasia Filipovna, the heroine runs away on the eve of her wedding, becomes hysterical and sick. The "final" version in the notes, according to Dostoevsky, is the following: her cousin, the officer moneylender and fiancé of Masha, "sells" her to the uncle's son in order to get her off his hands. But just as the son, a compassionate and good person, is about to make his feelings known to the heroine, the uncle (his father) makes her an offer. The heroine is consequently "sold" to the father. Engaged to the uncle, the heroine wants to have an affair with the son, but he refuses. From spite she turns the head of the Idiot and runs away with him on the eve of her wedding to the uncle. The uncle then demands that the heroine marry the Idiot; the heroine agrees, but the marriage does not go through. The uncle himself plans to marry Mignon (possibly from frustration), but he dies from a liver attack before the wedding takes place. He wills all his money to the Idiot and Mignon, but they give it all away to the heroine and the son.

The heroine treats the Idiot's love with contempt and exacts trials of his devotion. He is, according to her, ripe for "horrors, crimes, villainy." The Idiot suffers her contempt and cruelty without murmur, but he tells Mignon that he is going "to pay her back." When he finds out that she is having an affair with the son, he wants to kill her. His love for the heroine looks on the surface to be generous and forgiving: thus, if she marries another man, his reaction would be "Let her marry him, I will love her just the same." He will love her if she becomes a whore and if she marries another man. But Dostoevsky refers to this as "the last degree of pride and egotism." Dostoevsky seems to be giving to the Idiot the ability to love or to sacrifice, or to do virtuous acts from pride and self-will. Thus, when he gives up the money the uncle leaves him, he does so from a voluptuous feeling of renunciation.

Dostoevsky describes the main lines of the heroine's character as follows: "She is extraordinarily proud, she rides roughshod over all the conventions, and *therefore* the worst extravagances of the Idiot neither shock nor outrage her (once he almost killed her, another time he broke her hands). But once such moments are over, she flees in aversion. These moments arise partly out of her terribly abnormal and incongruous position in the family. In general, she is unquestionably of an original, frivolous, capricious, *provocative* and poetic nature, superior to her environment." These lines might pass as description of the Nastasia Filipovna whom we meet in the final version of the novel itself: her disdain of conventions, her attraction to the power and destruction of Rogozhin (here embodied in the Idiot), her capricious, provocative, and poetic nature, which reveals itself so powerfully in the evening gathering when she throws the hundred thousand rubles into the fire and bids Gania retrieve them. Indeed, the attraction the heroine feels for the uncle's son, a forgiving, gentle nature, who at one point is identified with Christ, anticipates the alternating attraction that Nastasia Filipovna will feel and act on between the destructive, self-willed, instinctive, and brutal love embodied in Rogozhin, and the compassionate, forgiving, spiritual love embodied in the Idiot. The son, though engaged at one point to the heroine, seems to bear little love for her; rather he feels a compassionate love for the oppressed, fallen Mignon, anticipating perhaps Myshkin's love for that part of Nastasia Filipovna which had been bruised in childhood and wounded unto vengeance.

Although the essential dramatic situation and the main lines of the character of the heroine are already anticipatory of Nastasia Filipovna's situation and character, the heroine's motives are vague and unclear. We don't know why she acts in such a capricious, vengeful, spiteful, and cruel way. There are a few vague references to her impossible situation; but Dostoevsky seems either uninterested or unable to give us the grounds that would make her extraordinary actions believable. Nastasia Filipovna's motives are extraordinary, paradoxical, and inconsequent, but they are not unclear. They are complex but knowable. Mignon, who in part anticipates Nastasia Filipovna's character, has also a heart filled with revenge and hate; and some of her actions are as paradoxical as the heroine's, as, for example, her quiet unmurmuring acceptance of the Idiot's rape. But the motives for her hate, desire for revenge, and possibly for her acceptance of the Idiot's outrage lie in the oppressive conditions of her childhood and her life with the main family. She hates people because she has been hated, and she accepts the Idiot because he too has been hated by the family.

Dostoevsky had already caught in this plan—and was to hold throughout many plans—the essential dramatic posture of Nastasia Filipovna in the actions of the heroine, and to a lesser extent in those of Mignon. It is another story with the Idiot. The Idiot here is not the Idiot of the final version. For the most part, he is proud, cruel, vengeful, contemptuous, fiercely independent, and self-willed. The following quotation is characteristic: "*The Idiot's* passions are violent, he has a burning need of love, a boundless pride, and out of pride he means to dominate himself, conquer himself. He takes delight in humiliation. Those who do not know him make fun of him; those who do know him begin to fear him." The Idiot does what look like generous, sacrificial, noble deeds: he renounces the inheritance he receives from the uncle, he suffers the contempt and outrages of the heroine's love, he supports a family that laughs at him and a mother who hates him. But it is clear that he does these things from the voluptuous sense of pride and self-control. Still, Dostoevsky sees the possibility of the opposite in the Idiot: "N.B. *The Idiot's basic character.* Domination of himself out of pride (not morality) and rabid self-license in everything. As yet, however, self-license is but a dream, whereas at the moment he has only convulsive impulses. Consequently, he could turn into a monster, but love saves him. He becomes imbued with the most profound compassion and he forgives faults in others. (This had already become evident when he forgave the father. *The father's death.*) In compensation he progressively develops a high moral sense, and performs a heroic action." And it is possible that the heroic action Dostoevsky has in mind is the marrying of Mignon, for these words follow immediately after: "Mignon's wedding." Dostoevsky sees the possibility of the Idiot's saving himself by sacrificing himself for the outraged heart.

Many of the traits attributed to the Idiot are used in the final version for other characters: his passionate and self-punishing love for the heroine reminds us of the love that Rogozhin and Gania bear for Nastasia Filipovna; he burns his finger for the heroine as Gania will do for Aglaia; he is proudly disdainful of the money that the uncle leaves him, as Gania will proudly turn his back on the hundred thousand that Nastasia Filipovna offers him. The Idiot is different but the situations are not. It is as if what was important to Dostoevsky were the situations themselves. He is uncertain who should embody what, but he is less uncertain about what should be embodied.

Near the end of this section, Dostoevsky writes the following:

Notes for the second plan of the novel
The second plan of the novel
Chronological Pattern

What follows for a few pages (three in the original notes, two in Sakulin's edition) is an unimportant variant of what has come before.

The Russian editor, following Dostoevsky's own notation, makes this the second plan, but I am including these few pages in the first plan for substantive reasons: the cast of personages is the same, the actions and situations are virtually unchanged, and what is changed is less significant than the variant renderings Dostoevsky has given us within the first plan.

The interest in these few pages may lie largely in the insight they give us into Dostoevsky's creative habits. He reviews the action of what he has already written in a rapid shorthand summary, seizing on key words to recall situations for him. Here is a characteristic example: "The incident of the theft, wandering throughout the city; the rape; the business of the theft is arranged; the uncle receives the Idiot, who amazes and overwhelms him. The wedding of the fiancé and Masha." Each of the phrases is the nucleus of a situation he had worked on in the notes preceding this part. "The incident of the theft" refers to the theft committed by the downtrodden and degenerate father, and for which the Idiot is blamed and cast out of the house. It brings to mind also the Idiot's magnanimity in not blaming the father, and the loyalty of Mignon in leaving the house with him. The next phrases, "wandering throughout the city; the rape," refer to the sequel to the theft. After being chased out of the house, the Idiot and Mignon roam the city for three days, talking in a half-delirious way about wealth and gold, and about Mignon's desire to enter a brothel. "The rape" refers to the paradoxical relationship between the Idiot and Mignon. The Idiot seems to rape Mignon from frustration, perhaps from being chased out of the house, perhaps from the cruelty he suffers at the hands of the heroine. "The uncle receives the Idiot, who amazes and overwhelms him" recalls the uncle's opinion of the Idiot, which changes from regarding him as an idiot to regarding him as more intelligent and finer than himself. "The wedding of the fiancé and Masha" summarizes not only that unimportant relationship, but perhaps recalls also the family's financial dependence on the overbearing officer moneylender.

The variations are minor, and the notes concentrate largely on the heroine and her lovers and on the outrages she perpetrates upon them. She has apparently turned the head of a senator to whom she has become engaged, and whom she suddenly rejects, possibly because everyone approves of the match. She becomes engaged to the uncle, but is also attracted to the uncle's son. She flees from the uncle with the Idiot on the eve of her wedding, and then holds him with a punishing and cruel love. Dostoevsky is apparently trying to make more precise the dramatic situation of the heroine, but there is still no hint of a motive for her strange actions. He also attempts to make more precise the grounds for the Idiot's actions, turning in one note to *"His relations with his mother.* At one time he used to weep. His mother remembers that once he threw his arms about her. But now, when his mother *tries to approach him before the theft,* he scornfully repulses her." But nothing more is made of this.

List of Characters for the First Plan

Family of Ruined Gentry
Father
Mother
The handsome youth (the elder son)
The Idiot (the younger son)
Masha, a daughter, engaged to the officer
Mignon, a foster daughter

The Uncle's Family
The uncle, younger brother of the father of the family of ruined gentry
His son

The Fiancé's Family
The fiancé, an officer
His father
His mother
His sister, an old maid
His cousin, the heroine, also called "the beauty"

14 September 1867   Geneva
14 September[1]
22 October[1]

   An impecunious family of landowners (of good stock) have ended
up in Petersburg. Despite their impoverished circumstances, they
put on a bold front, especially the mother, a woman worthy of respect, of a noble but capricious nature. The family includes a son
(a handsome young man spoiled by his mother, who adores him,
but capable of appreciating his position). He is job-hunting, well
mannered, with a very middle-class nature, but he has some claims
to originality and even to poetic talent. Carries himself with an air.
Supercilious, mocking. Has a delicate constitution. *Is in love with*
a young girl, a distant relative, and engaged to her. [N.B. He is not
at all in love. Before the wedding he says he does not know how to
get rid of her.] She visits the family. A harsh, sarcastic girl.
   The sister (M.) on her own initiative has found herself a fiancé;
she gives piano lessons, which her fiancé tolerates. Silly, cruel, and
middle class. Her mother has kept a strict hand over her. Her fiancé
is an officer who lends out money on pledges. He writes letters, keeps
well out of the family's way, eats pears and grapes. ("Make me some
coffee.") Finally, there is the father of the family, who has run off
from them and is traveling abroad, where he is nonetheless pursued
by his debts.[2] When he returns to his family, he at first tries to brave
it out, then he quickly collapses in his last-ditch, desperate efforts
to get hold of some money. So long as such people have any money,
even though they are *not intelligent,* they manage to keep up appearances, but without money they go to pieces fast.
   The fiancé's cousin (the heroine), an extraordinarily beautiful,
arrogant girl, visits the family. (The fiancé's mother is friends with
the mother in the other family. One of the two old ladies is a typical
landowner's wife; the other is a typical wife of a Petersburg bureau-
crat.) The father is a libidinous old fellow (he is friends with the other

---

[1] These last two dates are written in a different ink.

[2] Debts: Dostoevsky himself, having left Russia in order to escape his creditors,
was unhappily aware of how their threats and vexations could pursue one across
frontiers.

old man); they were once schoolmates, and the two old boys ramble about together. The fiancé's sister is an old maid; there is a girl cousin; and so forth.

The main family also includes an adopted child, the stepdaughter of the mother's sister—the wrathful Mignon, a Cleopatra. [Olga Umetskaia.] And finally there is the *Idiot*. He was dubbed an idiot by his mother, who hates him. He supports the whole family, but in their opinion he does nothing for them. He is an epileptic and has nervous seizures. He has never finished his university studies. He lives with the family. He is in love with the fiancé's cousin—secretly. She detests him and treats him worse than an idiot or a footman. (*On the street as he is accompanying her, he kisses her.*) Seeing that he is in love with her, she teases him, for lack of anything better to do, and sets him beside himself. She is twenty-four. *After one of these occasions* he rapes Mignon. *He sets fire to the house.* On her command he burns his finger. *The Idiot's* passions are violent, he has a burning need of love, a boundless pride, and out of pride he means to dominate himself, conquer himself. He takes delight in humiliation. Those who do not know him make fun of him; those who do know him begin to fear him.

His mother detests him and constantly complains of him. The fiancé and the sister have insulted the mother. The favorite son, his fiancée, and the others agree in a family council to behave more decorously to one another, no matter what. [N.B. The novel opens with this scene.] The fiancé's cousin and his mother are on their side. (They abuse Mignon atrociously, they treat her worse than a servant—this is a mean trait in the mother. Mignon is in love with the handsome brother and hates his fiancée.) [Entirely out of envy.] (N.B. When the Idiot raped her, she said not a word, uttered not a single reproach; but when the father of the family tried it out, she struck him.)

At the family council (where at *great* length they discussed *the uncle*), they had hardly come to any decision when the Idiot pinned the right labels on them. A tremendous scandal. The fiancé wrote letters demanding that the Idiot be turned out of the house, otherwise he would provide nothing for their maintenance; he was contributing fifteen rubles a month. Shortly before this the fiancé had found a post for the Idiot in an office. For three days the Idiot went there, then he got into an argument and left; descriptions of how they were quarreling, and how the Idiot sat there a long time just copying (*his fine penmanship*[3]), then, seeing how they were all trembling before the director, the idea seized him of spitting in the other's mug. Within the family circle they were saying: "This is what happens with him—sometimes he is humble and compliant, then he suddenly rebels." N.B. All his idiocy was in reality merely his mamma's invention (his mamma's character), so that when answering the uncle's queries they began to ask themselves, "Is he really an idiot?" To their surprise, the family could not understand where this reputation originated and how it became established. The elder brother (the handsome youth), however, held to the opinion that he was an idiot, "Yes, he is so strange."

Mignon is terribly downtrodden and terribly timid, but inwardly she is dreadfully spiteful, insolent, and vindictive; she hates the handsome youth's fiancée. Mignon's history is altogether like that of Olga Umetskaia.

They have given up waiting for the father of the family to return from abroad. But in Petersburg they finally learned (through former agents, neighbors, and businessmen) that their estate has been completely liquidated, squandered, and that the father of the family has not only run through everything he owned while he was abroad but is also being threatened by many huge debts, and finally that even abroad he is subject to judgments against him for suits brought in Russia. (To the handsome youth's question, "Is it possible for this to happen to someone even abroad?" the uncle replies, "Indeed, it is!")

At last they decide to appeal to the uncle. [The first news of *the uncle's son*. The uncle's wife had died a long time ago. They had quarreled all their lives.] They call his steward in (a former family serf, now a prosperous clerk); the meeting of the mother of the family and the former serf; at first she did not ask him to sit down, and he drank his tea standing, but when the handsome youth came in, he was shocked and had the clerk sit down. The conversation; news of the Idiot and of Mignon. Finally, the uncle gives them to understand that he will come, and he fixes on an evening. General confusion. Tea. Mignon even has an attack of hysteria. They proudly announce to the fiancé that the uncle is coming and that now they

---

[3] Penmanship: calligraphy was a special interest of Dostoevsky, and in the manuscript pages there are numerous calligraphic designs and doodles of human faces, Gothic church windows, and so forth.

will have a support, a protection, and finally that they will deal with the Idiot. The fiancé coldly replies that he himself has done business with this uncle and that they are friends (though this is nonsense).

The uncle is the chief character in the whole novel. A hypochondriac, with a very deep-seated vanity, pride. He suspects everyone. A cultivated man. Fundamentally, he is even magnanimous, but everything in him has been warped and corrupted. He has suffered a great many painful wounds. A usurer living a solitary life, but a usurer with a certain poetry in his nature. As a child he was badly brought up, poorly developed. An unloved child. He had been sacrificed to his brother, the first-born. The mother of the family had at first been engaged to him, but then had been given in marriage to his elder brother. Finding himself on the Petersburg streets, he had amassed a fortune, penny by penny, working by the day. Now he is probably worth a million and a half. He gives nothing away to anyone. (The count and he.) He is absent-minded and careless; an eccentric fellow; once he attempted suicide. At times splenetic. There is no one he loves. He dreads being with people for fear his heart might be revived and bound over to someone through love.

The gist of the conversation was that the uncle agreed to pay over a very small monthly allowance (25 rubles). The fiancé, who had boasted of his acquaintance with the uncle, said a hurried goodbye, then became embarrassed and did not leave. Both he and Masha remained standing at the door listening. (Riabtsov was throttling her, all in fun, for they were on perfectly good terms.) While the uncle was preparing for the meeting at this hour (exactly one o'clock) he was in great agitation, though outwardly he seemed hard and icy and haughtily abstracted. He was apprehensive at the idea of seeing his former love. But the impression he made proved comic, and he departed in gloom and vexation, full of self-scorn.

The mother of the family then burst into a tirade. It turned out that the uncle had known little of the father of the family (his brother). For the first time in his life he had learned a number of details, for until then he had been living so much apart from the family. His attention shifted to Mignon, and they told him her biography, *in her presence,* saying that she was the daughter of a landowner, that no one had troubled to see that she was fed, that she had tried to hang herself and had been cut down. The beauty (the heroine) then arrived. The uncle turned his attention to the Idiot, for they were already hastening to explain about him. He listened absently. (His handwriting. The clerk had already told him

<about the Idiot>.) "I'll have to deal with him; I have a whip. How can he be an idiot? No one knows this for a fact." The handsome youth's fiancée. Everyone jeered at the Idiot. He went away.

Mignon is in love with the handsome youth and hates his fiancée. And she hates the heroine, because the latter hovers round the handsome youth; but since she is extravagantly beautiful, Mignon kisses her hands and feet when left alone with her (and because of that intensifies her hatred). She even kisses her feet for the special purpose of hating her the more. "Therefore I will hate her all the more fiercely." Mignon is envious and proud. One could chop her into mincemeat, but she would not ask forgiveness; yet she trembles like a coward (out of nerves). She could hang herself, but if no one gave her a crust she would never beg. Her desires are naïve, to revenge herself on everyone, to swim in gold. She makes common cause with the Idiot. Her friendship for him is passionate to the point of enslavement, though they are on terms of equality. Mignon worships him. Once when the handsome youth was already engaged, *he made an attempt* on her while in his cups, and Mignon nearly killed him in a fury of pride, taking it as an insult, despite the fact that she was in love with him; but when the Idiot violated her, she gave in to him (without love) and never even referred to it again. Once done, neither gave it another thought.

Now and then the Idiot and she would meet and talk, she with her naïve daydreams, he gloomy and incommunicative. Mignon tells him all her dreams. She daydreams incessantly. She hates the family; she is extremely intelligent and observes everything. They meet as a regular thing and talk of the day's happenings. Then she begins imagining how she will take her revenge. The Idiot talks to her, gazing at her, and sensing his power over her. He leaves the house and wanders through the streets of Petersburg, where he has many haunts. The secondhand dealer. Capital. Mignon hides his capital away and guards it.

The Idiot takes up work as a copyist in the uncle's house. The uncle had almost forgotten him. His handwriting. A week goes by, they meet. The uncle alludes to his whip. The Idiot stares at him derisively. The office correspondence. This he wrote. The uncle is struck by this and invites the Idiot to dinner. The Idiot speaks haughtily, laconically (he pretends to be an idiot out of mockery); he puts the uncle in the wrong and shows off how well-read he is. "Well, I never gave myself out as an idiot. I did not finish my studies; I was an auditor."

Meanwhile the father of the family arrived unexpectedly. He is flabby, with a pock-marked face and a womanish build. At first he brazens things out. He did not praise the cook. She smelled bad. She fired right back at him. Later on he tried to make it up with her. He had come in hopes of influencing his brother and extracting some funds from his wife, who as he surmised still had some money. At first he even played the *galant-homme* with her. In the beginning he treated Mignon like a young lady, then turned harsh. "Take off my boots." The fiancé's superciliousness. Explanations about money. "I would have liked to stay out of all this, so that Masha would not marry her fiancé." At her fiancé's instigation, Masha had talked harshly to her mother that morning. They tell the father of the family about the fiancé. "My dear, I've blown in out of the blue, to be sure, nonetheless, matters have to be looked into."—"Well, now you. . . . . . ." Recounts the quarrels (as they are taking coffee). All this has to be managed cleverly, with style, so as to display his nobility. He has an abject regard for money. *He has been borrowing.* The fiancé considers this a crime. Each of them goes off to his own room.

The father would have liked to take an authoritative stand, but the fiancé gave that a stern veto. The handsome youth dissociated himself from the whole thing with an air of indifference. The mother began to cry and reproach the father. He set off for his brother's; his brother refused to give him any money and laughed at his shady proposal, showed it up as a swindle. Falling on his knees, the father began to implore him for 4,000 rubles; *the uncle* did not give it to him. Once back home, he made advances to Mignon on the spur of the moment, but she scratched his ugly mug. He and Mignon had been left alone together. "I used to know your father." "Well, what of it?" "What a charming creature, she's scratched my eyes out." Then he called for a piece of sticking plaster. The cook had seen everything and reported it to everyone in Mignon's presence. The mother of the family demanded of Mignon: "Is this true?" Mignon was impudent to her. The mother hit her, the father rushed in to intervene. The mother of the family: "You needn't think I did that on your account."

For the old man's arrival the mother had made an elaborate toilette; before the rest she even behaved as if proud of him; it was only in private that she gave rein to her exasperation.

Meanwhile (coincidental with the arrival of the father of the family), the once humbled Idiot found himself alone with the heroine and began to kiss her violently, though until then he had behaved with meekness. She did not protest; but from then on she coquetted with him now and then. "Do you love me very much?" He burned his finger. That same evening he raped Mignon. After the uncle menaced him with the whip, the Idiot kissed the heroine and then burned his finger that very night.

Vexed at the uncle's advantageous circumstances, the fiancé brought his money to show his own worth. The lost wallet. They accused the Idiot of having stolen the money. The uncle drove him out of the house: "Where did you get the money?" The handsome youth had seen him in the attic; he had already come across the money. However, it was the father of the family who had put it there. The housemaid and Mignon had seen him in the act. The fiancé insisted that the money must be found. The handsome youth found it and returned it. The engagement period was cut short. The handsome youth took up his sister's defense in his own way. They have things out in a characteristically rude and middle-class fashion. In any case, the Idiot was not to attend the wedding. N.B. They banished the Idiot, the uncle *turned him out of the house.*

Day and night Mignon and the Idiot wander in the Petersburg streets. Three days of roaming about. Mignon too has rebelled and taken flight. "I am of age." In the rain and cold, at night, they converse about gold, about wealth. Mignon wanted as soon as possible to become a woman of the streets. He gave her food, revealed his own golden schemes.

Finally the handsome youth smooths things over; he says to the uncle that it was not the Idiot who had stolen; he tells the Idiot to keep quiet, the mother understands, she weeps heartbrokenly, the Idiot says they should pity him and *he restrains the handsome youth,* who was about to tell everyone that the father was the thief. The mother is astounded. He proudly ignores her amazement. The heroine becomes pensive.

Mignon does not want to return to the house. The Idiot takes an apartment for her. [N.B.] His *first* serious and proud conversation with the uncle. The uncle sees that this Idiot whom he had menaced with his whip is infinitely deeper and finer than he himself is. The uncle questions him about Mignon, whom he had seen with the Idiot in the street. The uncle goes alone to have a look at Mignon. N.B. A fantastic encounter. He talks with Mignon. She tells him that as soon as she gets her revenge on them all, she will kill herself at once. The uncle soon leaves her. The Idiot boldly requests his salary. The uncle gives some money for Mignon. The uncle has a severe attack of hypochondria. Shall he hang himself—or marry? Marry the hero-ine. (He has heard that the Idiot is in love with her, and knows this to be a fact.)

[The heroine hates the handsome youth's wife. (N.B. Fabricate these characters.) After she gets engaged, she becomes involved with the handsome youth. She seduces him. The uncle finds out. Jealousy and a scandal. Rejection. The fiancé comes to his sister's defense. "Well, would you object to marrying the Idiot?" She retorts scorn-fully, "Why not?"]

N.B. *The Idiot's basic character.* Domination of himself out of pride (not morality) and rabid self-license in everything. As yet, however, self-license is but a dream, whereas at the moment he has only convulsive impulses. Consequently, he could turn into a mon-ster, but love saves him. He becomes imbued with the most profound compassion and he forgives faults in others. (This had already be-come evident when he forgave the father. *The father's death.*) In compensation he progressively develops a high moral sense, and per-forms a heroic action.

Mignon's wedding.

N.B. N.B. N.B.

(*The main point.*)

1) The uncle's wild infatuation with the Idiot, after what was at first an aversion. When he caught the Idiot in the street after the theft, he already felt a love for him. He made his will in favor of the Idiot and his fiancée Mignon. Everything went to them, and only 25,000 rubles to his son.

2) Just at that point the uncle's son arrived. His character. He is unloved and unacknowledged by his father.

3) One of the heroine's strange traits: though engaged, she made the Idiot fall in love with her out of spite, rousing him to fury and jealousy; but when the uncle's son came, suddenly, *to spite* them all, she ran away with the son on the eve of her wedding, thus shaming the uncle.

Or else (N.B. N.B. N.B.): the heroine finally succeeds in breaking off the handsome youth's engagement (the characters, *the love affair*) and becomes engaged to him.

At this point the uncle succumbs to her fascination; he buys off the handsome youth, pays him (with the Idiot's approval) for releas-ing his fiancée, the heroine. The heroine consents, forced by her brother's despotism and *her fiancé's* reproaches that she is beholden for the bread she eats, also by the scorn and despair that seize her when she discovers that *the handsome youth* has sold her off. But step by step she evolves a plan for avenging herself: having found out that the Idiot had endorsed the uncle's scheme and agreed to his purchase of her from the handsome youth, laughingly assuring him of success, she resolves to avenge herself on the Idiot and drive him utterly out of his wits. Since family *gossip* [N.B. *About the gossip.*] has it that the Idiot is groveling to the uncle and has got him under his thumb in expectation of huge benefactions to come, she determines to force them into a quarrel once and for all; therefore on the eve of the wedding she runs away with the Idiot, who has quite lost his mind, and thus she shames the uncle.

Then she laughs straight in the face of both the Idiot and the uncle.

She acts this way because of her character, without a great deal of reflection on her part.

The fiancé and the family confront her with fury. The uncle demands that she marry the Idiot. She retorts: "Well, what could be better than to marry you!" For three days she acts as if out of her senses: now she curses the Idiot, repulses him, laughs at him, now she weeps, begs him to love her, his future wife, *she flatters him, caresses him.* Finally she falls gravely ill. Meanwhile, the uncle's anger, his marriage to Mignon, who goes out of her mind once and for all.

The Idiot listens and instructs the uncle as to what he is to do. Meanwhile the uncle has a liver attack [in his ravings] and dies.

N.B.　N.B.　N.B.　N.B.

N.B. *Or perhaps like this:* Though she laughs at the Idiot immediately after running away with him, still she is so far gone in her madness that she is ready to go off to church with him at once. They go through the marriage ceremony. At first he tries to dominate her, but eventually he gives in. Meanwhile, the uncle marries, or plans to marry. The heroine is beside herself (now she derides the Idiot, now she caresses him). The uncle comes, accompanied by the Idiot. The uncle has a liver attack. (She runs away somewhere with someone or other), and so forth.

Finally: N.B.　N.B.　N.B.　N.B.　N.B.

Or like this (definitely): There is a son who has arrived from Moscow. They sell her off (the fiancé); but just as the son was about to make his feelings known to his father (that is, to the uncle), the father makes his own offer. (The son is an extremely noble person.) Not wanting to strike his father such a blow, the son hesitates, then withdraws. Meanwhile, the family despot, the fiancé [Trace in the novel the picture of family despotism; his wife Masha; it must be more comical.] forces her to accept, and *she* says *in spite* and wanton vengefulness, *"Yes!" to the uncle.* In scorn of the *son*—because he had withdrawn. They have sold her outright. Now that she is engaged, she has an affair *with the son* and insists that he take her away. The son cannot decide to deal his father this wound, and he renounces her. Meanwhile, the Idiot has turned up at her door: in two days' time she turns his head completely, and he carries her off on the eve of the wedding. Thereupon she laughs at them both.

At this point the uncle demands revenge and arranges the Idiot's wedding. (It is absolutely out of the question for her to marry the son.) In a state of hysterical defiance, she says: "Well, all right, then." Now she is doubly enraged with the son. (N.B. As yet they are *not* married.) At this point she falls ill, cursing and beseeching. Meanwhile, the uncle's wedding, so that the preparations should not go for nothing. Mignon. All this is fantastic and grips the imagination. She falls ill. The uncle has a liver attack. The Idiot and the uncle are reconciled on the latter's deathbed. The uncle dies. He wills his estate to the Idiot and Mignon. Instead of her avenging herself (as she meant to when she was seething with rage), Mignon *gives it all away* and *abases* herself to everyone. The one thing she cares for is elegance. The uncle dies. His whole estate goes to the Idiot and Mignon. They give the entire estate to the son and the heroine. But the Idiot and Mignon go away together: the prouder, nobler course.

Sequel. At this point, when the uncle is drawing his son and the Idiot together, the Idiot finds out that the son is in love with the heroine. He spies on him. Explanations between the two men. The son is in despair at the heroine's frivolity. The Idiot says he has no need of any guarantee; however flighty and faithless she may have been, it is really all the same to him.

The heroine begins to love Mignon. A strange friendship develops between the two girls. The son is preparing to become a lawyer. It can be foreseen that even if the Idiot is to die, he will not give her up.

N.B. The heroine behaves amiably to the uncle (so as to facilitate the son's petition). But the uncle himself catches fire, assuming that

this display of affection is on his own account. He does not know that
his son is his rival.

Invent some terrible episodes for the Idiot's stay with the uncle.

Sequel. Invent some terrible episodes for the Idiot's stay with the
uncle. (Between the moment he is seen to be innocent of the theft
and the uncle's wedding.)

The uncle is simply fanatically attached to the Idiot, with a mania
typical of a hypochondriac. He even offers him his whole estate. The
latter *tyrannizes* over him and repulses him brutally. *Their psychological relations.* He feels a voluptuous delight in disdaining wealth.
"I am above all that, I have more pride." It is not love, but a feeling
of despotic vanity that motivates the uncle; he wants to bend the
Idiot to his will, force his own way on him. "You yourself do not
know what you are demanding," the Idiot tells him, "if I give in to
you even a little, you will instantly throw me over. . . . . . ." The Idiot
mocks him cruelly with these words; he analyzes, criticizes, the
other's whole existence. In one of his paroxysms the uncle wants to
hang himself—but suddenly he gets married.

N.B. Throughout the whole novel there is a continual struggle
with the son.

N.B. The wedding is a piece of madness, a way out of the dilemma,
come what may.

Sequel. Ever since the theft and the Idiot's expulsion from the
house, right up to the hour of the uncle's wedding, the Idiot has
been in love with the heroine. This is love—it is love and likewise
the supreme satisfaction of his vanity, his pride. This is the highest
point of his ego, his kingdom.[4]

Meanwhile, though the heroine was being humiliated and treated
despotically by the family, she suddenly displays herself in a remarkable and astonishing manner. Captivated by her beauty, a rich man—
a senator and a count, by no means an old man—falls in love with her
and asks her hand. The wedding arrangements are nearly completed;
the fiancé and the family are already trumpeting victory and triumph;
and then she abruptly breaks off everything under an odd pretext.

The family nearly tear her to shreds; the fiancé wants her turned
out of the house; she does not give in. At this point, scenes between

---

[4] Kingdom: the Russian word here is *tsarstvo,* having both a concrete and an
abstract meaning.

her and the Idiot, conversations between her and the Idiot; she merely laughs at his love, haughtily and contemptuously; her contempt
for him swells to loathing; she shows a striking indifference to the
Idiot's suffering, which counts for *nothing* to her. Meanwhile, she
wants to exact major services on the Idiot's part. N.B. N.B. He is
ripe for horrors, crimes, villainy. (One day he visits Mignon: "I'm
going to pay her back!") Suddenly he finds out that she is having a
secret love affair with the son. He wants to kill them. All this part
is romantic and episodic.

The Idiot's love is of a strange kind: it is simply a spontaneous
sensation devoid of all reason. He nurses no dreams, does not calcu-
late, as, for example, Will she be his wife, is that possible? . . . To
love is the whole of his necessity. If she married another man, likely
his reaction would be quite different from what one would expect:
"Let her marry him, I will love her just the same." If she were a
whore, it would come to much the same thing: "But I will love her
just the same." Eventually he begins to lose all sense of reality. He
even goes to the son and talks about her without concealing his own
love, yet as if supporting the son, so that the latter marvels and begins to believe him out of his mind. His pride even reaches the point
of his not noticing that she considers him insignificant. "It's all the
same to me, you know, I love her for my own sake." The last degree
of pride and egotism.—At this point the uncle, having heard about
the senator and taken seriously her affection for himself, proposes
to her just at the very moment when the son is about to lay his own
cause before him.

N.B. The son opposes him, says he is independent of his father,
and quarrels with him, but she tries to reconcile them.

They make an appointment; the uncle comes with his offer, but
she takes the son's part. Abruptly, the uncle forestalls her and declares his own suit.

She cannot bring herself to hurt the son. The family press her on
the uncle's behalf.

The main point is that the son withdraws.

She is *at a loss* as to what to say, and the last word remains the
uncle's. But suddenly she insists on the son's taking a firm stand.
"Now it is out of the question for you to give your father such a blow
and shame your own father."

Then she appeals to the Idiot to take her away. The Idiot is not at all her slave, on the contrary. (Their relationship is a far more romantic one.)

Sequel. Instinctively, she disbelieves in his love and therefore assumes that it does not count for *anything.* As a matter of fact, while she does not understand him, somehow she senses that his *independence* of her is boundless and that to him she is necessary only in so far as she intensifies his own self-assertion. In suggesting that he take her away, therefore, she is out of her mind. But later she is afraid of him.

The main point. *Nota bene.*

From the outset he frightened her *to such a terrible degree* that she would suddenly be seized with an urge to run away from him and hide; but also she would have a sudden urge to play with fire or leap off a tower: the voluptuousness in a sinking of the heart. She would exasperate him to frenzy, then dart out of reach, as it were, keeping her distance, gazing avidly at him yet dreading to approach him. *The lines of her character are emerging.* She is extraordinarily proud, she rides roughshod over all the conventions, and *therefore* the worst extravagances of the Idiot neither shock nor outrage her (once he almost killed her, another time he broke her hands). But once such moments are over, she flees in aversion. These moments arise partly out of her terribly abnormal and incongruous position in the family. In general, she is unquestionably of an original, frivolous, capricious, *provocative* and poetic nature, superior to her environment. She understands, for example, that one can set the house on fire. But *the son* produces an extraordinary impression on her.

About the son, his character.

Sequel. Nota bene.

N.B. *Projection of the son's character.*

1) Perhaps the son has but little love for her.

2) In his talks with the Idiot the uncle describes his son as a *socialist.*

3) But he is not a socialist; on the contrary; he finds in socialism little besides an unrealizable ideal. Economic redistribution, the problem of bread.

4) He says he pities the uncle, that one should pity the uncle, and forgive him a great deal. The Idiot retorts that this is precisely why the uncle detests him.

5) The uncle detests him also because he refused the money. The son preaches about how there is a great deal of happiness in life, that each moment is a happiness; self-expression and self-awareness. (Other peoples have undergone a long period of scattered energies, then a sudden concentration.)

6) The son is struck by the idea of Mignon as fiancée. When the uncle dies, the son stands by Mignon. (Compassion. The son soon becomes close friends with Mignon. Develop this scene more brilliantly.)

7) Christ. To an extent, the son has already impressed the Idiot some time earlier. Suddenly the latter becomes forthright with him. But the Idiot is carried away on the full tide of passion.

8) The son confesses that he is not yet a man, that he is preparing to be a man. (He is carried away by his compassion for Mignon.)

He even wonders at his former love for the heroine. The heroine, however, is enthralled by him, and his indifference merely inflames her the more. Once she runs to see him, but the Idiot waits for her on the stairs. Tragedy is in her soul, but she jests and quips with the Idiot on the stairs.

9) This is why the son at the last moment is hardly willing to steer the heroine back to his father. She flings herself at the Idiot, not understanding what the matter is. "Marry the Idiot."

10) Then everything subsides in her because of a crisis and an illness. The Idiot triumphs over her. The stepmother (Mignon) triumphs over the son.

Main point. Nota bene.

Perhaps she is already married to the Idiot.

At first he acts like a despot to her, but later she begins to love him. Mignon gives everything away and goes out of her mind. Her fantasies, one stranger than the other. The uncle is the subject of all her fantasies. The son adores Mignon and through her *is reconciled with his father*. The father dies and bequeaths Mignon to him.

Or else: the heroine deserts the son and clings to the Idiot, though the Idiot would have surrendered her to the son.

The one thing in the world is spontaneous compassion. As for justice—that is a secondary matter.

4/16 October

Geneva

Notes for the second plan of the novel[5]

The second plan of the novel[6]

Chronological pattern

The entire beginning as in the first version.

1) The family council. N.B. The only difference is that an old civil servant's wife tells the mother of the family under the seal of secrecy that the heroine *has won a sort of victory over the senator.* The clerk talks of the son; the heroine questions him, and so on.

The heroine after her victory appears at the evening party. This victory—some sort of amusing story *(to be invented)*[7] [*to be invented*] delineating the heroine. [They have moved from the villa.] The Idiot is much struck by this story. She laughs. The handsome youth would like to accompany her: "You have your fiancé, but I have my adorer." She leaves with the Idiot (during the evening, the incident with Mignon, which amazes the heroine). On the way the heroine discusses it with the Idiot. They digress, change the subject to love; all along the way the heroine teases the Idiot. He burns his finger [stay at my house], there are matches. He actually does burn it, and the heroine runs away in fright.

2) Details concerning the Idiot. N.B.? A letter from the father of the family. An official invitation to visit the uncle, conveyed by the handsome youth. They treat Mignon harshly, the Idiot intercedes. Incident with the headmaster. Letters (from the fiancé). The little labels. The fiancé behaves all the more airily because the senator actually does propose marriage.

3) The evening with the uncle. Everything as before; he gazes at the heroine (already engaged to the senator) and is greatly taken with her. The fiancé and Masha do not appear. The letter from the father of the family. The whip. Mignon creates a scene. The Idiot again takes the heroine home. "Advise me: should I marry or not?"

4) Suddenly the heroine breaks off with the senator. The father

---

[5] The "notes" do not appear on this page of the manuscript, but on a later page, where Sakulin, the Russian editor, deleted a passage describing an epileptic attack Dostoevsky suffered in Geneva on the night of 17-18 October 1867. Above this entry of 4/16 October is written "Notes of seizures," also deleted in the Russian published text.

[6] In Anna Grigorievna's handwriting is added, "The Idiot."

[7] *"To be invented"* is written again in the margin with emphasis.

of the family arrives. The commotion. The fiancé. The whole incident with the father. The Idiot visits the uncle; the uncle is amazed. The uncle and the son. The uncle alone. The uncle wants to propose (after his conversation with her). He does propose.

5) The incident of the theft. Wandering throughout the city; the rape; the business of the theft is arranged; the uncle receives the Idiot, who amazes and overwhelms him. The wedding of the fiancé and Masha.

6) Meanwhile the heroine has become engaged. Her whim of summoning the son. The son makes a deep impression on her. After a painful scene of jealousy between the uncle and the son, she says to the Idiot almost on the eve of the wedding. "Take me away." Their crazy flight. She is in a constant state of hysteria, weeps and laughs.

7) A terrible general upheaval. The family are horrified at this turn of events. (They begin saying that she set the father and son to quarreling.) Even the mother disapproves. The fiancé and Masha firmly show her the door. The uncle is astonished and hurt. Having stirred up trouble, she is seized with alarm, but she braves it out, laughing hysterically. "Well, then, I'll marry the Idiot. I will marry him! I will marry him! The uncle gave me the idea." The wedding.

8) The Idiot. After having married him, she is frightened and disgusted by him (10,000 rubles). Both their natures become apparent. The Idiot is beside himself. He and the uncle. She consults the son. She confesses to her husband that she loves the son. She finally rushes to her son and vows she will not marry. The son and the Idiot. (She would like to seduce the handsome youth.) N.B. At the same time, the romance of all the other characters in the novel.

9) Meanwhile, Mignon lives with them. She becomes close friends with Mignon. The meeting between Mignon and the uncle. Her counsel. The uncle grows attached to her.

10) Suddenly the marriage of the uncle and Mignon is announced. Mignon gives everything away.

11) The heroine comes back to him. The uncle dies. The son and Mignon become close friends.

Notes for the second plan of the novel.

1) *His relations with his mother.* At one time he used to weep. His mother remembers that once he threw his arms about her. But now, when his mother *tries to approach him before the theft,* he scornfully repulses her.

2) His attitude to his brother (more affectionate).

3) His brother is not engaged. He is courting the heroine. He is not engaged, but he aspires to a girl with money. The handsome youth berates her but keeps a hold on her in any event. The mother spends extravagantly on her.

4) While accompanying her home the Idiot asks the heroine (who had spurned the handsome youth during the evening party and made him accompany *his fiancée* and the mother home): "Does she love my brother?"

5) The handsome youth subsequently marries his fiancée and acquires a fortune.

The Second Plan

(Written about the middle of October, 1867. The date October 17 is to be found in the manuscript.)

Dostoevsky tries, in this plan, to connect more dramatically and organically the economic and romantic situations. They are loosely knit in the first plan, and their relationship plagued Dostoevsky throughout the various plans and even into the final version. Dostoevsky also attempts in this section to render more precise the character and motives of the heroine and the Idiot.

The economic situation of the main family is still prominent. As in the first plan, the family is impoverished gentry, ruined perhaps in large part because of the dissolute habits of the head of the family (recalling perhaps the situation of the Ivolgins in the final version). They continue to rely in part on the uncle's help, but mostly on the outcome of a lawsuit, the character of which is never defined. The lawsuit fails, and the handsome youth—still adored by his mother—who had intended to marry the heroine, prudently marries the daughter of the strong-minded mother because of the girl's fifty thousand ruble dowry. The economic situation of the main family and their attempts to recoup their fortunes are conventional and unintriguing. When the handsome youth marries the daughter of the strong-minded mother, the dynamics of the situation are brought to a halt.

As before, the romantic situation involves the Idiot, the uncle, and the heroine; Mignon (Olga Umetskaia) plays a less significant role. An attempt is made to interweave the economic and romantic plots through the handsome youth's courtship of the heroine. It is unclear why the family should encourage this courtship, since there is no mention of the heroine's being financially well off. It is possible that the lawsuit concerns an inheritance she expects. This becomes explicit in later plans, but is not clear here. When the lawsuit fails and the handsome youth and the family are again reduced to bleak prospects, the heroine throws over the senator (presumably a wealthy suitor) and offers herself to the handsome youth. The situation anticipates that of Gania (a handsome youth of an impoverished family) in the first part of the novel. There, it will be remembered, Gania must choose between Aglaia, whom he loves, and Nastasia Filipovna and the seventy-five thousand rubles Totsky is offering to get her off his hands. In the notes the handsome youth must choose between the heroine and the daughter of the strong-minded mother, who has a dowry of fifty thousand rubles. Gania, of course, loses both women.

Dostoevsky also gives us in these notes an early analogue to the "bidding" that takes place for Nastasia Filipovna in the first part of the novel. The handsome youth apparently goes to the uncle to borrow fifty thousand rubles as a means of being paid for marrying the heroine. He does not accept the fifty thousand from the strong-minded mother until he is refused by the uncle. The uncle himself, in one note, offers a million and a half for the heroine's hand. And later the Idiot thinks of taking five hundred thousand rubles from the uncle, presumably as payment for marrying the heroine.

The heroine's character is still unclear. The basic situation is repeated again and again: she is unable to commit herself to any man and yet is driven to provoke their love and their attentions. After the heroine is refused by the handsome youth, she promises to marry the uncle, but once again flees with the Idiot on the eve of her wedding. In several variants she is afraid of the Idiot and returns to the uncle. Dostoevsky brings no new insights to an understanding of her character.

He seems to be having a bit more success in understanding the Idiot. Much remains the same: he is still the unloved son, still apparently suspected of some theft that he did not commit; he still feels compassion for Olga Umetskaia (Mignon) and wanders the streets with her; he still loves and hates the heroine. But there are significant changes. In the first plan Dostoevsky spoke of the Idiot's impulse to kill the heroine when he learned of her affair with the son; now he makes the possibility more explicit. We have the following: "She runs to the uncle: 'Save me.' (Perhaps the Idiot will kill, but likely there will be a fight and he will not kill.)" And, "The main point: the reader and *all the characters* in the novel must remember that *he can kill the heroine* and that everyone is expecting him to kill her." The possibility that the Idiot will kill the heroine is an early sketch of Rogozhin's threat to kill Nastasia Filipovna. In this early note and in the final version the possibility of murder holds us in suspense throughout the action.

It is sometimes suggested that the Idiot's character is all pride, self-will, and cruelty; but Dostoevsky had already suggested in the first plan, and here develops with emphasis, the possibility of the regeneration of the Idiot. The Idiot's violent emotions, his pride, his voluptuous pleasure in self-control and the control of others come from a distortion of his "spontaneous thirst for life and for seeking his identity." Dostoevsky characterizes him in this way: "But manage in this fashion: (N.B. 1) Let him be oppressed; and (2) show what kind of man it is who has been oppressed. In the 1st place he is oppressed; and in the 2nd, he has a spontaneous thirst for life and for seeking his identity in self-indulgence, in every instance spontaneously, *without reflection.* For the sake of his own peace of mind, that is, so as not to reason and vacillate, he seeks a solution in pride and vanity; and in the absence of the genuine delights for which he longs so much and the chance of enjoying them, he has converted his intense pride into poetry and the pleasure this brings him, and thus raises pride to an apotheosis. For the first time, love urges him along a new path; but love has a long struggle with pride, and ultimately it too is converted into pride. This savage pride captivates the heroine. (Nevertheless, she perceives that on occasion and under extreme provocation he is capable of a crime. The heroine is carried away with him and at the same time she is terrified of him.) And finally, in the *third* place (3), the spontaneous force of development impels him eventually *to reflection and to a new path in life."*

The Idiot in these early plans is a double character: the traits of satanic pride, vengeance, hate, and self-will are dominant and persistent; the possibility of a regenerated Idiot is faint and sketchy, but just as persistent. From the very beginning Dostoevsky looks for his good and beautiful character, not only in the possibility of a transformed Idiot, but also in the Christ-like traits he gives to the uncle's son and the beautiful character he gives to Gania in subsequent notes. He is never able to effect the change in the Idiot from hate to love, but he eventually solves the problem—the insight begins in the seventh plan—by making the Idiot good and beautiful and by putting him in a world of hate, vengeance, hurt, and self-seeking. In the earliest plans a proud and self-interested Idiot was apparently destined to confront a beautiful Idiot; in the novel itself a beautiful Idiot confronts a proud and self-interested world.

List of Characters for the Second Plan

Main General's Family

Father in retirement
His mother
His wife
His son, the handsome youth
His son, the Idiot
His daughter Masha, engaged to the engineer
Olga Umetskaia

The Second General's Family

The general
The general's wife
The elder son
The younger son (the murderer)
The daughter, aged twenty-five

The Fiancé's Family

The engineer, fiancé of Masha
His father
The heroine, engaged to a count or senator

The Strong-minded Mother's Family

The mother
Her daughter, in love with the handsome youth

The Uncle's Family
The uncle
His son

New and definitive plan

[N.B. bene]

The general's family are in Petersburg. (The general is retired.) The old mother, who adores the general; his silly pretentious wife (she still flirts and dresses elegantly), not devoid of character and good traits, however; two sons—the handsome youth and the Idiot—one daughter, Masha; and Olga Umetskaia; the governess; and so forth. Pretentiousness. About the lawsuit. They are convinced of the successful outcome of the lawsuit. The daughter's fiancé is an engineer; though he is a born sycophant, at the same time he flies off the handle at the least cause. Then there is a lieutenant-general and his family; they have a high opinion of themselves. In this family there are 2 sons, the elder is promising, and the younger—a murderer—and a daughter aged 25. (The engineer's father is a landowner, a retired cornet,[1] an old man who lives abroad and is a friend of the retired general's.) Then, besides, there are the strong-minded mother and her daughter, who has 50,000 rubles in cash plus expectations; she is in love with the handsome youth. But the retired general is counting on the success of the lawsuit, and therefore in his inordinate affection for the handsome youth he promises to ask the heroine's hand on the latter's behalf. ("Though she is not rich, she has connections.") Altogether, they are a pretentious lot.

[N.B. bene]

The uncle. The general's brother (*a well-known story*). They receive him with condescension, but he is personable and well bred, and *he bides his time*. They treat him superciliously, though they have borrowed 10,000 rubles from him. Nevertheless, the uncle knows his own mind. The Idiot has made an impression on him and on Olga Umetskaia. [The uncle's prayers.]

---

[1] Cornet: in a troop of cavalry, the fifth commissioned officer who carried the colors.

[N.B. bene]

(Supply more details about the uncle; present him frankly as the main character.) For the moment, his *adventures* with the Idiot. Pride. Humiliations. Out of pride he does not justify himself. *The penknives in the flea market.*

Some sort of a base and scandalous deed. (N.B.: a theft.) At first they accuse the Idiot, but it turns out that the handsome youth is the guilty one. To avoid scandal, they make the Idiot the scapegoat. In secret the Idiot is passionately in love with the heroine.

N.B.: *strange conversations between them.*

The finger. (His relations with Olga Umetskaia. He kisses her feet.) The uncle is interested in the Idiot. *Relationships and inter-relationships.* At the time of the base deed (when the Idiot is thrown out into the street with Olga Umetskaia), the uncle repudiates him, but later he calls him back. The family is happy moreover because the uncle consents to take him on at least as a clerk.

[N.B. bene]

The senator-count proposes to the heroine.

Rumeur. The family are offended, especially the grandmother and the mamma, because they had intended her for the handsome son. The family make representations to the uncle to enlist his support for their side. His half-mocking reply. They quarrel. They almost show him the door.

[N.B. bene]

The quarrel is short-lived. Suddenly a terrible blow befalls them: they lose the lawsuit. They are all at the uncle's. (The strong-minded mother begins declaring: "I foresaw that you would lose, I expected this.") The heroine immediately breaks off with the senator (knowing that now the handsome son is utterly out of the question); she expects and demands that the handsome son *should take her.* They all go to the uncle's: 100 rubles. They are full of indignation, they accept.

(N.B. There follows a swift and progressive downfall.) The handsome son goes to the uncle, who laughs and refuses. The handsome son acts prudently and marries the strong-minded mamma's daughter with the 50,000 rubles.

(N.B. At first the Idiot does not accept the uncle's money under the conditions. Romantic relationships.)

[N.B. bene]

The uncle, tortured because of the Idiot, wants to kill himself. Suddenly he decides to marry. He goes to the heroine. "Let's see whether they will not give in." The uncle does not know of the Idiot's passion. *The heroine* is bullied by everyone at home because she has broken off with the senator. A million and a half. The promise to the uncle. Beside herself and in a paroxysm of nerves, the heroine consents.

[N.B. bene]

Having got engaged, she goes on a wild carouse. The uncle's patience is worn out. On the eve of the wedding she runs away with the Idiot *out of spite and nerves.* She runs away and disappears, madness and delirium.

[N.B. bene]

The family say: "Marry the Idiot." "300,000 rubles." "I accept."
The Idiot and the family gathering, the Idiot with the heroine. The uncle and *Olga Umetskaia.* The fiancée (*Olga Umetskaia* and her transformation). The uncle has a liver attack, dies.
The Idiot gives up the heroine.

[N.B. bene]

Perhaps like this: in terror of the Idiot, the heroine takes refuge with the uncle (whom she had insulted and who was already engaged to Olga Umetskaia). "Forgive me, protect me, take me in." The uncle forgives her. (The Idiot gives up the heroine and goes away with Olga Umetskaia.)
(Incomplete.)
At first, with his teeth bared, he says to the uncle: "Well, I will take the 300,000" (but he does not accept any conditions).
But when the heroine ran away—he did not take the 300,000. He hesitated: should he play out this farce with the uncle, take the money, or not?
The household will not receive the heroine, and she is installed with the family (who are already deeply disintegrated and are eying the Idiot with amazement and fear).
She runs to the uncle: "Save me." (Perhaps the Idiot will kill, but likely there will be a fight and he will not kill.)
But within the family, before her flight to the uncle, he is silent

and accommodating, but in such a way that everyone trembles at him. At times the heroine tries to laugh at him, then she screams at him in frenzy and rage. In essence he agrees that she will never be his wife. He is ripe for some mad act, some atrocity. She takes fright and runs to the uncle.

[N.B. bene]

The main point: the reader and *all the characters* in the novel must remember that *he can kill the heroine* and that everyone is expecting him to kill her.

[N.B. bene]

Perhaps he tells the uncle when the heroine runs away: "Well, show her that you love her boundlessly; as for me, I am showing that —I am giving her up. (N.B. bene) And I am not about to kill her. Marry her, forgive her." N.B. Then the uncle surrenders the heroine to him. The heroine is overcome and falls in love. Mignon dies. The uncle by now is excessively in love with Mignon. They are all reconciled.

N.B. The heroine's character must be developed.

New plan

N.B. From a seignorial and lordly way of life, a great comedown. They lose the lawsuit, finish off and torment the debtors. Then the swift downfall. *They are debtors.* (The colonel has a mania for talking about the people to whom he has lent money and in all the secret details, so that exposure means more to them than the money itself.)

N.B. *Add to the new plan.* The Idiot gets into a tremendous quarrel and a fight, in the heroine's presence, in which he displays a boundless firmness of character.

N.B. As a child he used to weep when they scolded him, but in time he grew hardened and *derisive.* The incident with the headmaster.

New plan

1) He is ashamed of everything and of everyone, of his intimate feelings, he is a wild downtrodden creature. He does mean things out of spite and thinks it necessary to do so. (N.B. N.B. N.B. He seeks the solution and his salvation in pride.) He ends up with a sublime deed. (N.B. Trace the thread of his character, that will be fascinating.)

2) If he is merely an oppressed character, nothing will come of it but oppression. An old, worn-out theme, whereas the new and major idea of the novel vanishes.

But manage in this fashion: (N.B. 1) Let him be oppressed; and (2) show what kind of man it is who has been oppressed. In the 1st place, he is oppressed; and in the 2nd, he has a spontaneous thirst for life and for seeking his identity in self-indulgence, in every instance spontaneously, *without reflection.* For the sake of his own peace of mind, that is, so as not to reason and vacillate, he seeks a solution in pride and vanity; and in the absence of the genuine delights for which he longs so much and the chance of enjoying them, he has converted his intense pride into poetry and the pleasure this brings him, and thus raises pride to an apotheosis. For the first time, love urges him along a new path; but love has a long struggle with pride, and ultimately it too is converted into pride. This savage pride captivates the heroine. (Nevertheless, she perceives that on occasion and under extreme provocation he is capable of a crime. The heroine is carried away with him and at the same time she is terrified of him.) And finally, in the *third* place (3), the spontaneous force of development impels him eventually *to reflection and to a new path in life.*

Nota bene

1) When the Idiot and Mignon are wandering at night through the city, a discharged soldier, a Polish tramp, attaches himself to them and does not want to leave them.

2) The heroine pities the Idiot and does not believe he has stolen.

3) The scene in which the father borrows 5 rubles of him.

4) The father realizes that people know he has stolen. His wife (the mother of the family) lets him know that she knows and that others do. Scene with her. Having borrowed the 5 rubles, he tries to tempt the cook. She is sitting there knitting a woolen sock and laughing at him with the unceremonious openheartedness of the common people. He goes away muttering, he would like to get drunk, but he goes off to bed. His death. N.B. He *almost* confesses. He dies a good death. N.B. At home they have always hidden things from him and kept things locked up. This ⟨incomplete sentence⟩[2]

---

[2] Here the text breaks off because of a tear in the page. Sakulin believes that an entry on page 16 of the manuscript dealing with *Crime and Punishment* may properly belong here: "1) He has robbed, and 'he has to return.' What a strange

17 October

Notes for the main plot

[N.B. bene]

1) In the begining they treated the Idiot as if he were a madman in a physical sense, short of flogging him. They looked on him as a nonentity. They talked about everything before him. Not even the needs of nature deterred them in his presence.

His own attitude conduced to this treatment by the family. He remained silent, peering up at them all, though inside he was seething. (He read a great deal; they saw this, but out of stupidity took no notice of it.)

2) N.B. *Later,* when the uncle asked him: how could he allow such a treatment of him, *he replied vaguely but let it be understood* that he was quite aware of his own delight in this inordinate humiliation and the thirst for revenge it incited. "I have subdued myself." That's voluptuousness. He was awaiting his chance for a reckoning; in Petersburg, so it seemed to him, this would be a possibility. The incident with the headmaster.

3) They punished the Idiot. He broke the cane and pushed the hand away. He did not want to get himself arrested. Arsenic. Aloes.

---

story. 'Sacre nom d'un Caniche.' He returns. Goes to bed. Dies well. Confesses to the theft. His borrowing of the 5 rubles and the story of the stockings had happened before this. At the tarts last of all."

The Third Plan

(Written in the second half of October, 1867. There are two dates in the manuscript: October 18 and October 22.)

Dostoevsky calls this plan the "definitive plan for the novel," but the words "definitive," "final," "last," are dispersed throughout his manuscript, representing more wish than fact. The very repetition of these words perhaps points to the sense of frustration he must have felt before the ever-elusive "definitive" plan. The same four groups reappear: the general's family, the uncle, the engineer, and the strong-minded mother. The second general's family, which appeared in the second plan but played no role in the action, disappears from this plan. It is an example of that peripheral life that nudges its way into the world of the novel, but, finding no place, disappears only to reappear at a later time.

Relationships are fluid in Dostoevsky's plans, and he redefines them repeatedly, seeming to test them for dramatic implication. The heroine has moved from the fiancé-engineer's family to the general's family, where she is apparently a governess. As before, the heroine is courted by most of the main characters, and, as before, she rushes from one to the other and stays with none. In the previous plan it was unclear why the general's family was urging their handsome son to court her; in this plan Dostoevsky provides a motive by telling us what the portentous lawsuit is all about. The lawsuit concerns a two-hundred-thousand-ruble inheritance that the heroine expects, but which apparently fails to materialize. The handsome youth is presumably interested in her because of her inheritance, but when this fails he takes money from the uncle as a bribe to give up the heroine. The uncle pays suit to her; as before, she finds this repulsive, indulges in an orgy, and rushes off with the Idiot, whom she fears and from whom she also flees.

Olga Umetskaia, as before, is an oppressed girl. Her heart is filled with vengeance against her family, and then with vengeance against the general's family, where she visits for a long time. Her role has been consistently overshadowed by the heroine's, and in most cases she is either married to the uncle—when he loses the heroine—or goes off to live with the Idiot, when he loses the heroine.

The most important alteration concerns the Idiot, who is changed from being the son of the general—and thus the brother of the handsome youth—to the son of the uncle—and thus the brother of the uncle's son and the competitor with his father for the heroine's hand. Dostoevsky seems unable to decide whether he is the actual son, the natural son, or the stepson. Dostoevsky does very little with this new relationship. As before, the uncle and the Idiot are competitors for the heroine's hand; as before, the uncle offers him three hundred thousand rubles, presumably as payment for marrying the heroine. The Idiot accepts the money disdainfully and then returns it.

For the most part the Idiot acts as he had in previous plans: he carries off the heroine on the eve of her wedding to the uncle; he frightens her with his passion and threatens to kill her if she deceives him; he is compassionate and kind to Olga Umetskaia, as he has been to Mignon-Olga throughout the notebooks; and his idiocy is only apparent and not real. There are changes, however: the Idiot is now actively an intriguer who works to set everyone against everyone else. Dostoevsky says:

> He incites the heroine against them all.
> He incites everyone in the household against the heroine.
> He sets them all to quarreling with the general's wife.

He reveals to the heroine that the handsome youth has been bribed into deserting her and that the uncle has bought him off. He arouses the hostility of the heroine against the uncle, to whom she is engaged, and "speaks ill of the heroine to the uncle." Perhaps his most serious intrigue is the slander he spreads that the general has been in love with the heroine. This brings the general to misery and provokes him to challenge the Idiot to a duel, which never takes place. Dostoevsky explicitly compares him to Shakespeare's Iago, and at least for a while thinks of making him something of the same kind of plotter and intriguer:

Plan for Iago

The Idiot's character—an Iago. But he ends up divinely. He renounces, and so forth.

N.B. He has slandered everyone, carried on intrigues in full sight of everyone, he has got what he wanted, money and his fiancée, yet he renounces it all.

The reference to renunciation brings us back once again to what has haunted Dostoevsky in every plan up to this point: the possibility of a regenerative change in the Idiot. The Idiot's passion, pride, and self-will are seen here, as in the last plan, as a misunderstood and mis-applied thirst for life. The regeneration was apparently to take place by way of love for the heroine. The Idiot was to perceive that love need not be brutal, passionate, and vengeful: "The Idiot, always cold-blooded, suddenly frightens the heroine with the violence of his passion, a passion as steely and chill as a razor, the maddest of mad-nesses. This passion is not love but the passion of gratified vanity. N.B. *But when he really feels and perceives what love is, he renounces her and immediately sends the heroine back to his brother.*" And a little later we find: "The Idiot confesses to her that he has hated her and that he has wanted to avenge himself on her by putting her in this situation. But now that he sees she will perhaps love him, he is ready to give his life to her, but if on the other hand she is going to deceive him, he will take her life also."

The possibility of an act of sacrifice, of change from hate to love, vengeance to sacrifice, plotting to sympathy, is insisted upon. A simi-lar change takes place in his attitude toward the uncle's son, who is in this plan his brother. The uncle does not acknowledge the son as law-ful. The son, as before, is simple, ingenuous, and virtuous. He is horrified by the heroine's suggestion at one point that he take her away when she is engaged to his father. The two brothers meet on a train—our first reference to the situation that will begin the final version of the novel—and the Idiot conceives a hatred for his brother.

He plots and intrigues against him, but then is won over by his simplicity. At one point the son agrees to marry the heroine, when she has been rejected by others, anticipating perhaps Myshkin's offer to marry Nastasia Filipovna, a "fallen woman."

This was not, of course, to be Dostoevsky's last plan, though it must have felt like his last. He seems to be pirouetting in place, refining again and again the same basic situation. The Idiot's hate-love for the heroine and the heroine's flight from suitor to suitor are the magnetic core of the drama. Something refuses to give itself to him, something implicit in the drama, but something that Dostoevsky is unable to raise to consciousness.

List of Characters for
the Third Plan

The General's Family

The general
His young wife
His son, the handsome youth
Another son
His daughter
The heroine (governess, ward, the beauty)
Olga Umetskaia

The Uncle's Family

The uncle
His son
The Idiot (stepson, real son, or natural son)
Kostenkinych and his wife, the uncle's shop assistant or clerk

The Aunt's Family

Aunt Sofia Fyodorovna
Her husband, the Jumper
Her daughter

The Engineer's Family

The engineer
His father (a major without legs)

His mother

His sister (Olga Umetskaia)

The Strong-minded Mother's Family

The mother

Her daughter

Or else he is a stepson
Definitive plan for the novel

The heroine loves (or imagines she loves) the handsome son. Earlier she had a romance with an engineer. The senator proposes to her in the uncle's presence. She refuses him. The uncle does not interfere. She is furious with the uncle because he is keeping the handsome son out of the running; the handsome son is afraid of vexing him.

N.B. They are exasperated with the heroine because it is impossible to treat her like all other governesses.

The lawsuit fails. The heroine hopes that the handsome son will propose to her. But then the strong-minded mother and the others suddenly begin to harass the heroine: why has she rejected the senator?—What business is it of theirs?—Evidently they are angry that she is eating their bread. At this point the uncle proposes. Despite the general's defense of her, the heroine is obliged to accept his proposal.

From the very beginning the Idiot won over the father's fiancée. In the general's family it suddenly appears that he is no Idiot. (His birthday.) He accidentally runs into Umetskaia.

N.B. Scene with the heroine—the finger. *Little old men.* The senator. The uncle is glad at having ridiculed the senator. The engineer's father.

As he was returning home from the evening party, the uncle storms at him: how could he pretend like that?

Romantic relations with the uncle.

The Idiot and Petersburg. Umetskaia. The Idiot's convictions. The uncle offers him money, he accepts disdainfully. The uncle and Umetskaia. (Prayers, the funeral, and so forth.)

The lawsuit fails. (Meanwhile the catastrophe involving the uncle and the Idiot.) The uncle's proposal.

The heroine's indignation at the handsome son. The general. They accuse the general of being in love. "There's nothing to be done, you have to accept the uncle."

The heroine goes on a wild carouse. The heroine's flight with the Idiot (with the stepson).

The uncle's wrath: "Let her marry the Idiot."

N.B. At first the heroine *mocks* the Idiot.

He has no hope of her ever coming to love him. He infuriates the uncle and the handsome son, at first by saying that she was living with the general. Then he incites the uncle into proposing to her. This puts him in the master's seat. "She was making fun of me."

The heroine is ill, she runs away before the wedding: "Save me."

The general and the uncle stand up for her, they take her in.

18 October

Definitive plan for the novel

Meanwhile, the uncle and *Umetskaia.*

He wants to kill the heroine—but gives up the idea. The uncle dies *of a liver attack. The theory of happiness on earth.*

The uncle has two sons: the Idiot is his natural son, but the uncle does not want to recognize the other one as his legitimate son; they live apart; he visits him. A hypochondriac; before the brother's arrival he wants to blow his brains out.

The general has a young wife. The children—one is a Petersburg diplomat; then there is still another son and a daughter. (The engineer is courting her, but he is also courting another girl.)

They have a ward. She is to inherit 200,000 rubles. It is hard for the general to get her to marry the son who is a diplomat; it would be believed that the reason is money. For the moment she is a governess. Orgy. The engineer was at their house in the province. <He proposed> *to her.* And was refused. But he again urges himself on her. The senator. (They are prepared to refuse him.) The uncle (he only tries).

Until the Idiot's arrival, things have gone well with her.

The Idiot hates the son and plans to disparage him to the uncle, but very cleverly.

They all meet at the uncle's house.

The Idiot tells the general and the others that there is something going on between the general's wife and the son (they had known the son before).

He also says to the general that the latter is in love with the heroine.

He incites the heroine against them all.

He incites everyone in the household against the heroine.

He sets them all to quarreling with the general's wife.

When the lawsuit fails, the general forces the diplomat. At this point they declare that he is in love with the heroine.

The Idiot declares to the heroine that the man she loves (the diplomat) has been bribed into deserting her for the wilful daughter.

It is the uncle *himself* who has bought him off (on his own initiative, without asking the Idiot).

The Idiot outwits the uncle.

At this point the heroine dies.

The Idiot has an aunt married to a Jumper,[1] an old man. (?N.B. The theft.) She has a daughter. The engineer. They live a secluded life. There is still another *son,* who speaks with a French "r."[2] Under the seal of secrecy he confides that he is the uncle's natural son. This is very hard to prove. He wants to prove this to the uncle. The engineer has a mother, a sister, and an impoverished father, a major, who has lost his legs.

Olga Umetskaia.

With the Jumper, the aunt's husband, he visits the tarts.[3]

The Idiot has *his own money.*

The Jumper at the general's house.

Olga Umetskaia is the engineer's sister.

The Idiot has installed Olga Umetskaia in the general's household.

N.B. As soon as the general's family arrive in Petersburg, they invite Olga Umetskaia *to be their guest.* They have already been acquainted with her in the province.

---

[1] Jumper: a member of a heretical religious sect which sprang up in the 1860's. The more extreme were flagellants and induced a state of ecstasy by wild dancing and leaping until they collapsed, after which unrestrained orgies ensued; the milder practiced a form of communism. The word Dostoevsky uses is *Prygunchik,* derived from *prygat,* the verb "to jump."

[2] The French "r": the Russian word is *kartav,* derived from *kartavit,* "to burr" or pronounce "r" incorrectly; the indication here is that he speaks with an affected accent.

[3] The tarts: the Russian word is *kameliia,* or "camellia," perhaps associated with Dumas' play *La Dame aux camélias.* It is a milder, less offensive term than *sobaka* ("bitch") or *bliad* ("whore"), words Dostoevsky also employs in the notebooks but never in the published text.

This manuscript page corresponds to pp. 62–63, beginning with the date "18 October" and ending with the phrase "This is very hard to prove. He. . . ." One is struck by the controlled neatness of the handwriting and the disruptive movement of the subject matter. We have also at the top and sides of the page specimens of Dostoevsky's calligraphy.

N.B. Olga Umetskaia settles herself in the general's family in order to accomplish her revenge on her own family. But then she begins to hate the general's family and to scheme revenge on them as well. Their treatment of her is all a mockery, and they intend her for the Idiot. "A fiancé! A fiancé!" She is in love with the diplomat.

As soon as Olga Umetskaia is installed in the general's household, she begins to talk about the Idiot. "At once! Let him come! Let him come!" They correspond.

Nota bene.

Stepson or son, *but no ordinary man.*

18 October

Nota bene. (*For the definitive plan.*)
Nota bene. (*For the definitive plan.*)
N.B. bene. *The Idiot* (to the uncle): "I sensed that I was necessary to you so that you could talk to somebody about how unhappy you were."

2) In some way the uncle hurts him; [incident] apologizes; torments himself.

"I am necessary to you so that you can gratify your pride at my expense."

The uncle asks: "What sort of a girl is Olga Umetskaia?"

When he was a young man, 20 years ago, he was the cause of his wife's death.

Something happens which tragically affects the uncle and the Idiot. At this point the heroine loses the lawsuit and refuses. Her relations with the family are extremely chilly.

The general does not dare protest at the barbarous way the household treats Olga Umetskaia, for he has already aroused the family's jealousy.

N.B. The general comes *to complain* to the uncle that the mother and son are accusing him of being in love with the heroine. The uncle then makes his offer for her. And when the general shows alarm, the uncle says: "Perhaps you yourself are in love with her."

[N.B. bene]

(*The main point.*) Before the heroine is carried off, even before his own betrothal, the uncle gives 300,000 to the Idiot. The latter accepts and merely laughs at him. He begins with a poignant account of Olga Umetskaia's story.

P.S. Perhaps he is *a stepson.*

18 October

[Nota bene.] *(For the definitive plan.)*

The Idiot is the uncle's son. The 2nd and main point.
The uncle parts from the woman he had been living with.
By chance the Idiot gets acquainted with Olga Umetskaia.
"If I am not your son, so much the better for both of us."
The Idiot has been living in the uncle's house only recently.

[Nota bene]

The main point. The novel begins thus: "You are already 22 years old." And he takes him into his brother's house.

When he carried the heroine off: "I was joking, here is your money." He returns the 300,000.

Plan for Iago

The Idiot's character—an Iago. But he ends up divinely. He renounces, and so forth.

N.B. He has slandered everyone, carried on intrigues in full sight of everyone, he has got what he wanted, money and his fiancée, yet he renounces it all.

Plan.

Again a new plan. Ptitsyn.[4]

N.B. *He* enlightens the uncle. "How is it possible you do not see their plot?"

Ptitsyn.

22 October[5]

II

The Idiot, always cold-blooded, suddenly frightens the heroine with the violence of his passion, a passion as steely and chill as a razor, the maddest of madnesses.

This passion is not love but the passion of gratified vanity. N.B.

---

[4] Ptitsyn: derived from *ptitsa* ("bird"), the name conveys to the Russian ear an idea of mediocrity and commonplaceness. In the published novel the name is assigned to the young moneylender who courts Varia Ivolgin.

[5] Again this date has been written in a different ink.

But when he really feels and perceives what love is, he renounces her and immediately sends the heroine back to his brother. Duel with the general, who has seriously compromised himself by his indignation and his intervention on the heroine's behalf. [Conversations about decapitated heads.—There is no God.]

N.B. When the uncle proposed to the heroine, he did not in the least suspect the Idiot's true feelings, but even asked his advice.

22 October

He takes every word of the heroine's as her never-ending mockery of him. In the general's household they ridicule both her and him, *in a highly innocent manner,* saying that he is in love with her and that she is his betrothed. He himself pretends to take all this as a joke. (His image of himself is that of an extraordinary man, and once when this was remarked in his presence, he felt flattered.) But actually he is in love, but he conceals this fact; yet he burns his finger and frightens the heroine terribly. At the same time he has vowed himself to implacable hatred. The uncle gets married (he proposes), for he regards all the jesting about the love affair between the Idiot and the heroine as having no significance. He is the first to take it as a joke.

He worships the Idiot.

N.B. Perhaps like this: the Idiot rouses the hostility of the heroine (already engaged) to the uncle (the general), and speaks ill of the heroine to the uncle. On the eve of the wedding the heroine runs away with the Idiot. The Idiot flaunts his capital. Sofia Fyodorovna. The uncle contributes 300,000. "Let the Idiot marry her." The Idiot proudly returns the money. The heroine behaves tenderly to him. She is half triumphant.

The Idiot confesses to her that he has hated her and that he has wanted to avenge himself on her by putting her in this situation. But now that he sees she will perhaps love him, he is ready to give his life to her, but if on the other hand she is going to deceive him, he will take her life also. Seized with fright, the heroine abandons everything and runs to the general's. (The uncle has married Umetskaia at the engineer's house.) The general proposes and marries her.

The finale of the Idiot.

The Idiot has a mother and an aunt, Sofia Fyodorovna. The interview. The funeral of Sofia Fyodorovna. He is her heir.

N.B. The general's son (the brother) had already met the heroine abroad (though without admitting this). He did not take her away from his father. The heroine has run away from the Idiot.

This manuscript page corresponds to pp. 66–67, beginning with the date "18 October" and "[Nota bene.] (For the definitive plan.)" and ending with the words "but even asked his advice." This manuscript page has, in beautifully calligraphed letters centered about one-third of the way down, the words "Plan for Iago," pointing to Dostoevsky's brief consideration of the Idiot's character along Iago's lines.

Beside himself, the general challenges the Idiot to a duel. The latter laughs at him and declines. (Or else he lets the general fire at him, while he himself refrains from firing.) He gives up the heroine to his brother because *he despises* a love that is not total. He remains single. Umetskaia lives with him.

He challenges the son (his brother). "Marry her now if you like." On learning of *the son's* deed, the uncle acknowledges him, makes him his heir, and asks him to marry the heroine. The son agrees, amazing the Idiot by his lack of squeamishness. The family council at the uncle's. His confession. The uncle dies. The Idiot takes Umetskaia to live with him. "She is the only one who loves me."

Develop the relationship between the two brothers.

He and Olga Umetskaia (*the decapitated heads*).

22 October

Especially nota bene. Early autumn.

In the railway carriage. The general, the family (the fiancée or young wife). The beauty.—The son. They meet for the first time in their lives. Recognition. The general likes him, they get acquainted, and want to continue the acquaintance. They promise to be in Petersburg in the autumn. The general tells a story *about the brother*. (At the station. Cigars.) From his point of view. He outlines his character and explains it. 1½ million. [The beauty.]

The natural son. He is traveling with the son. They get acquainted. The natural son knows that the other is also a son. The latter has only heard it said that there is a natural son. He is timid and morose on meeting the general's family. Incident. He is hit on the head. He keeps in the background, where he is unnoticed. They all say: "How odd he is!" The son: "Yes, but he doesn't seem to me to be stupid. He is odd, that's true." "He's a regular *yurodivyi*."[6] Again they meet in the railway carriage. The son and the natural son. The latter does not confide in the son but draws him out instead.

They meet at the uncle's. "How reserved you are." However, the natural son would like to make himself attractive to the son, and he does attract him.

---

6 *Yurodivyi*: an untranslatable word meaning literally "foolish" or "cracked," a beggarly and weak-minded devotee, sometimes rendered as "God's fool," "a fool in Christ," or even "a religious maniac."

Thereafter the uncle. Disgust. Petersburg. Sofia Fyodorovna. The engineer. [He fetches Umetskaia at Sofia Fyodorovna's.]

The son's aunt. Umetskaia. Sketch in the character of the natural son.

The relations between the uncle and the son. (Incident.) The son's observations. [They set fire to the house.]

The general and the family. The uncle. The son. (Incident with the Idiot.) The uncle takes the Idiot to the brother's.

Success at the general's. Scene at the house with the uncle. [He is very enigmatic.]

A long time before he made his appearance at the general's, the Idiot placed Umetskaia in the general's household. (The lawsuit. To the son, apropos of the lawsuit.)

By the son's arrangement, the Idiot without undue haste presents himself to the general. The latter says to the son: "You remember this young man at the station?" The others beg the uncle, "Bring him here, bring him here!"

For some time Umetskaia has been reporting everything *to him*. (She is naïve, not very intelligent. Big-hearted.)

The Idiot is wholly sincere in all his suspicions and errors. He is entirely convinced that the uncle and the rest hate him. Sofia Fyodorovna.

?N.B.? Though the Idiot has slandered the son, still, oddly, the son is *ingenuous* (Fedia) and the Idiot is more and more taken with this ingenuousness. And finally by the gentleness with which the son forgives him. The Idiot *grows enamored* with the son, though he laughs at himself. *The heroine* is in love with the son, who is oblivious of it. "The Idiot slandered him." Intrigue. The Idiot surrenders the heroine to him. (His struggle with generosity; the passion of friendship is almost stronger than his love.)

The theme of the 1st Part: the unmasking of the Idiot's heart. His increasing hatred.

The plot as a whole: the uncle is glad that after 4 years his son, the son of his flesh, is being embraced by everyone. But the Idiot is *apparently* pretending to be an idiot. The uncle's despair. At the general's the Idiot *triumphantly* shows that he is not an idiot, as if what he wanted was *to feed his vanity* on this futile triumph over the uncle.

Moreover: the relations between the Idiot and the son. The evident struggle in his heart and the ardor of his feelings. His feelings

die down; except for Umetskaia, his relations with them all are iron-
ical.

His attitude to Sofia Fyodorovna and to his own shame.

He took the money and lent it out on pledges. *Hatred.*

His daydreams about the general and the handsome son, dreams
without any object, yet they become the crux of his existence, as a
simile of his social relations with the rest of society. Pride. He visits
the general's family and watches them superciliously.

The dead.—

On the eve of her wedding to the uncle, the beauty proposes to
the son (on the Idiot's advice) that he take her away. The son refuses
in horror.

In the beginning he tries to harden himself by hatred and strenu-
ous scheming. But then he slackens. *Anguish:* he does not believe
in the heroine's love. Not until the end does he himself catch fire.

He says of the uncle: "What a strange man."

But he gives in to his brother and ends in despair and *anguish.*

Essential points in the 1st Part

N.B. bene

The railway carriage. Getting acquainted. (The incident.) Conversation. Friendship is born. The encounter with the general's family. Romantic assumptions on the part of the two young twenty-two-
year-old men. Clash with the general and his wife. (A prank.) When
he meets the general, he finds out who his companion is. From the
son he finds out everything about Sofia Fyodorovna. He restrains
himself and keeps silence. The son is rather frank. (About young
people, the new society, and so forth.)

Furthermore: the Idiot *has been deeply impressed* by the beauty
and by the general and his wife. A fleeting expression on his face.
The son says, speaking of him to the general: "He is so queer."

Petersburg. The uncle. Their second coming together. Kosten-
kinych and his wife. About Sofia Fyodorovna. He resents them all.
"He is an absolute Idiot."—The uncle. The uncle and the son. The
Idiot is already dining at another table. The uncle and the Idiot.
Again the uncle and the son. Strange scenes.

The Idiot and Sofia Fyodorovna. The Idiot seeks out the son.
"You're a sly one." But the son is always like that with him. "Either
he is so haughty that he despises me or else he is very foolish, that

This manuscript page corresponds to pp. 70–73, beginning with the words "The theme of the 1st part" and ending with "the uncle marries Umetskaia." The page is a good example of Dostoevsky's neat untidiness. The vertical material is evenly lined, even when it has to skirt the head of the gentleman. The head of the gentleman in the center of the page bears a slightly caricatured resemblance to Dostoevsky himself. Male heads and Gothic churches are the characteristic subject matter of Dostoevsky's drawings.

is, sincere." The son takes him to the aunt's. He introduces him to the engineer. The Jumper. Umetskaia. [With Umetskaia. The fire. About Sofia Fyodorovna: "I don't respect myself." Scenes about the penknives.]

The son is sad. The Idiot makes him confess that he has quarreled with the uncle. "I don't need his money if he has . . . . my mother." He is being very serious *sans que cela paraisse.*[7] He begins to like the son. (The uncle finds out about this, and questions him about how it happened.)

The general in Petersburg. The son's remarks about the general and the beauty. (He was impressed.) The son says in talking with the uncle at the general's: "He is absolutely not an idiot." The uncle is amazed. "Bring him to us." He goes to the general's. He lays his plans. He wants to be taken for an idiot. The reception at the general's. The uncle is amazed. Subsequent scenes, and so forth. It seems to the Idiot that they are all laughing at him. Envy, wealth, and revenge, and so on.

Finale. (He surrenders her to the son after the uncle marries Umetskaia.) A unique plot. The first signature.[8]

---

7 *Sans que cela paraisse:* "without appearing to be so."

8 Signature: *Russky vestnik,* the monthly review in which *The Idiot* was published, was composed of sixteen-page signatures or "sheets." Dostoevsky was paid by the signature, and he constantly measured his progress on a novel by estimating the number of signatures completed or planned. Thus he reckoned here that the plan so far laid out would come to one signature.

The Fourth Plan

(Written in the latter part of October and the beginning of November, 1867. The dates in the manuscript are October 27, 29, 30, and November 1.)

Dostoevsky refers to this plan in the opening lines as the "unique plan." The cast of characters is essentially the same as in the third plan, but these changes are important: the handsome youth is now named Ganechka; the Idiot is back in the general's household, as is Olga Umetskaia, who is now some kind of relative. Ganechka (diminutive for Gania), as the handsome youth, has had a role from the first plan. He has consistently been adored by his mother, courted the heroine, and unworthily rejected her, usually for monetary reasons. In this plan he receives not only a new name, but also a new character. The character of Ganechka–handsome youth was previously vague, prudential, and self-seeking; now it becomes Christian, forgiving, and virtuous. Dostoevsky seems intent on giving these qualities to someone, and up to now he has given them largely to the uncle's son. He describes Ganechka this way: "*Ganechka.* Pure, beautiful, virtuous, strict, very nervous, with a profoundly Christian, compassionate lovingness. He is anguished because of this, for, despite his *ardent compassion,* he is sensible, devoted to his duty, and unshakable in his convictions. In his ideas he is neither profound nor arrogant, though intelligent; he is well educated and reflective. But *feeling* dominates his nature. He lives by feelings. He lives ardently and passionately. In a word his is a Christian nature." Dostoevsky adds later: "(Ganechka, too, must be made the most charming, gentle, and strong personality throughout the novel.)" Gania in the novel is anything but this: he is, in the first part of the finished version, vain, proud, vengeful, weak, and self-seeking, and toward the end of the novel, petty and plotting. This is another example of the fact that names and qualities live in these notes in a fluid relationship. Ganecha's qualities here are Myshkin's in the final version, and some of the Idiot's qualities here are Gania's in the final version.

The plot remains essentially unchanged. The general's family continues to suffer financial hardship and the economic situation continues to hover about the romantic situation without adequate justification. The Idiot, the uncle, the uncle's son, Ganechka, and the general continue to sue for the heroine's hand, with the same predictable and indecisive results. One might note that the general has progressively become more prominent in the romantic situation. Up to now he has been the cause of the financial disarray of the family, largely because of his degenerate and somewhat pathetic character. In this plan Dostoevsky attempts to make him stronger and more important. He is tormented because he must depend on the family for his upkeep and because he is "a harsh, despotic, gloomy, passionate character." In the third plan the Idiot had accused him, with some justification, of being in love with his ward. Now it is clear that he is in love with the heroine, and his love is both a mark of shame to him and an obstacle to Ganechka's wooing of her. He finally comes to view his love for the heroine "with consternation," while the family regards it with horror. If the general, as seems probable, is an early model of General Ivolgin in the final version, this bypath leads nowhere. But, as we shall see, Dostoevsky will return to the stronger general and his illicit passion more than once in the notes that follow.

The Idiot's role in this plan overshadows everyone else's, and indeed the plot itself. Dostoevsky seems to be tiring of repeating again and again the variations on the heroine's spiteful abandoning of her suitors. He seems to sense that he is not getting anywhere and to sense that the trouble lies in the Idiot's character. The Idiot continues to play the intriguing, plotting, almost prankish Iago-role of the third plan. He urges the uncle to become reconciled with his son and yet incites one against the other; he opens the heroine's eyes to the diplomat's (Ganechka's?) attention to other women; and he kills the general by revealing that the general is in love with the heroine: "He *tortures* the uncle, he tyrannizes over the general's

wife, *and surrounds the heroine* with a web of intrigues, all for fun."
He is seeking a "causeless" revenge on everyone, possibly because
"He himself, furthermore, was brought up outrageously among tyrants." He continues proudly to disdain the money the uncle gives
or offers him to marry the heroine. He sets fire to a house with
Umetskaia, shames her (possibly the rape repeated so often), and
burns his finger, presumably as some test of his love for the heroine.
The main line of action in the novel is the following: "seeing that
he can make no headway with the heroine, he rouses them all against
her, the uncle, the son, the father. Revenge, but of a vaudeville kind,
and *sudden* passion." But true love lies in the shadow of his vengeful
love: "N.B. All the time he did not love her, all the time he hated
her, he only wanted to avenge himself on her. But as soon as he
carried her off, he fell in love with her."

Dostoevsky seems intent on formulating the main idea of the
novel, and the main idea seems to lie hidden in the recesses of the
Idiot's character. He tells us unhelpfully: "N.B. *The entire novel
is built on the struggle between love and hate.*" And of the Idiot,
he says: "N.B. *Boundless pride and boundless hate.*" More helpfully,
he tries again: "*The chief idea of the novel:* how much strength,
how much passion, in contemporary youth, yet they are unbelievers.
Boundless idealism together with boundless sensuality." The Idiot,
the embodiment of the younger generation, has a boundless desire
for life that has been frustrated by aimlessness, by distortions of love
(sensuality), and by restlessness. Dostoevsky attempts to account for
the distortions in the following way: "As a child he ought to have
had more beauty, more impressions of loveliness, more encompassing
love, a better bringing-up. But now, though he has a thirst *for beauty
and the ideal, at the same time he has no belief in the ideal,* or rather,
he does have belief but no love for the ideal."

Dostoevsky continues, perhaps now even more energetically, to
seek for some kind of redemptive act, some regeneration of the Idiot.
He seems to sense instinctively that he needs a purified character,
but he seems unable to effect the transformation. He has not found
the lever by which he can turn the proud, cynical, hating, volup-

tuary, and later bored, aimless, restless, prankish Idiot into a purified and regenerated hero. But he tries in this plan by detailed outlines such as the one that follows to take the Idiot through vengeful self-love and passion to a lofty and redeeming love:

> Dominating all these characters is the Idiot, an anguished, contemptuous, endlessly proud personality who delights in his own superiority and others' worthlessness, he hates and despises his success and his pleasure to the point of loathing, *in the end he is agonized by his own role,* and suddenly he perceives a solution in love.
>
> In the beginning:
>
> 1) Revenge and self-love (a *causeless* revenge, he himself sees this, and that it is *characteristic* of him).
>
> Then:
>
> 2) Frenzied and merciless passion.
>
> 3) Lofty love and regeneration.

But the alchemy refuses to work, and the vengeful and passionate Idiot stubbornly refuses to become the purified lover. Dostoevsky schematically expresses the translation from one to the other, but his dramatic instinct apparently continued to balk at producing another Raskolnikov nudged improbably from hate to love.

List of Characters for the Fourth Plan

The General's Family

The general
His wife
His son Ganechka
The Idiot
The daughter Masha
The heroine, a ward
Olga Umetskaia

Levinka
Kostenka

The Uncle's Family

The uncle
His son
Kostenkinych, the shop assistant

The Engineer's Family

The engineer, Masha's fiancé
His mother, aged

The Strong-minded Mother's Family

The mother
Her daughter

Main points

27 October ~~November~~

Ganechka.[1] A unique character. A unique plot.

The general's son by his first wife. He is hated by the whole family. *He has grown up at a distance from them.* He makes his appearance in the family. He hates them all, chiefly the heroine.

An episode with the general's wife; he is unjustly turned out of the house. (A tale.)

The uncle takes notice of him. He has no respect for the uncle. *The uncle* invites him. They get acquainted. The general offers the Idiot a distinguished post; the latter declines and takes a clerk's job. Indignation.

The Idiot makes friends with the uncle's son. The uncle's son is in love with the heroine. He takes the Idiot into his confidence. The caricature of the general's wife. He leaves the house. Ganechka.

More and more the Idiot astounds the uncle. He will not accept any money.

---

[1] Ganechka: written calligraphically, as it is in the heading that soon follows; this is the first time the name appears—the only proper name in this notebook besides Ptitsyn that is retained in the published text.

He urges him to be reconciled with the son and at the same time he incites the one against the other.

He astounds the father. The father comes to see him.

The heroine and the diplomat. The diplomat courts now one girl and now another. The Idiot opens the heroine's eyes. The lawsuit is lost.

They intend her for the senator. The senator loses out. She is in love with the uncle's son. She refuses the diplomat. The diplomat sells her off to the uncle.

Ganechka

The uncle proposes. The son cannot press his suit because the Idiot has convinced him that the uncle is in love with her.

(The whole trouble between the son and the uncle originates entirely from the fact that the son insists that his father acknowledge that his mother is indeed his mother; each of the two is prodding the other's pride, but it is mainly the Idiot who under the guise of friendship has prevented them from being reconciled.)

When the general insists that the diplomat fulfil his promise, the Idiot advises the latter to say that the general himself is in love.

Family scene.

On learning that the uncle has proposed, the son goes into hiding.

The heroine is furious, she is in the Idiot's hands (the finger has already been burned). He gives the uncle his promise.

Melancholy, sadness, fury. On the eve of the wedding she runs away with the Idiot.

The general says to the Idiot: "Marry her!" The uncle gives money. "To the devil with the money." He is alone. He torments the heroine with his frenzied, passionate love.

The main points. N.B.

The uncle has long been on special terms with Umetskaia. Along with the Idiot, she set fire to the house, the Idiot shames her. The uncle wants to marry Umetskaia. He has a liver attack and dies.

He sets the heroine free on learning that she does not love him.

He takes Umetskaia, gives back the uncle's money.

N.B. All the time he did not love her, all the time he hated her, he only wanted to avenge himself on her. But as soon as he carried her off, he fell in love with her.

He released her out of generosity (pride and disdain). He released her to the son. Umetskaia gave her fortune to the son.

The main line of action in the novel: seeing that he can make no headway with the heroine, he rouses them all against her, the uncle, the son, the father. Revenge, but of a vaudeville kind, and *sudden* passion.

The 18-year-old brother devoted himself to him.

2nd Signature

In surrendering her to the son, the Idiot does not ask any gratitude. His pride alienates him from them all.

N.B. He has a terrible love for the son. A queer passion.

N.B. Queerest of all, he loves the uncle too.

N.B. *The entire novel is built on the struggle between love and hate.*

One example of the young generation, a man in process of development.

N.B. He says at the finale: "In everyone's eyes I am a criminal, but there's no one I have to beg pardon from."

N.B. *Boundless pride and boundless hate.*

The chief idea of the novel: how much strength, how much passion, in contemporary youth, yet they are unbelievers. Boundless idealism together with boundless sensuality.

Notes. *Well, now there opens up a new path.* What is to come now?

(To be inserted into the conversations between the uncle and the son.)

1. He cheats and schemes, yet throughout the entire novel he regards this as petty and mean on his part. At moments he reflects that in the abstract *it would be better to forgive but that this would not cost him much* and would not be anything to be proud of, everything would remain as before, and that therefore he might as well go on with the *vaudeville* (he himself called all this a vaudeville), he is depressed and wearied. [He burns his finger, but then he says, "You will pay me for this. *Le jeu ne valait pas la chandelle.*"[2] The roots of passion were in him, but as yet he did not love.]

---

[2] *Le jeu ne valait pas la chandelle:* "The game wasn't worth the candle."

He himself puts the question to himself: "Is it really revenge that motivates him? How silly if so! On what should he avenge himself? Especially since no one has perpetrated so tragic an outrage on him, yes, people are too commonplace. Well, uncle perhaps, a funny fellow, amusing, at any rate. I might go visit him."

He chats with the uncle about various things, about a suicide pact, about Christ. Out of boredom he sets fire to the house and rapes Umetskaia. The uncle and Umetskaia.

Ergo: the whole problem lies in this, that a nature as powerful and as frustrated (with a bent for love and revenge) has a need for life, for passion, for a goal proportionate to his strength; and *that is why* in the end, having dropped the vaudeville, *that is, having carried off the heroine* in hatred, he suddenly sees that the heroine is yielding herself to him, she caresses him and promises love. In a flash he catches fire, he sends them all packing and renounces the money. But the heroine is terrified of his passion, of what may come of it. In grief and disenchantment, she abandons him.

As a child he ought to have had more beauty, more impressions of loveliness, more encompassing love, *a better bringing-up.* But now, though he has a thirst *for beauty and the ideal, at the same time he has no belief in the ideal,* or rather, he does have belief but no love for the ideal. Even the demons believe, and tremble.

Memento: the chief point of the novel is the uncle and the son, those two characters.

Memento

The Idiot is received at the aunt's house because he is the uncle's favorite.

29 October 1867   Notes[3]

Psychological points and divisions of the novel

The very beginning. The Idiot is waiting expectantly and anxiously, as if there were something he had to do. He bestirs himself energetically and thus drives his sadness away by deluding himself. (N.B. As if he had a goal, though he has none.)

He is very disturbed by the general and his wife, and by the hero-

---

[3] This annotation appears in the handwriting of Dostoevsky's widow, Anna Grigorievna: "I gave this notebook of F. M. D. to my grandchildren, Fyodor and Andrei Dostoevsky, on 28 January 1909."

ine—not because he had any aspirations toward a career or any love for the heroine, but because of a feeling of *combativité*. He is especially interested in the son and questions him (though the son makes a certain impression on him). From the moment he arrived he has been deceiving the uncle—without being aware of it, he has become his enemy—though with no particular purpose. Sofia Fyodorovna, and so forth.

At the general's house he scores a triumph (but at the same time he is ashamed of this triumph). Then solemn conversations with the uncle, then *an escapade and a scene,* then the burned finger, the heroine, then trouble, then the house is set on fire, and Umetskaia is raped.

Afterwards a sudden total apathy. Why? To what end? He does not even *dream* of the heroine, he does not even *desire* her.

Le jeu ne vaut pas la chandelle.

He closes his door to everyone and wanders about endlessly. The uncle goes out to find him. Suicide.

And that's how he got into all this mess because he had nothing to do. He *tortures* the uncle, he tyrannizes over the general's wife, *and surrounds the heroine with a web of intrigues, all for fun.* But this game costs him dear. Suddenly, jealousy. So as not to fall into the clutches of the son, he turns to the uncle. Love.

And then all at once, the heroine is in love with him. Frenzy, madness.

The end of a great soul.

The three stages of love: revenge and self-love, passion, a loftier love. Man becomes purified.

N.B. He subjugates the uncle to the point of enslavement and crazy fanaticism.

He torments Levinka.[4]

He subjugates the general and torments him by suggesting that he is in love.

He completely dominates the general's wife.

The engineer, the diplomat—they are all in his hands.

N.B. Draw the son in sharper outline. ~~The son cools toward him. But he warms to the son.~~

N.B. The uncle's main concern is *the son.*

He constantly complains and takes counsel of the Idiot.

---

[4] Levinka: the diminutive form of Lyov (Leo), the name later given to Prince Myshkin.

Also, the son does not accept the money.

He made the son suffer by the way he brought him up.

Or else: they are all virtuous, highminded, and magnanimous, but unjust to him. He is a natural child. They are especially kind to him. This rouses hatred in him.

Periods.

The general—a well-known character. Has hopes from the uncle. His wife—of good family. He installs the elder son with the senator, and so on. Looks after his career. The Idiot was always considered an Idiot. Envy and pride.

The uncle.

The ward.

The daughter Masha <illegible>.

The engineer.

The general's debts.

Where does the Idiot come from? (They all give him to understand that he is a burden to them.)

"In our house no victuals can be had for nothing." The Idiot arrives from somewhere with a letter from his godmother's heirs; she was the old woman he used to live with in the country because people did not like him, and she had died without making any will. He had been living idly, reading a great deal. For some time the heirs had kept him on, then had sent him <to Petersburg> (demanding money), setting forth his good qualities; he was contesting <the will>.

The general was expected to arrive from somewhere; in his household there was an upheaval brewing.

The character of the elder son: sensible, egotistical, with poetic inclinations, his mother's pet, vain.

The ward possesses 200,000 rubles.

A typical mother, and a daughter who is her mother's pet.

N.B. The novel begins half a year before the Idiot's arrival. The whole situation is already outlined, with all the hostilities . . . . (in dramatic form).

The Idiot keeps his silence. The kind of job he had—in the story.

He has insulted the mother. He has insulted the brother's fiancée.

They are awaiting the uncle—their last hope. The uncle decides to visit them.

The engineer's tricks.

"Well, I've got a whip."—At the uncle's house. Kostenkinych writes papers.

N.B.? (Levinka had robbed the engineer.—The Idiot has *his own* money, is in trade) *not needed.*

When they drive him out because of the ward, he declares his love to her and burns his finger.

The beginning. An upheaval is imminent at any moment, they are all upset, everyone resents everyone else. About the engineer's story. *The Idiot prepares to accuse* the general of being in love with her. He tells her that they are keeping her on because of the legacy. The lawsuit is lost.

30 October

Initial theme

The family.

The general. A harsh, despotic, gloomy, passionate character. He has just been in court. Has lost everything through his own fault, because of his petty wilfulness, which intensifies rather than lessens, the worse the circumstances become. Deals with his creditors. Wants to keep his family in despotic and enslaved subjection. *A figure out of times past.* He himself sees that the old ways are no longer possible. He depends on the family in a material sense, and this is his torment. He conceals his gratitude under a stern severity, though *in reality* he loves them and is grateful! He protects the ward, and only toward the end, when the lawsuit has been lost, do the mother and son suspect him, with horror. He finally realizes with consternation that he is in love with the ward. His relations with the brother.

The general's wife. Likewise a despotic character, but she silently bows to circumstances. Not without magnanimity. Everything is for Ganechka. She tries to persuade him to another marriage (Ganechka will have none of it), she is awaiting the outcome of the lawsuit. Being the Idiot's persecutor, she detests him. (Especially because of the uncle's sympathy for him.) In her own way she courts the uncle.

Ganechka. Pure, beautiful, virtuous, strict, very nervous, with a profoundly Christian, compassionate lovingness. He is anguished because of this, for, despite his *ardent compassion,* he is sensible, devoted to his duty, and unshakable in his convictions. In his ideas he is neither profound nor arrogant, though intelligent; he is well educated and reflective. But *feeling* dominates his nature. He lives by feelings. He lives ardently and passionately. In a word, his is a Christian nature. He loves the Idiot and forgives him, but does not agree with him. *At moments* the Idiot loves him passionately, but *in general* he is spiteful, sneering, obdurate, and rejects him. The idea that the general is in love—this in the main is what inhibits him. *Still only an unofficial fiancé.* In a fit of rage ~~passion~~ the heroine *herself* rejects him. She runs away from the uncle with the Idiot, and so forth. Charming—gay—high-spirited—a frivolous and fascinating character.

The Idiot. The child of a prior marriage. From the country. Well educated—he hides everything. Breaks down the despotism by his insubordination. Pierces the general's heart; insults the general's wife. Loves the heroine, but considers himself unworthy of her and therefore he hates her. N.B. He hates her without being able to explain it. He plots and slanders. He has opened Ganechka's eyes and also the general's wife's eyes to the general and his love. Though he had no standing when he entered the family, he dominates them all. The heroine is struck by his love. His magnanimity in the Levinka affair impresses her. Then she grows afraid of him [? invent].—N.B. At first the Idiot incites a rebellion in the family. When he arrives, he perceives merely a nascent desire to rebel, but then he himself instigates revolt on his own account. Then he becomes everyone's confidant. He exerts an ascendancy over Ganechka. N.B. He simply wants to ruin the heroine; he discovers that he is in love with her quite by chance, after the flight.

The uncle. A well-known personality. Marries Umetskaia.

The Idiot surrenders the heroine to the brother. He becomes intimate with Umetskaia. N.B. *He knew her before in the country.* *The general* dies. (N.B. If he is to be drawn as a happy person, then he must be made a noble one, with magnanimous and charming attributes.)

(Ganechka, too, must be made the most charming, gentle, and strong personality throughout the novel.)

The engineer, Masha, Levinka, the old mother, the Idiot's parents [the Umetskys], Ganechka's employers, the senator, the diplomat, and *the incident?????*

The main theme of the novel:

Dominating all these characters is the Idiot, an anguished, contemptuous, endlessly proud personality who delights in his own superiority and others' worthlessness; he hates and despises his success and his pleasures to the point of loathing; *in the end he is agonized by his own role,* and suddenly he perceives a solution in love.

In the beginning:

1) Revenge and self-love (a *causeless* revenge, he himself sees this, and that it is *characteristic* of him).

Then:

2) Frenzied and merciless passion.

3) Lofty love and regeneration.

N.B. (After her flight he installs the heroine with his relatives, *the Idiot's relatives?* N.B.)

Notes for the theme of *30 October.*

1) When the uncle comes to the Idiot and says that he remembers a great deal and that revenge certainly. . . . . . .

The Idiot replies that he has *nothing* to avenge himself for and *no one* on whom to wreak revenge (his characteristic).

He himself, furthermore, was brought up outrageously among tyrants. He had known Umetskaia, *one of his own kind.* (Was he brought up by his relatives?)

2) The general is a man who has been struck to the heart in his self-esteem.

Wounded in what is best in him. A despot, paradoxical, unjust, stoical, chivalrously honest, gloomy, violent. Never manages to overcome what lies within him, he feels this, and acts to excess in everything, a trait from which he suffers all his life. The idea instilled and developed by the Idiot that he is in love with the heroine kills him.

3) In the beginning, as before, *the general and all of them* were living in brilliance and glory. At that time they tormented (?) and repudiated the Idiot. Now, *at the beginning of the novel,* he appears among them at a moment when they are being humiliated.

4) The novel begins with the family wrestling with huge difficulties and with the Idiot's arrival.

5) The general *and the family extricate themselves from those difficulties* successfully enough to live better and *entertain.* Masha *wants* to give lessons, against the wish of the whole family.

6) The Idiot allies himself with the diplomat (proposes the heroine for him), attends an evening party of the ~~Grand-Monde~~ at which the general and his wife are present. A remarkable evening, the brilliance of the Idiot, the marvel of all, especially the heroine. But the general takes offense and drives the Idiot out. The latter out of revenge but *mainly out of jealousy* pushes the heroine at the diplomat. (Or else he does so for the sake of spying, because the heroine is in the senator's good graces and is flirting with the diplomat. The general's jealousy on this account.—The Idiot is carrying on all these intrigues.)

7) The general and the senator are long-standing enemies dating from the time when they were in service, and they bait each other.

8) He pushes the heroine toward the diplomat out of *secret* jealousy. He would like (paroxysm) to cover the heroine with shame, make her a whore.

9) The uncle's high esteem for him, formerly the uncle's secretary. He masters and subjugates the uncle and rules over him out of *pleasure in ruling him.* But the uncle moves him by his affection. The confrontation and struggle of the two characters. A crazy, jealous, and lunatic friendship.

(Explain and delineate *more precisely and more clearly.*)

10) The episode of the fire, the finger, the rape, everything happens abruptly and, as it were, unexpectedly. So as to show in the novel what the Idiot is capable of.

N.B. Without explanation.

Ganechka has a very good post, this has to be appreciated.

The general has been traveling in the province. He recently returned. In his absence, signs of rebellion.

Debts (4,000 rubles), "Get them wherever you like," to the brother.

The uncle won't give 4,000 rubles. But will give 100 rubles a month. Insulting to the general. "Don't accept." A scandal in the family on this account. The Idiot turns up. Levinka's 4,000 disappear. They drive the Idiot out of the house. Scandal (disrespect to the general's wife). On the family's urging him to do so, the general agrees to accept the 100 rubles a month.

The special relations between the general's wife and the uncle. They taunt each other incessantly.

The general's relations with the engineer. The general's fury.

The general returns and *he himself* brings the Idiot with him. This is how the novel begins. A letter had come beforehand saying that he would return with the Idiot.

In his absence the general's wife had embarked on dealings with the uncle. (The heroine's lawsuit.)

On the general's return they decided to conceal from him the fact that they were receiving 100 rubles a month from the uncle. The uncle often visits them. The general decides to go to him in the morning and request 15,000, then 4,000, rubles.

1 November

Impromptu. Matters progress. The downfall.

The evening party at the general's wife's. Ganechka and the

mother. "Don't marry, don't get engaged." She quizzes him: "Didn't you propose to her?" Noble response on Ganechka's part. The mother weeps. He comforts her, about the father and about the rebellion. Incidentally, about Masha and the engineer. The Idiot is listening in a corner. The engineer's letter about the label, he urges them to send the Idiot away. (Levinka)—Kostenka, who had arrived bringing the heroine, whom he is pursuing, says that the senator is in love with her; then he leaves. At the gate Levinka is waiting for him. Young people's talk. They come to an understanding. They threaten the Idiot with the uncle. Ganechka says a few words to him (with all respect) reproaching him for pretending to be an Idiot. Though the mother declares that he is pretending to be one, at the same time she treats him like an idiot. *Embarras de richesses* in reproaches and accusations. Masha's rudeness as she passes through the room. Masha and the engineer at their place. Fruits.

Everyone is in an uproar because the general is soon to be there. At this point the heroine is announced.

The uncle arrives. The mother's frankness is a fraud. Outpourings and tears. The 100 rubles a month, in secret from the general; about his imminent arrival, his misfortunes, and his despotism. The mother behaves meltingly to the uncle. The special elegance of the general's prestige. (In passing: recapitulation of the family's relations with the uncle.) About the engineer and the Idiot. Full account. The engineer asks to be allowed to present his respects (how did he, not by letter?). The engineer appears and complains. Stories about the Idiot. *"I have a whip here."* The heroine goes away. The engineer leaves with heightened politeness and indignation and with a deep respect for the uncle. The uncle is disturbed on the heroine's account, conversation about the heroine. The heroine's story and her relations with the family. The uncle prepares to go home, suddenly the general.

N.B. *Interim.* (The Idiot sees the heroine off. Conversation. Encounter with Umetskaia and Levinka. He returns home.)

The general makes an appearance. An unexpected meeting with the brother. About the 100 rubles—concealed. He is firm and dignified, but flattered. The uncle hastens to leave. The engineer says goodbye. Masha, the son, and the Idiot. The whole family in conclave; the general: "Yes, I've lost everything. How is one to eat. But I don't want to lose my authority." In a few words he explains his material situation. To get hold of some money [the debts]. Finally, inquiries on the family's part: about the uncle, quickly. (They conceal the business about the 100 rubles), about the engineer and Masha.

The general's rage. He refuses. Masha's rebellion. The mother keeps silence. Ganechka intercedes. Piano lessons. Mashenka says: "I will get married, on my own." The general shouts that he insists on his authority, that though he is a beggar, still he will be master. Sarcastic sallies about the power of children. "I'll call in a midwife." About the Idiot. (P.S. The general has the idea that he has been unjust to the Idiot.) It was for the Idiot's sake that they called the uncle in.

(The Idiot's scene at the time of his rebellion.) Full account of the Idiot and the engineer. About the fact that the Idiot is disrespectful. The Idiot is—an Idiot. About Masha and the engineer.

Certainly the main business is about the heroine. Why did she become a governess. She herself didn't want to. She goes off to bed. About her pitiful situation. Might it not be possible to get some money.

The next day he is reconciled with Masha. A letter from the engineer.

About the general (details).

Ganechka and the heroine. The Idiot and Ganechka. (The poison begins to take effect.) ~~The Idiot.~~

The Idiot and his relatives. Umetskaia. Umetskaia's money is the Idiot's. Umetskaia's naïveté. Dreams. Kostenka and Levinka.

The Idiot at the uncle's. The uncle. (A strange character.) Relations with the Idiot. How the uncle saw the Idiot in the street with a picture. Kostenkinych; about the idea that he is not an Idiot.

Uproar about the 4,000. Stolen goods. The Idiot has money.

The general drives the Idiot out. So does the uncle.

Scenes with the Idiot and the uncle.

The Idiot and the general.

The Idiot and Ganechka.

The lawsuit is lost. Thunder in the house. He himself is in love. Discord. . . . . . .

1 November

No good.

The main idea as to the Idiot does not emerge.

Essential: that the Idiot should be the uncle's son.

The Fifth Plan

(*Written at the beginning of November, 1867. The following dates are found in the manuscript: November 1, 2, 3, and twice November 4.*)

The heroine's hysterical flights from suitor to suitor, a situation that dominated the early plans, are still present in these notes, but the emphasis is now on the Idiot's posture between two loves: the love for the heroine and the love for his wife. The Idiot was brought up by the Umetskys and married off to a girl who had already had a baby. Apparently the Umetskys believed they were deceiving him, but it turned out that he had known about the baby and had married the girl from compassion. His impulses toward his wife, however, are a mixture of anger and compassion, tenderness and cruelty. He torments her, confesses to her, loves her, and hates her.

His attitude toward the heroine is similar, but the reasons for his hate-love for her are different. The Idiot loves the heroine because others love her, because she is above him in station (she is perhaps a princess, whereas he is a Ptitsyn, the son of a moneylender), because she has mocked him, because she believes him to be despicable, and because for instants he really loves her and she him. "I never loved you," he tells her, "except with a hate-love." His love for his wife is different: it is based, apparently, on deep compassion and on her simplicity in accepting him wholly and without condition. He hates her because she is an obstacle to his career, because his marriage to her makes impossible a marriage to the heroine, and because he fears exposure and ridicule in being married to a woman who has borne the child of another man. Most of all he hates her because he feels compassion for her. Dostoevsky says of this love: "*Love for his wife and a rather naïve encounter: At first he informed himself about everything, then Umetskaia, then sternly, then little by little—but love, alternating with unconscious hatred.*"

The Idiot is poised between two kinds of love: vengeful love and purifying love. The wife sees him as good and as he wishes to be; the heroine sees him as despicable and as he fears to be. At moments he hates both: the mockery of the heroine because he hates himself as he fears to be and the love of the wife because he fears the burden of being what he wishes to be. He wants and does not want to be loved. If we look for an analogue in the final version of the novel, we will not find it in Myshkin placed between Nastasia Filipovna and Aglaia; nor even—though we would be closer—in Myshkin between Nastasia Filipovna and the Swiss girl Marie. Rather, the analogue is to be found in Nastasia Filipovna herself, because it is she—like Myshkin here—who is torn between the brutal and passionate love of Rogozhin and the purifying love of Myshkin; and she is fearful of both for analogous reasons.

The two loves act on the Idiot in this way: "In the beginning he courted the heroine and made himself attractive to her (just the sort of travesty he played with the uncle), then he renounced the heroine because he was falling in love with his wife, being moved by his immense compassion for her. But he torments her. He struggles with himself. He torments the heroine as well, because she cannot belong to him." He revenges himself on both of them, and sometimes on himself, and at least once on the innocent Umetskaia: "He torments his wife. (Her redoubled mockery at first. He burned his finger and took revenge for this reason.) N.B. *After the burned finger,* he raped Umetskaia ~~the heroine~~." The consequences are even more serious: he poisons his wife at one point (presumably in order to marry the heroine), and elsewhere in the notes his wife poisons herself, apparently from despair over his love of the heroine.

The Idiot is torn in love and hate between two women, and the loves objectify his double character: "The chief and paramount idea of the novel, on which everything hangs, is: namely, that he is filled with ~~and he sees with a mature mind all the paltriness of the people around him~~ morbid pride to such a degree that he cannot help considering himself a god, and yet *at the same time* he has so little esteem for himself (he analyzes himself with great clarity) that he cannot help despising himself intensely, infinitely, and unjustifiably. (At the same time he feels that for him to take blind revenge on everyone would be despicable, still, he acts like a scoundrel and he does take revenge.)" In the notes Dostoevsky speaks of *"The Dualism of a deep nature."* The Idiot wants useful activity, love, and compassion; he wants true pride and to do a beautiful deed, but he is always plagued by the "tongue in the mirror," an enigmatic expression standing apparently for the self-irony that corrupts his good impulses. He is drawn to compassion and true love for his wife, but he cannot help turning it into torment and cruelty. Similarly, something in his soul turns love into hate, compassion into torment, true pride into false pride. The thirst for life becomes the hatred of life, and the desire for self-worth becomes the fact of self-will. He is driven to torment others and himself, and every motive turns into its opposite. He has boundless pride and self-contempt, and he wants to make everyone suffer, or he wants to suffer for them in death on the cross.

Sakulin, the Russian editor of these notes, repeats over and over again—as have some American commentators—that Dostoevsky was wrong to give Christian motives to a character who is as proud and self-willed and vengeful as the Idiot. There is no contradiction, or rather there is a contradiction, but precisely the kind that leads Dostoevsky into the most refined analysis of his characters' motives. The situation he is struggling with here is one that he will take up again in *The Adolescent, The Possessed,* and *The Brothers Karamazov.* Dostoevsky harbors the secret dream of a hero who can wrench himself out of the trap of turning love into hate, compassion into torment, and nobility into baseness.

Throughout the various plans, Dostoevsky has tried to explain the character and actions of the Idiot—as well as of other characters—by environmental factors: the Idiot has been hated by his mother, abandoned by both father and mother, mistreated in childhood, accused falsely of theft, mocked by the heroine and others. Most of these factors are restated in this section, perhaps a bit more forcefully, and some new ones are added. The Idiot is married off to a "fallen woman," and his mother leaves the uncle (the Idiot's father) for another man. According to one set of notes she lives in filth, poverty, vice; according to another set she hangs herself; and according to yet another she reconciles herself with the uncle. The added environmental factors explain very little, and one suspects that Dostoevsky never intended them to explain very much. In the novel itself he gives such explanations of motives to superficial minds, such as Radomsky's. The Idiot's motives can be described but not explained, not even by himself: "To domineer over them all, to triumph over them all, to take revenge on them all (but for what reason—unknown)." The Idiot suffers from an outraged heart, but in Dostoevsky's world—and in these notes—the heart outrages itself, baffling the reason and frustrating the will.

List of Characters for
the Fifth Plan

The General's Family

The general
The general's wife
His son Ganechka
A daughter
The heroine

The Uncle's Family

The uncle
The Idiot, his son
The Idiot's mother
The Jumper, the husband of the Idiot's mother
The Idiot's wife
The uncle's son
Kostenkinych
Sofia Fyodorovna, perhaps the Idiot's aunt

The Umetskys

Vladimir Umetsky, the father of the engineer
The engineer
Olga Umetskaia
Levinka
The consumptive son

The Idiot is the uncle's son. (*See* No. 1.) The notes at any rate.

The most important scene: the Idiot at the general's. The Idiot captivates everyone with his childish naïveté.

N.B. (Incident, the relatives, and so forth.)

2 November

The Idiot arrives, he is rather apathetic, aimless, sunk in grief. At first, *he rambles.*

In reality, there is a kind of anxiety in him, but even to himself this is an obscure *and vague* anxiety.—His *distrustful wariness* toward the son in the railway carriage, and moreover his *dissembling* to the uncle show that he has been reflecting a good deal and at length, in solitude, regarding his situation, and in general, *in the abstract,* he has taken steps with a view toward the future. But after taking the first steps he shows signs of anguish, a malignant consciousness of his egoism, a craving for self-assertion, and his pride. He wants to take *steps,* make a *career.* He envies the son. He speaks with hatred of the general to the son, and he can hardly imagine that he would ever be able to make a place for himself there. *The son tips him off about that.*

He visits his former relatives (from Kostenkinych he learns that they are in Petersburg and that Kostenkinych *had met them*). (He is an old friend of Umetskaia's.)—Natural children. The son discusses natural children with the father.

[N.B.? The figure of the uncle dominates everything. *This is the major point.*]

Sofia Fyodorovna. *His* mother hanged herself.

Several times Vl. Umetsky makes attempts on Umetskaia. So does the son.

At any rate:

Conversations between father and son.

N.B. Outspokenness as to the role of the moneylender, of the count, and so forth. Such frankness has always been disagreeable to the son, for the uncle always evinces a feeling of painful pride and an expectation of gratitude because of such frankness.

The son's conversations with the Idiot. The son *says of his father:* "He has always been a gloomy, strong personality. Now he is even gloomier and more voluble."

"The besetting sensitivity of an old woman," says the Idiot. The son defends the uncle—with dignity.

The son queries the Idiot as to a career. Conversation about usury.

The Idiot's conversations with the uncle. Though the uncle considers him an Idiot, still, on several occasions, *even before the general's arrival,* he had his doubts of him, and derisively he quizzes the Idiot with venomous disapproval.

The Idiot says to the son in response to the latter's broaching the subject of a career: "Probably you are interested in what share of the legacy I am claiming. Do you know, I am claiming nothing at all. I like to think that the uncle imagines that I need him, *that I live with him,* and therefore that I depend on him. Let him think so, let him think so."

The Idiot to the son regarding a career. The son: "How could you leave uncle?"

"With what resources? How?"

The Idiot: "That doesn't frighten me. I don't know. But one day uncle found himself alone on the sidewalk." (The son had already related the uncle's story *to the Idiot.*)

About the uncle and about usury.

????—*The Idiot's* ~~the son's~~ *attempts in the flea market.*

The enigmatic interview between the Idiot and Umetskaia.

Umetskaia: "I have my own money." (Stolen from the engineer.) They found the money at Umetskaia's. The Idiot took Umetskaia in. *Even before the general's arrival the Idiot had rented an apartment.*

[The Idiot's triumph at the general's was unexpected even to himself. He went there out of anxiety. But once there, inspiration. The scene with the general follows immediately after this. With Umetskaia. He slandered her. They set a fire.]

The next day after the visit to the general and his wife the uncle comes to him. About the King of the Jews. The uncle offers him everything and weeps. The latter laughs. About Umetskaia. After this, a little later, a conversation about suicide and marriage.—(The engineer had been robbed.)

The lawsuit having failed.—

N.B. (Here in the second Part it is indispensable to show somehow a clash between the general and the Idiot, their encounter at the son's?) (And the story of Levinka's theft.)—He allies himself with the general's wife.

He insinuates himself with the general.

Meanwhile—*Interim.*

The Idiot shuts himself up. Anguish. Torment. Delirium. Meet-

ings with the tenants, and so forth. (Story.) The death of Sofia Fyodorovna (the Idiot has some capital).

Last notation

The Jumper is a relative of the son's.

But the engineer's family (old Vl.) are distantly related to the Idiot.
Umetskaia is his sister (but by another father) ~~but by another mother~~.
Problems and enigmas.

Arrange it perhaps so that the Idiot's mother is still alive (character).

N.B.—The uncle has always despised the Idiot. He thinks that the
mother (is a trollop somewhere in the province). From <illegible>
the Idiot learns that his mother is in Petersburg.

The Idiot seeks out his mother, filth, horror, her character.

Or else: his mother has remarried. A strange family, impoverished.

The mother had actually run away from the uncle with a merchant, having abandoned the Idiot to the uncle. (But then she married an old civil servant. She looks after the old fellow.) But she
hides from the uncle. She has a daughter. Conversation with the
daughter about science. *The reasons why they are in Petersburg.*

"That's the merchant's son."

"Once I came very near marrying a prince."

N.B. *The main point.*

The old husband is a toper. He visits *the mother*. The Jumper ~~the
prince~~ supports her, this is where the engineer is, the relative of the
son. (Umetskaia is also with them.)

But if the Jumper, he protects the Idiot. He robs the engineer and
his family. But principally it is the merchant who comes to the
mother's (the merchant and the Jumper). He learns further that
through Kostenkinych the uncle is supporting them.

N.B. Without the Jumper, just the merchant, with the uncle's
assistance, while the Jumper hangs around out of a long-standing
habit.

Sofia Fyodorovna is there too.

But Umetskaia? That ~~family~~ among whom he was brought up.

The engineer is the son of Vl. Umetsky. They have a daughter,
Umetskaia, and a natural son. These are acquaintances of the uncle.
The Jumper belongs to the son's family (the engineer fiancé at the
Jumper's house). Levinka is there too, also a tuberculous old official.

T H E   I D I O T is the uncle's legitimate son and blood brother to the son, but he has been an outcast since childhood and has never seen the son. (Interesting young man.) He was brought up at the Umetskys. The son has his own family. (The son is the elder. The Idiot is the younger.) [Masha.]

2 November

Hurry up

He is the uncle's legitimate son, though he is unacknowledged. An Idiot. They married him off at the Umetskys. Then the uncle sent him to Switzerland. All his life the uncle has been struggling with this doubt: *Is he his* son or not? The Umetskys knew the answer to this. He got married in a special state of mind.

At the Umetskys he lived in a particular manner. He was in continual conflict with them and enjoyed seeing how they always gave way to him.

Switzerland—sad, gloomy. He used to read. Envy and malice.

The railway carriage, and so on, as before; the two brothers.

N.B. (Later): "Please let's say 'thou' to each other."

The elder son tortured by the uncle is on bad terms with him because of the mother.

On leaving for Switzerland and on returning from there, the Idiot ordered the Umetskys under threat of his wrecking everything (N.B. "I won't support her any longer or give you any subsidy") not to dare to inform the uncle but to keep matters hushed up. On his return they moved (and on their instance) (the engineer) (on trial). His wife and Umetskaia went to live with an old lady related to them.

Umetskaia is a *yurodivaia,* an avenging angel. The wife was finding out. . . . . . .

He arrived and imposed silence. He gave his wife 15 rubles. (Did he tell his brother?) He does not live with his wife.

All the vacillations as in the first Part, the melancholy, the revenge, scenes with his wife, as before.—Explanatory conversations throughout all the novel and scenes with his brother and with the uncle, as before.

His rapture at his success with the general and his family.

Then his dejected withdrawal into himself. His wife's torment. Sometimes he seems close to her, sometimes he pushes her away. He detests her, yet is jealous of her. (His characteristic.)

Then he taunts the uncle with his marrying.

(The uncle goes to the wife and to Umetskaia.) He leaves them,

This manuscript page corresponds to pp. 96–97, beginning with "Problems and enigmas" and ending with "The Idiot is the younger." This page contains drawings of characteristic Gothic motifs; they are neatly lined up along one side of the page. The handwriting is of various dimensions on the page but is characteristically neat and evenly lined. The variations Dostoevsky permits himself are always framed and controlled.

and suddenly he gnashes his teeth, rushes to the general, to the heroine, he does not like the heroine. But then. . . . . . . To domineer over them all, to triumph over them all, to take revenge on them all (but for what reason—unknown). (He is a natural son.)

He drives matters to such a point that the heroine runs away. The wife and the heroine at the Umetskys. He openly loves the heroine, *and then* he gives her up. (In some strange way.)

N.B.? Or else: *No one* knows about his wife, neither the heroine nor the uncle, nor his brother. Only *toward the end* does Umetskaia declare this to the uncle.

The chief point. He wants to subjugate everyone—first his brother, then the uncle (he tyrannizes over his wife and Umetskaia), then the general and his family, then the heroine.

The Idiot relates to the son why he has been reputed to be an Idiot. He was ill in his youth. "The Umetskys kept writing that I was an Idiot, extorting money for doctors. *Never could anyone have harassed the uncle as I did then.*" He even vowed that he himself would run down the true facts, but he verified nothing personally nor did he send anyone else to do so. Before his departure for Switzerland, they married him off while he was drunk. (Then it appeared that he had married out of compassion; he was supporting them.)

No one knows he is married until the last moment. *He is a legitimate son.*

Kostenkinych sent him from Petersburg to Switzerland when the opportunity arose. The uncle was away.

He considers that his wife has spoiled his career. But he enjoys tormenting her.

He is apprehensive of everyone, out of pride. He wants 1st place. He does not want to accept anything from the uncle.

N.B. The heroine continually harasses him with her gibes and her coquetry. She loves the son without realizing it, problematically. Suddenly, at the very last moment, she confesses to him that she loves him.

He turns on the heroine and takes revenge on her because of her *gibes* and because he could not get her. He does not believe that she could love him.

He imagines that his face and appearance are horrifying, and he does not believe it when they tell him that he is even *very* attractive.

In Switzerland only 2 years.

He embraces his wife, kisses her, confides his depression to her, and then rejects her, charges her with being responsible for the fact that he loves the heroine. The latter loves him to distraction. He says jeeringly to her: "I am a monster."

The Jumper is a likely candidate for being his father.

N.B. (Think this over.) N.B.?

Through a confidential letter, the Umetskys have learned how much the uncle values the Idiot, perhaps he will acknowledge him and make him his heir.

They arrange it with him that, when he has gained the uncle's good graces, he will inform the latter that he is married.

When he carried off the heroine, he told her and Umetskaia: "Don't tell her," and he stayed by her when she was in agony and delirium.

"I heard her confession."

The heroine is a princess. Her people are distinguished. But he is simply a Ptitsyn.

The Idiot has a post in the general's chancellery.

[Is he a Ptitsyn?]

N.B. At the station a comic scene had taken place between him and the heroine. They remembered and asked the uncle to bring him back.

He says to the uncle: "You repudiated me and my mother; now I repudiate you."

Then he came into possession of a document proving that he is *legitimate* [legitimate] but he did not want to show it to the uncle and pretended that he was illegitimate.

His mother hanged herself.

Only to him did it seem that the heroine loved the son. Instead she loved him. The son informed the uncle when the latter made his own offer. [Afterward.] [?]

Umetskaia is not his sister.

They married him off to a young girl who had had a baby. They had brought her there from Saratov.[1] They beat her severely and married her to him. They believed he did not know about all this. But he did know that there was a baby kept hidden. Umetskaia went to see her. He went too, and fondled the baby. He told the uncle that

---

[1] Saratov: a town on the Volga in the province of that name. Many kinds of religious sectarians, mystical or rationalistic, flourished among the peasantry of the Volga Valley. A great many Germans had settled in Saratov, and their influence here and elsewhere promoted the rise of the Stundists, a dissident sect rather like the Presbyterians.

the son loved Umetskaia. [The uncle marries Umetskaia, so that the son will marry.]

It appeared that the heroine loved him, but he continued to reject the heroine, yet he could not leave her alone, he was in love with her, his boundless vanity.

The baby kept hidden. The mother does not know. Umetskaia knows.

He supported the baby *in secret*.

Long ago the heroine had told the son when he proposed that she loved the Idiot.

When the uncle wanted to pay his court to the heroine, the son told the uncle that the heroine loved the Idiot. "Let them marry." The uncle marries Umetskaia (whom he knows).

The Idiot says it is impossible—he is already married. He loves the heroine but gave her up. He was struggling with himself.

The struggle of revenge with love.

He brings the heroine together with the son.

The uncle dies.

In the beginning he courted the heroine and made himself attractive to her (just the sort of travesty he played with the uncle), then he renounced the heroine because he was falling in love with his wife, being moved by his immense compassion for her. *But he torments her.* He struggles with himself. He torments the heroine as well, because she cannot belong to him.

The Idiot's conversation with the son about *useful activity*. The Idiot hears him out, silently but with indifference, as if the subject being discussed were quite other.

The chief and paramount idea of the novel, on which everything hangs, is: namely, that he is filled with ~~and he sees with a mature mind all the paltriness of the people around him~~ morbid pride to such a degree that he cannot help considering himself a god, and yet *at the same time* he has so little esteem for himself (he analyzes himself with great clarity) that he cannot help despising himself intensely, infinitely, and unjustifiably. (At the same time he feels that for him to take blind revenge on everyone would be despicable, still, he acts like a scoundrel and he does take revenge.) [All this analyzing with the uncle, the son, his wife, and with himself.]

He feels that he has no cause for revenge, that he is *like everyone else*, and ought to be satisfied. But since he demands more than others do, out of infinite vanity and pride (and at the same time he thirsts for truth), nothing suffices him.

From his upbringing and his surroundings he early imbibed this poison, which had penetrated his very bloodstream. His magnanimity and his yearning for love derive in general from an infinitely outraged heart. He has never <been able to heal those wounds>, and therefore he has retaliated and revenged himself on all those he would have liked to love without limit and to shed his very blood for all those *dear* to him.

Instead of useful activity—evil.

For the future, a plan: "I shall be a banker, King of the Jews, I'll keep them all in chains under my feet. Either to dominate them like a tyrant, or die for them on the cross—that's all there is or can be for me, given my nature, but what I don't want is just to wear myself out like this." (His *casual* remark to the son.)

Or else he sat down one day and wrote out his will. He wanted to kill himself, but didn't, instead he began an intrigue.

They set fire to the house.

N.B. "For what reason am I obliged to love a woman I don't love?" But when they insulted her, he defended her unconditionally.

Envy of the heroine.

N.B. "If you only knew how I despise human glory! But if you knew how I *trembled* at presenting myself to the general's family and how often I shuddered at the thought: but what if they knew I am married!"

"What is a career to me? But I have been tormenting my wife on account of career."

He won a triumph and gained the heroine's recognition, and *for the first time* he possessed his wife—then he rejected her.

His wife has a long-suffering, naïve personality (an *actual* character).

A precious question and answer:

"You will end up either by committing a great crime, or by performing a great deed"—says the son to him.

"God willing!" he replied quite seriously, and faintly, "But more likely by nothing of the sort."

(He is yearning to do some noble deed, so as to distinguish himself and surpass everyone else. They set the house on fire, and the burned finger.)

"I can't take money from a usurer."

(He loves the baby terribly, the baby dies. Sitting at his wife's feet, by the baby's coffin.)

He confides *everything* to her about the heroine (he is beside himself), but he confides only his cursing her, only his raging fury at her, only that he hates her. How she insults him (in anguish, his wife comprehends that he is in love).

But suddenly the heroine proves to be wealthy and aristocratic (she turned down the diplomat for having put her up *for sale* to the uncle, on the Idiot's instigation).

The heroine flirts with everyone and with the uncle and with the son, and rejects them all. The Idiot suspects that she loves the general, and he spreads this idea about. She goes to the uncle, and then suddenly to him. . . . . . .

He had always *hated* her, but at times he gave up and shut himself away, alone. He raped Umetskaia. It appeared that Umetskaia had always loved him and had been sacrificing herself completely *to him and his wife*.

His brutal defilement of her was both an overwhelming happiness to her, and death itself.

She became obsessed with the idea of universal brotherhood. She captivated the uncle. So that the heroine should give herself to the Idiot and declare that she would marry him—she had to surmount so many obstacles that in frenzy and hysteria she simply ran to him, and suddenly she found that he was married.

The Idiot abandons her, half dead, to the son. The uncle dies.

N.B. Precious questions and answers—by the Idiot to the son.

The son: "But why do you abase yourself and run yourself down and despise yourself so? I have always noticed this with amazement. Why can't the heroine love you and marry you?"

The Idiot with surprise: "A monster, an awkward creature, outside their circle, not one of them, the son of a moneylender, despised and detested by everyone?"

The son: "Who detests you? You are a millionaire's son. You can be whoever you want to be."

The Idiot: "Everyone who does not understand me detests me. I know this for a fact. I haven't the same belief as they do. I am not a millionaire, but a beggar. I can't help being detested, because I long to be above them, but since this is impossible, I hate them, and since this is so, they must hate me for it. Finally . . . . . . when I look deep within <illegible> I cannot help perceiving that I am a base and vile person, and therefore I know I deserve to be hated." [Is he a Ptitsyn, or is he a legitimate son? (definite decision). But in the dénouement he shall perform a striking deed.]

The son (to himself or later in conversation with the heroine): "He loves her intensely and demands too much from love." Not perceiving any love *around him,* he hates. Instead of the sacrifices *of love* (which occur daily and are therefore in his opinion trivial), it seems better to him to act like a scoundrel, to inflict torment, to take revenge. This is the reason he despises himself. He has a need of heroism.

The Idiot (thinking as he left): "Strange. In those questions and answers in discussing with the son why the heroine cannot belong to me, I did not once think of the fact that I am already married."

How is it that the uncle speaks of him as an Idiot?

The son says he is mysterious.

"Bring him here."

In taking him to the general's, the uncle says: "I warned them that you were an Idiot."

After the evening party, the general takes him immediately into his service. The son also furthers his advancement, describing him as an extraordinarily strange man, a thinker.

N.B. The uncle at first says to him: "You must serve the general."

"You are a *Ptitsyn,* and you have to earn your rank in the service."

The uncle's conversation with the general's wife.

The sequel to this conversation: "Bring him to us."

He. He comes. The general is surprised. "What, is it you."

The uncle: "He is an Idiot."

Or else—an idea:

When he carried off the heroine, he ordered his wife to keep her silence (the baby's coffin has already been described). His wife, who had been ailing, suddenly dies. Symptoms of poisoning. The heroine and the uncle *attack him.* He states simply: "Yes, I killed her." Umetskaia keeps silence, but ultimately she shows her letter.

"*Nevertheless, I killed her,*" says the Idiot.

He leaves the uncle. Umetskaia is with him. The heroine is at the son's. The uncle has a liver attack. The legacy goes to the Idiot, with a fraction to the son. The Idiot renounces the whole inheritance.

The Idiot with Umetskaia ~~the heroine~~.

"I had happiness—I didn't recognize it."

In the night, in the storm, by the tomb with Umetskaia.

Before this he was wandering through the city.

Umetskaia goes looking for him over all the crossroads.

"It must be better," he said, not understanding what he was saying, and he smiled oddly.

"Yes," said Umetskaia, devoutly.

"Let's go away!" he said to Umetskaia.

And together they went off to an unknown destination. (Another happiness.)

N.B. (Vl. Umetsky persuaded the uncle that he had done the poisoning.)

Umetskaia had withheld the letter for some time.

The letter—in the style of Holbein's "Madonna."[2]

Before then—a frightful tirade to the uncle about *the King of the Jews.*

Enthusiastic conversations with his wife, his wife is filled with inspired veneration for him.

Once he let fall these words: "I talk to you because it seems to me you are the only one who understands me."

N.B. (He runs into a group of contemporary young people attending a sermon about useful activity. The whole evening. He kept silence and did not even think about it.)

Umetskaia reads the *New Testament*. In her demented state, she sermonizes. She disconcerts the uncle. (*Umetskaia's naïveté is boundless.—This is the chief trait in her character*.) About heads being cut off, about fingernails being torn out, in the beginning she had set a fire—.

She has been too downtrodden, she is a regular *yurodivaia*.

"In Switzerland—we used to read the *New Testament* often, and after Renan's book[3] I questioned the doctor *about the cross*. (We were strangely at one on the subject of fingernails torn out and needles.)"

---

[2] Holbein's "Madonna": this is *The Madonna of Burgomaster Meyer*, which was then in the Royal Gallery of Dresden and was Holbein's copy of his own original (1525–26) in Darmstadt. The figure of the Madonna is an example of ideal Nordic beauty, with flowing golden hair, an oval face, and a high forehead, with the eyes cast down. Interestingly enough, the model, Magdalena Offenburgh, also posed for Holbein's *Venus* (1526) and *Laïs Corinthiaca* (1526), whose faces have a seductive expression absent from the perfect modesty of the Virgin. The latter two portraits Dostoevsky must have seen in the museum at Basle, but he may not have known that the same model posed for all three pictures. In the published version of *The Idiot*, Aleksandra Epanchin reminded the Prince of the Madonna (Part I, chap. 6).

[3] Renan's book: *La Vie de Jésus* by Ernest Renan (1823–92) was published in Paris on 23 June 1863, shortly before Dostoevsky's second journey to that city. It created an immediate sensation and quickly ran into many editions—one of the earliest of a long line of "demythologizing" portrayals of Christ which continues to the present day.

Umetskaia's speculations about what thoughts flash into the head of a man about to be decapitated.

Tableau.

"She's addicted to all such pictures,"[4] says the wife! "What she sees in the city is a regular miracle! Not what enters other people's heads. *For instance,* how the cemetery pervades the city! But the passion on the cross shatters one's mind." "But He has triumphed over mind."

"Was that a miracle then?"

"Certainly it was a miracle, nonetheless. . . . . . ."

"What?"

"Nevertheless, He gave a terrible cry."

["What cry?"]

["Eloi! Eloi!"].[5]

"There was an eclipse!"

"I don't know—but it was a terrible cry."

The account of Holbein's "Christ" in Basle.[6]

How the martyrs dug shelters for themselves deep in the earth.

About revolution.

About the devil's tempting Christ. ~~In him there is the beginning of a profound Christianity.~~

The tongue in the mirror.

N.B. He loves Umetskaia. A strange and *utterly* childlike friend-

---

[4] Pictures: this reference and the one immediately above it to "decapitated heads" allude to the question Myshkin poses in the published version of *The Idiot* (Part I, chap. 5) as to what can be the last thought passing through the mind of a man about to be beheaded. Myshkin speaks of a picture illustrating this idea. It was one Dostoevsky himself saw in the Offentliche Kunstsammlung in Basle by Hans Fries (1465–1518?), a Swiss contemporary of the elder Holbein. The subject is the beheading of St. John the Baptist (*Die Enthauptung das Johannes des Taüfers* of 1514). The right hand of the executioner lifts the sword, while the left grasps the hair of the martyr, whose eyes are open and fixed in an intense but enigmatic expression.

[5] "Eloi! Eloi!"—"And at the ninth hour Jesus cried with a loud voice, saying, Eloi, Eloi, lama sabachthani? which is, being interpreted, My God, my God, why hast thou forsaken me?" (Mark 15: 34.)

[6] Holbein's *Christ in the Tomb* (1521): wood, 30.7 by 200 cm., also in the Basle museum. It is a terrible depiction, devoid of any spiritual connotation: a rotting corpse, jaw dropped, the flesh spotted with a bluish decay, the eyes rolled upward in a grimace—the image of the denial of immortality. A reproduction of this picture is placed over a doorway in Rogozhin's house in the final version of *The Idiot*. Myshkin's comment on seeing it was Dostoevsky's own, as Anna Grigorievna records it: "Why, a man's faith might be ruined by looking at that picture!"

ship with the *yurodivaia*. "He always brings up matters like that when he talks with her."

She never instructs him as to his duties toward his wife, she merely acts.

In the country she had *twice* set fire to a barn, so as to be like Olga Umetskaia.

She set a fire in Petersburg, too.

Perhaps it would be far better to make him a legitimate son.

"Ever since childhood <I have had> the idea that I am going to be a man who is superior to everyone else."

Then Umetskaia says to him: "You are going to be a man who is superior to everyone else—you must not falter before some heroic deed."

Or else during a conversation with the son: "I should think along the same lines, if I were legitimate. I would reject the whole thing, along with the 100,000 rubles."

The main point.

He incessantly appraises himself: and says he is not at all unhappy, and not at all offended.

He is not at all unhappy, not at all offended, but *everything* is out of proportion in his view, everything is oppressive.

Also perhaps:

The son knows his secret: but he says nothing to the uncle, he does not tell [forewarn] the heroine—*not knowing, not suspecting,* how much she loves him.

The Idiot too is unsuspecting and is jealous of the son. "Let him get along without her," and he sets about matchmaking on the uncle's behalf.

Having conveyed her consent to the uncle, she suddenly declares to the Idiot that she loves him and runs to him.

Overwhelmed, he gives in to her.

At first, wild passion, then reflection, then love—.

("There's the great exploit that has been awaiting me!")

He goes to the son, he goes to the uncle, he tells him about the son and his love. (The general, the uncle, and Vl. Umetsky testify regarding the poisoning. But actually he had obtained the poison somewhat earlier from *the natural son* (who knew an apothecary). They found it at his house.

He is a Christian yet at the same time he does not believe.

The dualism of a deep nature.

N.B. *The tongue in the mirror.*

Conversations and evenings at the wife's, at the Idiot's, at Umetskaia's, and at the son's. "How after such talk can one *not believe!*"
He was jealous of the son's relations with his wife.
He had still another apartment.
N.B. (Think over the comic incident on the railroad.) All of a tremble, he entered the railway carriage and surprised the son.

Sequel

3 November

The main point: From the very beginning he does not imagine that *he can love* the heroine, and furthermore he does not consider this is within the bounds of possibility. N.B.
N.B. *The son* on the other hand falls instantly in love with the heroine and imparts this to the Idiot, who is unconsciously and laceratingly being devoured by jealousy. Throughout the entire novel he imagines that to dream of the heroine is not for him. It does not go with his ugly mug.
Even in conversation with the son (with whom the heroine was beginning to flirt, as was her way, but to whom in a mysterious talk she had confessed in a sudden flood of tears that she loved another man, though she did not *confess whom*—perhaps she was ashamed of it; it did not occur to the son that it was the Idiot, though he had thought of others)—nor did it occur to him when he queried the Idiot on the subject: "Why do you rate yourself so low?"—to compare him to the heroine, and when the Idiot suddenly asked: "But what if I fell in love with the heroine, would she marry me?"—he responded in confusion: "But aren't you already married?"
"That has nothing to do with it. What if I were free?"
"I don't know." (In greater confusion; the Idiot's face showed secret amusement, though he was not amused) "I don't know. In this case—in this case . . . . in any case, if you were a royal prince, you would love anyone you liked. . . . . . . However," he added hurriedly, correcting himself, "Why not then, why not?"
"Well, now, that's better," said the Idiot abruptly, "at first you were confused," and they both fell silent.
As the Idiot was leaving, though *he was expecting* precisely the reply he himself had evoked, but did not anticipate that it would be so insulting and spiteful a reply, he thought: "It's as if there were really something of the kind in me . . . . but perhaps he is jealous!

.... He does not know if the heroine were in my power and were attainable, I would not have married her."

N.B. *Perhaps.* But what if it happened like this: the heroine suddenly found out that he was married; she fell ill; then, desperately in love as she was, she married the uncle, ridiculed the son, and came in a rush to the Idiot, "Take me, let's run away, I love you......."

Hence it follows that this passion, this blazing love, must be explained *during the course of the novel* by means of episodes. He torments his wife. (Her redoubled mockery at first. He burned his finger and took revenge for this reason.)

N.B. *After the burned finger,* he raped Umetskaia ~~the heroine~~.

In the mother's case: "Ganechka must marry *for the sake of connections,* the princess is poor, but we have no need of money, whereas she comes from a distinguished family."

He hates the Idiot. Finds out that he is married; goes to the Idiot's wife and insults her. The Idiot intercedes.

Then comes a final row with the uncle.

Then after the mother's quarrel with the Idiot about his wife—the Jumper.

He behaves affectionately to the Jumper, so that the uncle takes it into his head that the Idiot is the Jumper's son.

To the Idiot the idea that he is the Jumper's son seems insulting and ridiculous. He mocks the uncle by suggesting that he is the Jumper's son.

All these insults accumulate in his heart. "Perhaps I am too young, and therefore am quick to take offense," he sometimes thinks.......

The mother is unconditionally reconciled to the uncle, so as not to remember, justify herself, which she considers would be base and unthinkable for her. She renews relations with the uncle as if she were doing him a favor....... The uncle, no one knows why, decides after 25 years to be reconciled with her.

The mother is jealous of the uncle because of the heroine (ridicule).

The Idiot (as before) has aroused the general's wife against the general by saying that the general is in love and that the diplomat, having rejected the heroine (who told the general that he was in love —the whole plot as before), had told the heroine that they had sold her off. The heroine herself had just confessed to the son only that she loved another man; however, the Idiot is married—the heroine's despair. (N.B. "Without the mother—I'll marry the uncle.")

What if she were the Idiot's mother, and the Idiot takes an apartment on leaving the uncle, and throughout all the novel there is a wretched warfare with the uncle in the mother's household on his account?

Major problem: Regarding this personality of the Idiot, is it more interesting, more romantic, and more graphic to express the idea that he is legitimate or that he is illegitimate?

N.B. *Most important of all:* In case he is legitimate, the mother tells him that evening with the uncle and the son present: "I don't understand what it means to love or not love—if we get along. . . . . . . You may be aware of that story. I have suffered too much on your account." (Then the uncle says: "Not on that account."—"Agreed: perhaps I behaved badly in deserting you: do you understand what I am telling you?") Perhaps he doesn't understand. He keeps silence: she is very much *the great lady.* Above all, the uncle is no old woman.

The Idiot gets rid of them with but few words.

If he is not legitimate.

The Idiot without his wife's knowledge is set up in the general's service by the uncle.

He arrives suddenly and inopportunely.

The uncle's reconciliation with the mother. The uncle is confused, the mother says: "I want to see him, that Idiot."

The uncle's talk with the son.

The Idiot's talk with the son. He is mistrustful, guarded, strange. But the son reassures him somewhat and interests him. His frequent companionship with the son. More and more the mother regards ~~repeats everything~~ that he is an Idiot, but she talks with him.

At the general's they rashly mentioned the Idiot. The mother interrupted, taking offense at this, and asked them to bring him to the house. The uncle frowns.

But the Idiot distinguishes himself. *Characteristic trait.*—At first the uncle is in rapture at his success, but then he falls into despair and prostration, recoils from him. The mother is likewise in a rage.

In case he is illegitimate—dreams of the heroine and of high society and of a career do not even enter the Idiot's head at first. Then everything becomes a vivid possibility.

N.B. Quarrel after quarrel. But the mother does not part company with the uncle for this reason, so as to arrange the heroine's marriage to the son first of all.

He is legitimate.

Greater pride.

Pride in demonstrating that he alone, without the aid of wealth or any other person, can triumph over them all.

N.B. After leaving the uncle he does not go to his wife but takes another apartment, where Umetskaia is awaiting him. Feverish conversation with Umetskaia.

The son was not acquainted with the general before the scene in the railway station. The general says to him: "Why are you mixed up in a quarrel? He's a strange man, your uncle." About a reconciliation, and so forth.

Afterwards. A major scene between the mother and the Idiot, in which she shows him that she is not obliged to him in any way.

She asks: "Perhaps you are refusing because of some kind of vexation?"

"Simply take the 100 thousand rubles. Don't get into a fight with me. . . . . . ."

"Take 300,000."

"He offered me 500."

"How?"

The Idiot to her: "I don't consider you are guilty of anything. I want to be alone."

She: "Hm. Pride still. *La Comedia!*"

The most important of all important things:

After she had refused the son, she suddenly went to the son and suddenly again to the Idiot: "Take me!"

N.B. (Poverty in the Idiot's house. Need of work. But Vl. Umetsky thinks: "Let him wait. He is being crafty, the clever dog! He wants the full half of the legacy while the uncle is still alive."

N.B. At first he inveigled the heroine away from the diplomat, then from the son (cursing his own baseness). The heroine accuses him of baseness. He answers her: "Well, yes, that's so; I did it because I love you!"

He (to himself) wanted to poison her; but suddenly she said: "But I love you!"

Important note.

She was always mocking and scornful to him and *never* did the idea occur to him that she could love him.

He hated her.

She makes an odd proposal to him: "Give up everything, your wife, I will give up the son, and let's run away."

He answers: "How can I do that?" He shrugs his shoulders and goes away in triumph and arrogance. Poison in his breast. And suddenly passion. He is frantic, ill. Before the wedding she suddenly appears in her wedding dress.

Problem and doubt: how justify the fact that all his activity is spent in love for the heroine?

Better for him to be legitimate (without a mother).

Having alienated the heroine from the son—and having induced her not to marry, he goes to the son and says that he did this so that she would not find happiness with him (and that she should marry the uncle).

"Do you love her?"

"I hate her."

Absolutely indispensable.

Sine qua non.

She does not *know* that he is married. The son has told no one.

He seized his wife by the shoulders and said: "You alone, perhaps" —and talks of the heroine to her. She listens quietly. *She is gentle,* like Holbein's "Madonna," and says: "Only don't be angry with me because you told me that."

And after the wedding she says: "If only you did not hate me!"

She was only 18 years old!

He was savagely jealous of his wife because of the man who had raped her (the father of the baby).

Last note: in the mother's presence, she broke off with the son. The heroine had gone to his wife. "I love him."

After this the wife dies.

As yet the marriage has not taken place. The heroine has not yet given her consent, she has taken back her word and said that she loved another man.

Then she had seen him. He went away, he rejected her.

But then passion and cursing, and suddenly his wife dies. Suddenly his wife dies.

Vl. Umetsky—he poisoned her.

The heroine—he poisoned her.

About the mother and legitimacy: "It all comes from hatred of the son."

It would be better for him to be illegitimate; then everything is explainable.

He hates everyone who looks down on him. The son's love for him, he loves the son. Then the mother's threats.

He spurns the uncle.

Envy of the son because of the heroine, his amazement at her love (the heroine's visit, and poverty).

His exalted bearing and his poverty amaze the heroine.

And he tortured his wife.

And for the last time the heroine comes to him with an avowal.

His wife's death.

P.S. "I have nothing to complain of; you were supporting me in Switzerland. You gave me 100,000 and now 500.—"

N.B. (The legitimacy of the other son was the reason.)

The illegitimate son: a terribly proud and tragic person.

N.B. Or else like this: he is legitimate but repudiated, he repudiates himself. A grand role.

But alongside his unaffected magnanimity of heart—vengefulness and envy.

Envy of the heroine [the son] (poverty), but he feels he cannot carry on, he turns to his wife. [Struggle.]

It seems to him that he is ridiculous because of his marriage and because of the Jumper Ptitsyn.

The heroine's love—he tortures his wife.

"You repudiated me—therefore *I want you all at my feet.*"

"*That's a fine thing!*"

Quite differently: a magnanimous but exasperated character, worn down.

He does not reproach his wife in the least because of career.

He repudiates everyone, just as they have repudiated him.

He is apprehensive about his being married [at first he concealed his marriage, then they all found out about it]. When the marriage was made known, the heroine wrote him (after the finger burning): "You sought me out, though you are married, you were ridiculous, you took a lofty attitude, you were afraid of letting your absurd marriage be known, you couldn't go through with it."

He replied: "Yes, you are right, I hated you, but I hate my marriage, this is all quite fair and completely sincere."

And she is in despair. The heroine loves him even more.

"Forgive me."

Then she went to his wife.

"Then, I love—."

Revenge on everyone.

Thereafter, the heroine, having already accepted the son, declares that she loves *the Idiot.*

She runs to him—(He: "I don't want or I want").

The wife's death.

"It's I who killed her!" "It's he who killed her!"

Byronic despair.

Love for his wife and a rather naïve encounter: At first he informed himself about everything, then Umetskaia, then sternly, then little by little—but love, alternating with unconscious hatred.

A letter from the heroine: "If I were indifferent, I would not have written a letter to you."

[I hated you at 1st glance more than anyone, first and foremost.]

[Why you? Because you shone among them like the sun; everyone sought you out, everyone adored you, but I hated them all. . . . . . . And you, the sun, you ridiculed me from the moment we met. I compared our situations: can I aspire to your level, can I evoke your love, claim your notice? . . . . And thus I began to hate you, and the more I perceived the impossibility of winning you and the more I seemed beneath you, the more ardently *did I desire you*. But all your reproaches and your mockery amount to nothing beside the reproaches and the mockery I heap upon myself. Everything you wrote is hardly the 10th part of what I know of myself. It's enough, let me alone. Now I've crawled into my den and it will be a long time before I show myself, but it's all the better for us not to meet for a long time. . . . . . . Oh, I understand how much baseness there is in all this magnanimity. But I didn't want merely to parade it. . . . . . . I was sincere at first. But I couldn't carry it off, I had too great a heartache. I never loved you . . . . except with a hate-love. Do you understand this? No, all the better. Goodbye. I thank you for your letter. You have shown me that you are not indifferent. I've grasped that much."

In reply he wrote her: "The idea I have grasped is that if you were not indifferent, there would have been no letter."

She took this for sarcasm posing as naïveté.

At first he himself was surprised that he felt such a hostility toward them all?

Then he clarifies his *role* to himself.

This was a painful question to him: why is he avoiding and rejecting them?

N.B. *Note:* Let them not think that he is suffering on his wife's account (that is, the readers, let the origin of his despair be made clear).

Characteristic trait. At first he has a morbid, cowardly fear (considering all the escapades and ruptures) of announcing that he is married. But now, since they have found it out, he suddenly holds up his head and prides himself on such a marriage and that he recognizes a different and higher destiny. . . . . . . And in the same moment he persecutes and torments his wife all the more.

4 November

He spurns everyone and even finds a relish in doing so whenever he encounters them, *whereas in all other respects he is quite sincere.*

He has acted *foolishly*(?) in marrying and wants to make it appear as a noble deed.

(He reproaches himself for his injustice, though the fact that he married *out of compassion and noble sentiment* counts for nothing *in his own eyes.* Why? Because in this society it will not be understood, not appreciated, it will not be valued, it will be thought laughable, and in so far as he does not esteem it as anything at all, he is even ashamed of it, inwardly he feels a slave to them all.)

He turns down the uncle's offer, and also the money. This makes him *frightfully honored and esteemed in the circle of the general and his wife,* though he did not do this on their account.

The plot develops, they learn his whole history. The loftiness of the figure he presents.

The son has also suffered because of the uncle. He was more frigid to him, but afterwards grew warmer.

Explanations now with the uncle, and then with the mother.

Now they have found out that he is married, ambiguous glances, derision. The mother fawns on the Jumper, the heroine is ill, and the letter. His reply, despair. He had turned to his wife, to the son, but suddenly he went again to the general and his wife and became their *âme damnée.* The heroine lost the lawsuit, he outwitted the diplomat, the senator————and so on.

He had wanted to outwit the son, but he managed something cleverer: he began to praise the son to the heroine and to scheme on his behalf (knowing the heroine's contrary character). The heroine dropped the son at the critical moment, but he tormented the heroine, the wife, the uncle, the mother and the son.

Note:

Within him a terrible struggle was going on: to avenge himself or not? His impulses are genuine, noble, but then his actions are evil. The prestigious role *he plays in society* makes him ashamed of himself. But when the absurd story of his marriage gets out, and the fact that he is in actuality the Jumper's son and that it was *not he* who

had repudiated the uncle *but the other way around*—he turned spiteful and irritable.

He does not justify himself, his generous deeds (they were—*invent*)
have been performed without any publicity—but he is still dissatisfied with himself, he judges himself and torments himself, because
his pride is not pure but only an expression of vanity.

It would be better, he thought, to forgive them all. "And my
Holbein Madonna—how pure she is, how beautiful" (now he understands her!), and then the crisis comes, he torments her, he schemes
to his uttermost at the general's, and, *after having sincerely accused
himself in his letter to the heroine, for that very reason he takes
revenge on the heroine.*

The heroine is no longer amused by him but treats him with
stinging raillery and at times with such scornful hauteur that she
even ignores him, while he glowers in silent rage. (He does not take
revenge on his wife, he keeps silent, but he is jealous of her and
avenges himself by his silence.)

At this point the heroine gives her consent to the son, but suddenly
she goes to see the wife.

This gives him an idea. He wavers: either ridicule, or else. . . . . . .
He wanders off as if in a delirium.

Unexpected tears and explanations between the heroine and the
son.

The heroine demands an interview. Confession of love. He rejects
her.

Passion. The little coffin, and the wife takes poison.

The heroine does not know that she poisoned herself, and she runs
to him. The coffin, and passion. Explanations beside the coffin. "I
won't let you go. . . . . . ." Vl. Umetski comes with an accusation,
the general goes to the heroine.

Beside herself, the heroine flings herself on the general: "It's I
who poisoned her."

Signs of poisoning; at the apothecary's.

"I poisoned her." Goes away.

Umetskaia's testimony. The letter. At first, because of the letter,
they let her go, but then the letter is read.

The uncle, the son, explanations of *his letter to the heroine,* full
confession. ("My passions were smoldering, they flared up within
me. I had taken the first step in my life.")

Goes to the cemetery.—"Let us go away!" Umetskaia says to him on the way: "Till the soil," and she recounts all his wife's life, various incidents, which made her heart bleed to remember.

He enters on a new way of life. *The first step.*

Note:

He is really noble, perhaps even great, the very image of pride, but—.

He cannot hold himself down, really the image of greatness and pride, *though he fully senses what genuine pride and greatness mean.* (By confessing he later made up for everything.) He avenges himself on the heroine, he loves her, *without loving her.* He was ashamed to love his wife, though he admired her and knew that she had cut herself off from everything for his sake, but yet, knowing this while she was yet alive and he possessed her, he did not value her.

Deep-seated feeling, demanding an outlet.

Nota bene. Of his own will, without asking the uncle or writing him, he left Fribourg. (A letter from his wife had reached him, the address had been got from Kostenkinych.) He surprised the uncle—confused and vexed him.

The mother was living somewhere in the province of Kaluga <south of Moscow>.

The mother said to him: "Of course they forced you to come."— "No."

He had never seen his brother, but two years before when Kostenkinych sent him to Switzerland, his brother was away on a visit to his mother.

Explanations with the uncle on meeting him.

Suddenly the uncle said ironically: "Do you at least know this, who is reigning over us, who our Emperor is."

"Who?"

"Alexander II."[7]

"Haven't you heard anything about the most important events of this reign? What did Alexander accomplish?"

"The emancipation of the peasants."

"Hm. He knows the answer. . . . . . ."

(The question was an even harder one: many things had been

---

[7] Alexander II (1818–81) reigned from 1855 until his assassination a few weeks after Dostoevsky's own death. It was in his reign that the serfs were freed by the act of 19 February 1861.

achieved in this reign, and therefore intelligence was needed to recognize them.)

But at the same time he saw to what a degree the uncle had under-estimated him—2½ millions. They were talking of ½ million. "I never asked you. You yourself volunteered this" (characteristic trait—"It's you who are the one concerned"). 4 days at home.

The son managed beforehand to appear at the mother's when the Idiot was announced; the son's amazement.

The mother: "What's this, allow me, allow me, what's this? What has happened, I'd like to know?"—"He came at 9 o'clock in the morning."—The mother was with the general and his wife; it was through the mother that they became acquainted with the uncle.

After the assault on her, Umetskaia had not a word to say to him.

The wanderer [He killed his wife, daughter.] each flower [re-joices].

The sister, an eccentric young girl, and his wife, the chamberlain A—v. The rather muddled business affairs yield 300,000. He wants (and hopes for) 400. The mother wants to insist. The daughter has been brought up by the mother.

The mother to the uncle. "When I married you, I had 50,000, in the 4 years of our union I hope (you were not so well off) I hope that in the 4 years of our union they have been of help to you and have grown to at least 100,000."

"Oh, far more, at least 200."

"Well, you are generous. . . . . . . Besides, you speak like a business-man, well, as for those 100,000, I accept them. Give Natalia 40,000 now, while you are still alive. This is absolutely essential."

4 November

Make the wife more poetic.

The general says in the railway carriage: "Oh, that proud man." The fiancé: "This much at least is known, that he is a businessman who does a great deal of good fundamentally."

"A practical man," said the general half ironically. "And besides his practicality, such idealism—."

"Well, now, we shall consider the daughter: Annushka will cer-tainly not blame me for this. She knows lots of things, though she respects him, because he. . . . . . ." "Well, you see, whatever I said of him, he certainly deserves respect."

The encounter in the railway carriage was a heated one, as is common, because they talked so fast *about so many subjects,* but mainly because the general held forth to the exclusion of the others.

The general's wife made a point of calling his attention to this fact.

The general: "Your brother: how unhappy they say he is—an Idiot."

After his success with the general and his wife at their house, a sudden revolution took place in him. He was ashamed of his success and in all sincerity broke completely with the uncle and the general, then—. Compact with the uncle <torn page of MS follows>

> with the mother, but only officially
> but with a desperate volubility
> they helped, but only poured oil on the fire
> —The illegitimate son. He had an affair with the
>   wife U—
> —The mother even reproaches then
> the Idiot ~~the son~~ gave his former mistress.
> The daughter came, the general came
> Kostenkinych at the Idiot's—"You must sit down
> When the general and his wife left—
>   and he announced
> —The general's wife
> at the Idiot's success at the general's
> already announced: "I
> He had been brought up

The mother's program. Exhortation to the daughter.

"Do your best to carry out your duty. Take me as your example in all this affair, you know what my life has been; do you likewise. I have tried hard to shape your life according to my own. I married when I was twenty-five. And I have kept you single until you were 25. The great thing is—duty. Don't listen to anything else. In this world don't contradict and don't judge. You have seen that I don't judge people in anything whatsoever. No use to prod people about trifles in this world, if you listen to what they say on the spur of the moment—keep yourself to yourself. You may object, but without bickering. Believe in God. Certainly the Ten Commandments are all very fine. As to this there's no use in arguing or reasoning; don't lie, don't steal, don't bear false witness, and so on. But above all, take me for your example. Have I ever offended anyone? Though I have led an unhappy life, I have never sinned against anyone. I've never opposed anyone."

About the fiancé: . . . . "they say that he composed. . . . . . ."

He is an empty-headed man, however, he may have other qualities that are meritorious, I never want to judge anyone. You will be happy with him, Daria. He seems like a good man, though shallow persons are seldom good—only so far as the first time they have to show intelligence. Therefore, don't rely on goodheartedness alone. That's even worse. However, all this is nonsense, beside the point, since you will be married in 2 months." (Here put in the business about the money and the uncle.)

~~The daughter's program. An undeveloped but deep-natured creature. A silent, firm character. Her mother has long seen but does not argue with her. She is waiting. The Idiot upsets her. Magnanimous character. Suddenly she broke off with her fiancé.~~[8]

N.B. Toward the end she rejected the Idiot, but later she understood.

This highly respectful *wooer of the progressives.*

"But that's exactly how it is."

"Which would be better? Tell everyone like that—

------

[8] This crossed-out section was found among Dostoevsky's notes for his novel *The Eternal Husband* (1870).

The Sixth Plan

(*Written November 6, 1867.*)

As in the last few plans, these notes are all tightly concerned with the Idiot's character. The deadline for submitting the first part of the novel is nearing, and the Idiot's character obstinately refuses to yield itself to him. Dostoevsky seems unable to decide facts as simple as whose son the Idiot is. He is now once again the son of the general and not of the uncle, but he is now the son by the first marriage. He has had once again a poor childhood: abandoned by the first wife, his mother, he is tormented and rejected by the second wife. Until the age of sixteen or seventeen he grows up in the uncle's house, where he is similarly mistreated, and then he spends some time with the Umetskys. Eventually he is sent to Switzerland, a circumstance that now recurs with persistence and will, of course, be in the final version. As in the fifth plan he has a wife and baby, and Dostoevsky uses this device to complicate his love for the heroine. Most often, the Idiot uses this fact to torment the heroine, revealing it after she declares her love for him, and once after she surrenders to him. His relationship with the heroine ends in torment for his wife, driving her, at least in some of the notes, to death by hanging, by drowning, and by poison. In other notes she dies a natural death. His wife forgives him and does not forgive him his love for the heroine. As in the fifth plan, he is poised between true love and false love, purity (his wife is called a Madonna) and passion. He cannot accept either.

The plot turns, as so often, on money and love. The general's family is again impoverished, and again when the lawsuit fails they encourage the heroine to marry Ganechka (an ideal and beautiful character), hint at a better suitor in the uncle, and apparently encourage her marriage to the Idiot, who seems to receive three hundred thousand rubles as a legacy or from the uncle. The Idiot proudly renounces the money, and at the appropriate vengeful moment renounces the heroine as well.

The Idiot's character shows no special changes throughout the piece: he is still filled with the poison of causeless revenge, still intent upon punishing the heroine, still attracted to Umetskaia, still loving and tormenting his wife, still proud and at times sacrificial. He tries to help the Ganechka-heroine romance, but with envy in his heart. He almost finds true love with his wife; more than once he falls at her feet and tells her he loves her. Despite the intimations of "regeneration" the change continues not to take, and the poison of revenge and hurt obliterates the impulses. Dostoevsky catches the essence of his character in the following brief outline of his character and situation: "Characterization. Magnanimous principles, childhood. *Envy*. Indignation."

The notes of this plan seem more schematic than most. Dostoevsky is still repeating the same situations: the Idiot's clerkship in the uncle's office, the heroine's (sometimes the family's) lawsuit, the heroine's mockery, the Idiot's social triumph, the rejected legacy, the burned finger, the rape of Umetskaia, the endless imaginary insults, and the flights (now more by the Idiot than by the heroine) from love to love. With the deadline approaching, Dostoevsky outlines the plan for the first part near the end of these notes. The action is supposed to start in the railway carriage, where the Idiot is to meet the heroine. His debut is not sparkling: he is rude in conversation, spills wine on her, and awkwardly flings down money and flees. The uncle still has a role in the plot, and the general still tries to borrow money from him. The Idiot—less than two months before Dostoevsky was to submit the first part of the novel for publication—has a wife, rapes Umetskaia, burns his finger, sets fire to a house, loves the heroine, and torments his wife. One must imagine Dostoevsky between boredom and exasperation as he rehearses the same situations.

Dostoevsky begins the sixth plan with the question: *"Enigmas. Who is he? A terrible scoundrel or a mysterious ideal?"* And he ends it with what seems to be a shaft of inspiration: *"He is a Prince."* And, "Prince *Yurodivyi*. (He is with the children.)?!" There is still no intimation that he will be the purehearted Prince of the novel, but the idea arises with full force in the next plan, and one can hazard that these few words are already the beginning of light. The enigma that has tortured him throughout the various plans is about to be illuminated.

List of Characters for the Sixth Plan

The General's Family

The general
The general's wife
His son Ganechka
His son, the Idiot (from the first marriage)
The Idiot's wife
The general's daughter
The heroine

The Uncle's Family

The uncle, the brother of the general's first wife
A son (Ilia?)

The Umetskys

Vladimir Umetsky
Olga Umetskaia

The family. Son of the first marriage. An arsonist from the beginning. The heroine is in the house. "I am furious. I carried her off on her wedding day." The uncle intervened and sent <. . .> abroad.

He returned from abroad.—They are totally ruined. They have lost the lawsuit. He supports the family and they all detest him. *His former mistress* is in love with Ganechka. The old man wanted to get out of the house. He is cool and polite. Suddenly a legacy of 300,000. They all turn away from him.

(All this time he was working in the uncle's office. The uncle quarrels with the family. The uncle and *he*. The uncle did not impress him.)

Within the family the former mistress began to be regarded differently when they received the 300,000. Especially the heroine. (Who is the heroine?) She insulted the young girl. The father was on her side. She herself rejected the son.

Enigmas. Who is he? A terrible scoundrel or a mysterious ideal?

Ganechka is an ideally beautiful person. (*Ganechka and she* turn away from the mother and father and turn toward the son for help.)

The uncle is not the general's brother but the brother of the general's 1st wife, who had hanged herself. The other is his nephew.

Or else. N.B. The uncle is vexed with him because he is not respectful (after returning from Switzerland) and gives him nothing except his wages. Meanwhile he has been brought up in his house (tormented), for the general at the urging of *his second wife* had repudiated him because his mother ran away. They behaved unjustly toward him. He possesses documents showing that he is legitimate. He does not want to subject himself to the new wife. (Is he an Idiot? The story of that idiotism.) The general is not poor but on the contrary is an important personage with prestige. (*The plot of the novel.*) The general had served in the province up until now. N.B.

N.B. Up to his 11th year *the Idiot* had lived with the general and his wife in Petersburg. When they went to the province, the uncle took the Idiot in (at the wish of the general's wife. The general checked up on him from time to time). The Idiot suffered in the uncle's house until he was 17 ~~16~~. Thereafter he was at the Umetskys. From the Umetskys he went abroad. He returned from Switzerland. (The Idiot) was working in the office. Meanwhile the general and his wife settle in Petersburg. The general summoned the son. (With them are the heroine and Ganechka.)

Perhaps: the uncle marries and the Idiot is married at the Umetskys.

(*Give me an idea!*)

N.B. When the general and his wife came back to live and serve in Petersburg, she wished to see him.

The uncle is *by no means* the brother.

The general and his wife *had in view* (as in the previous plan) marrying the heroine to Ganechka for the sake of social connections. But the heroine's lawsuit looks very doubtful of success. The general's wife wants a richer fiancé ~~perhaps the uncle~~ for her, to marry her to the Idiot, hoping that once the marriage is consummated the uncle will make him a gift.

6 November

It is more than likely that in the first place no word concerning a wedding between Ganechka and the heroine has been uttered aloud, and in the 2nd place that the general was too insistent that the heroine ought to become one of the family, and in the 3rd place that an end had come to the family quarrels with the general's wife, who had already found a fiancée for Ganechka.

Ganechka resists (an honorable and beautiful character).

The heroine receives the Idiot with a deluge of ridicule, having found out that they intend her for him.

The uncle visits the general's family (that is, he renews the acquaintance) *and is jealous of the Idiot.*

Plan

Sequel. The Idiot returned from Switzerland, *still an Idiot.* Meanwhile he is a clerk. The uncle understands and *is angry.* Several explanations. At the house of the general and his wife. The uncle *is jealous* in advance. At the general's house the Idiot is no idiot but on the contrary is highly esteemed. Charming and modest. (The general's wife—a type, especially benevolent.) The general is delighted. Impossible to be angry and there is no one on whom to take revenge, but his soul is filled with poison. The heroine greets him with venomous mockery, but by the end of the evening party she likes him (the daughter's fiancé—a chamberlain).

On returning the uncle creates a scene. He offers his friendship, but "to the devil with the legacy. I want to work in the office and I consider myself useful." The uncle is vexed, he agrees, but he is suffering. The heroine has bowled him over—he would be glad of—.

"You get married."—(Various stories about the uncle. Delineate the uncle, embellish him.)

Mysterious relations with the Umetsky family, Umetskaia, and the wife. The baby.

On the following evening Ganechka's visit to the general and his wife. Despite the fact that Ganechka has heard that he is intended for fiancé the heroine—he is charming and seeks his friendship. (He serves brilliantly in a post where no one does anything.) The Idiot is cool, but Ganechka's charm takes effect on him. (N.B. *The originality of the conversation.*)

He visits the wife. The wife makes an impression on him. But he is ashamed and is afraid of showing this.

The heroine goes on ridiculing him. The general, his wife, and the uncle are still full of hope. The heroine forces him into an explanation. He first tells her that he could never be her husband, has not the least *aspiration* to be, and has renounced all claim to the uncle's money. The astonishment of the general and his wife. He has his own apartment.

The burning of the finger. They commit arson. He raped Umetskaia.

As soon as the heroine heard that he had renounced both her and the money, she suddenly began to take an interest in him. Meanwhile Ganechka came to him, and he became Ganechka's and the heroine's mysterious protector and teacher. (His sister too was drawn to him and turned down the chamberlain.) The whole house is in a mess and an uproar.

His romance with his wife pursues its course in parallel and independently. Is he *frank* with his wife? With Umetskaia, *in his own way,* but he cannot live without Umetskaia. "When I came from Switzerland, I was different!"

Though he plays the role of Providence to Ganechka and the heroine, he is deeply jealous and is even *privately* jealous of Ganechka's relation to the heroine. Suddenly the heroine bursts into tears and declares to the Idiot that she loves *him*.

Then he says in malevolent triumph that he is *married*.

That he is married—at once the news spreads. Indignation on all sides. They stare at his wife. And so forth.

The heroine and the wife.

He torments his wife to such a point, though, as people are made to think, he is proud of her, that she hangs herself ~~drowns herself~~. (The uncle, who has fallen in love with his wife, goes to find her, together with him (scene) didn't she hang herself?)

Or else he goes to find her with the heroine. Here he finally recounts to the heroine how he tortured her. She did hang herself. (The baby had died before this.)

For the romance with the wife. N.B. On his return he is harshly insulting. But she is used to this. At first he is reserved in his reproaching her, but, seeing how she bows under them (like a Madonna) he begins to expand, confessing that he cannot live without her. In one such moment he throws himself at her feet and says he loves her. On the very verge of happiness. But then everything collapses. Pride overcomes him. And when he seduces the heroine—(he raped her).

Scenes with the general, the uncle, Ganechka.

He goes with the heroine to find the body of his wife. (The heroine runs to his wife.)

The wife's last words to them: "Love each other."

But while they are searching for her he was already confessing: "I don't love you."

For the epilogue

I have written a fantastic novel, but never more actual characters (thirst for love and for truth, pride and lack of self-respect).

(Incessant imaginary insults.)

He helps Ganechka and the heroine, but with deep-seated envy. The heroine sees through him and pursues him with her sarcasms (*but he himself is profoundly self-loathing*).

N.B.? (At one of these moments the heroine *surrenders* to him; his triumph; he tells her immediately after this that he is married.)

The heroine is ill. He is with his wife and the baby and makes her suffer. (The uncle; his wife is shown to him. The general.) He drives them all away. At this point the heroine comes to him. The baby dies. She hanged herself. (Umetskaia.) They search. Explanations in full: "*I acted thus out of envy.* I never loved you, I had lost her."

N.B. Or else *poison*. Accusations. The apothecary. Vl. Umetsky and so on. "Yes, I poisoned her."

The letter.

The scene in which they go out searching: didn't she hang herself? It was earlier, with the uncle. Then he falls at her feet and says, "I love you."

He found her with the baby and Umetskaia on the deserted bank of the Neva—near a rift in the ice. She had handed the baby to Umetskaia. He brought her back home. He falls at her feet: "I love *only you*." She forgives everything.

But she did not forgive the rape of the heroine, and she poisoned herself.

Characterization. Magnanimous principles, childhood. *Envy*. Indignation. It mounted in the general and his wife, in the uncle. He set fires and played tricks at the Umetskys. In Switzerland his bitterness swelled. He wanted to come back as a proud and magnanimous man. But he was deceiving himself, his envious pride served only to make him suffer. Self-contempt. His wife *exonerated* him of everything and consoled him with her forgiveness. The letter to him—*in case they detected poison.*

?N.B. Or else a natural death while out of her mind. The heroine is there. Letter to him written the week before at Umetskaia's. *She had been* well educated.

Plan of the 1st Part

1) The arrival. In the railway carriage. Interview with the uncle. Unuttered words.

The railway carriage. He watched the general and his wife. At the station. Stepped on the heroine's foot. Wanted to pay her a compliment. The heroine and the chamberlain aside. Several rudenesses during the conversation. Spilled the wine. Returned, flung down the money, and fled.

2) *At the Umetskys.* Harsh statement. Mutual demands. Characters. Explanations.

3) *Umetskaia and he.* At the wife's. His baby.—"Do you know my story?" (Briefly but clearly. Past and present aims and motives.)

The general and the uncle. To borrow money. Sees him and invites him that evening.

4) He and the uncle. (Explanation, the uncle discourses on the origin of idiotism. "What are your intentions?" Besides, he is somewhat jealous. He talks about the heroine.) "I am going in the morning, I'll stop by at 12 o'clock."

5) The following day. The Idiot's struggle and anxiety. Explanation with the father. Family morning. He charmed everyone. Stays to dinner. The uncle leaves, bowled over.

6) At the wife's. With Umetskaia. Fantastic conversations. Eccentricity. Hot, flaming impatience with his wife. About his plans, about idiotism. ~~Did he rape her? N.B. How many questions???~~

7) Explanation with the uncle, he refuses the money. Visits Ganechka.

8) Evening at the general's. The heroine. The uncle, ridicule. Rage, and so forth. Burns his finger.

9) He raped Umetskaia and sets fire to the house. Disappointment. "Better give up everyone and everything! I didn't arrive from Switzerland like this," and so forth.

2nd Part. (N.B. Don't forget the explanations with the general's wife and the sister and so on.)

The heroine's role is one of ridicule and defiance. The uncle's role (he reveals to the uncle that he is married. The uncle himself does not want to speak to the general about this.) Ganechka speaks his mind in his anxiety.

The chamberlain makes advances to him.

P.S. ? N.B. (Perhaps it is at this moment that he produces his wife.)

He is a Prince. Idiot. Everything is based on vengeance. A humiliated creature. The brother's wife [fiancée]. Refuses the uncle's money. In the office he sulks.

Prince *Yurodivyi*.[1] (He is with the children.)?!

He summoned them together for the sake of effect, so as to produce a dazzling effect, to repudiate the uncle and the general and the legacy. He had heard that the general was interested in him.

"How? You brought them all with you?"

"I heard of tortures."

He renounced the heroine, triumph.

"I am getting married." (Family evenings.) Scenes and sufferings. The heroine's mockeries.

To Ilia—"Get married."

"Very well."

He goes to the heroine (she is more affectionate and flirts with him. Pays no attention to the uncle). He proposes to the heroine. "I'll give up everything." She tells him: "I am going to marry uncle." Venomous letter.

He went to her: "There had been no marriage as yet." She fled, without knowing where, to hang herself.

They went to find her. They did find her. (The baby had caught cold.)

Crazy Ilia stood over her.

He replied to her (immediately after the heroine's letter):—

The Madonna absolutely rejects him. "Don't let me see you." Scenes with Ilia. Meanwhile, he works on the heroine. Ilia and the Madonna make wedding preparations.

He says to her: "Let's run away." She hangs herself.

Before the wedding the heroine says in a flood of tears: "I am yours, let's run away."

---

[1] Prince *Yurodivyi*: the word "Prince" is written in large calligraphy in the manuscript.

[Unable to control his passion, he rapes her.]

He rapes her. She dies. They seek her. She hanged herself.

He says to the heroine: "I did not love you. I do not love you, I hate you."

N.B. In the Entr'acte he broke off the sister's engagement with delight, and bewildered the general and the diplomat, advising the diplomat how to get free of the heroine. [Does he poison her?]

("You are my *bogatyr*"[2] to Ilia.)

She is half out of her mind with love of him.

But then before the wedding when

the Idiot comes back to her because the heroine

had refused him—she drowns herself.

Main point: envy and pride, exasperated pride, he recounts to the uncle (at his house with a group including Ilia and the Madonna) how he longed for gold when he was living with the uncle.

He is frank with the heroine, and that is how he seduced her.

---

[2] *Bogatyr:* a hero of Russian folklore, a valiant knight, and therefore a robust, vigorous, courageous man. Ilia Muromets (from the town of Murom in the province of Nizhni-Novgorod, now Gorky, on the Volga) was one of the most popular of the legendary *bogatyry*. In the epoch of St. Prince Vladimir, under whom Christianity was introduced into Russia (988), Ilia waged war against the pagan nomadic tribes threatening the young state. His exploits are celebrated in many folk tales and *byliny,* or epic ballads.

The Seventh Plan

(*Written between November 10 and the beginning of December, 1867.*)

The character of the Idiot is almost completely changed in these notes: he is humble, forgiving, sincere, Christian; he is, in short, the Myshkin of the final version, and in the passage that follows, his relationship to Nastasia Filipovna is sketched: "The Idiot was in the province of Saratov. When Nastia's seducer abandoned her, he took her in, she gave birth, and he took over the child, et cetera. In her anguish and rage at having been deserted, she inveighed against *him* and jeered at him, but afterwards she threw herself at his feet, and in the end she fell in love with him, he offered his hand, and she *ran away* ('I am furious, I won't ask pardon, I am defiled')." Dostoevsky senses the importance of this passage, and he adds: "*Absolutely has to be worked out:* He assented and believed as she did, so that he ridiculed himself, as if he were as distorted as she made him out to be. She is stunned by his *simplicity and humility.*"

We have in these passages the embryo of Nastasia Filipovna, seduced and defiled by Totsky, and forgiven and loved by Myshkin: the fallen woman and the purified love. We find also Nastasia's hurt and outrage, her pride, "I'm furious, I won't ask pardon," and her bruising humility, "I am defiled." We also find her ambiguous attitude toward the Idiot: "She inveighed against *him* and jeered at him, but afterward she threw herself at his feet, and in the end she fell in love with him, he offered his hand, and she *ran away.*" There are substantial differences, which are explained by the hold of past plans on this new conception. Nastasia Filipovna does not jeer at Myshkin in the final version, although there is some mocking condescension in her first meeting; the jeering is the legacy of all those past plans in which the heroine has mocked the attentions of the Idiot. Nor, of course, does Nastasia Filipovna give birth to a child in the final version, nor is the Idiot present at the time of her abandonment. In the final version Dostoevsky has given her more initiative, more self-directed vengefulness against others and against herself; in the final version she is more than a fallen woman saved by a magnanimous prince.

Despite the fact that the sketch brilliantly anticipates the essential lines of Nastasia Filipovna's attitude toward herself and Myshkin, it is hardly new in other respects. From the very beginning and throughout all the plans the Idiot had been drawn to the oppressed and tormented Mignon-Umetskaia, although curiously he had also raped her repeatedly. And in the plans immediately preceding this one, the Idiot had generously consented to marriage with a fallen woman who had borne the child of another man. What changes most of 'all is the Idiot's attitude toward the fallen woman and toward his own generosity. He no longer hates his own generosity, and his proud vengeance on his own compassionate impulses is gone. The purified love to which Dostoevsky had wished so fervently to bring the hating and loving Idiot is attained, but not as he had first foreseen it. The pure, noble Christ-like traits that had existed from the very beginning and had been given at different times to the uncle's son, to Ganechka, and to the Idiot's wife, are now centered in the Idiot himself. In the last few plans, the Idiot was poised dramatically between the pure love of his Madonna-wife and the vengeful-passionate love of the heroine; now Nastasia Filipovna is poised between the purified love of the Idiot and the passionate love of the son (Ganechka).

Dostoevsky now gives the Idiot's former qualities to the son: "This is the character that was formerly the Idiot's: magnanimous, bitterness, pride, and envy." He is the Idiot's antagonist for the hand of Nastia, and as such anticipates the role of Rogozhin in the final version: "She arrived at the Umetskys, there they seized her and beat her. The son intervened, *took her away to Petersburg* (he is to blame for this), and fell in love with her. She jeered at him and deserted him. A laundress. Then *she does indeed* fall in love with the son and resolves to lead a whore's life. To the Idiot she says: 'I look on you as on God, *but I love him.*' Rushes to the son in deep shame (storms, tears, and the Idiot's consolations; 'There, there, it's all right!' And suddenly she runs off to drown herself, and so forth." Nastasia Fili-

povna's flight with Rogozhin, her destructive love for him, her ideali-
zation of Myshkin, and her conviction that in going off with Rogozhin she confirms her fallen state are all anticipated in this passage.
However, the son does not have Rogozhin's brooding, brutal, and
silent character. He has impulses of generosity, and Nastia seems
more irritated with his youth than with anything else.

The son is also apparently a rival of his father for the hand of
Umetskaia-Ustinia. It is virtually impossible to distinguish between
these two, and Dostoevsky himself juxtaposes the two names and
crosses one out at one point. Dostoevsky seems to be experimenting
with some kind of parallel to the Nastia-Idiot situation. Umetskaia
has a baby in one set of notes, and Ustinia is a "fallen" woman in
some passages, seduced and apparently made pregnant by her father.
However, Ustinia's attitude to her fallen state is not the vengeful,
stricken, sense of defilement that Nastia feels. She seduces the son at
one point and then torments him by announcing that she wants to
marry the general for prestige. Dostoevsky seems to be experimenting
structurally with parallel situations so as to throw into relief differences in attitude toward the same situations. This is not an uncom-
mon device in his work, and indeed it is a structural analogue to the
psychological doubling that is so intimately a part of his view of the
psyche. Raskolnikov's and Svidrigailov's murders are paralleled, at
least in dreams, so as to throw into relief the differences of their
essential natures. Here both Nastia and Ustinia are mistreated by
their father, both are seduced and abandoned, and both are "saved,"
by the Idiot and the son. One seems to react to the seduction and
saving by a sense of self-defilement and outrage, and the other by a
sense of cynical self-profit.

The general's part in the love relationships adds other complications. As so many times before, he is hard pressed economically: "In
St. Petersburg the general thinks about a post. (Creditors.) Everything has collapsed. Before the Idiot's arrival, the 2nd part. (They
pawn the spoons.)" He has become, despite his economic setbacks,
more tyrannical and apparently more lascivious. In one of the early
plans the Idiot had horrified him, and the family, by suggesting that

he was in love with his ward; and in a later plan the general kills himself when he recognizes the truth of the accusation, presumably from a sensitive conscience. There seems to be no question of conscience now, only of profit. He is alternately in pursuit of a ward (the old motive) and of Ustinia (the son is horrified by his father's wish to marry her, because he has himself been seduced by her). It would seem that Dostoevsky was experimenting with two lines of development for the general. Even his love for the ward is worked out in two ways: in one scheme he marries her, and in another, the ward, on the advice of an aunt, refuses him. There is also reference to the ward's running away from him on her wedding day, paralleling what the heroine had done so often, and what Nastia does to the son.

It is just possible that Dostoevsky is experimenting with various structural doublings as a way of expressing what is painful to express directly: the seduction of a daughter by a father. This was a factor in the Umetsky case, and there are some hints that Umetsky slept with Ustinia. The seduction of the ward by the general, and his lascivious relationship with Ustinia, may be an indirect analogue to the seduction of Nastia and her impregnation. It is possible, in other words, that Totsky's seduction of Nastasia Filipovna in the final version, is a symbolic displacement of the father's seduction of a child. There is much in the final version to suggest such an analogue: Totsky does assume the responsibilities of the girl's father, after her own father dies; he brings her up, takes care of her, educates her, and then he defiles her. Even later, he assumes the "parental" function of trying to establish her in life by money and by arranging a marriage. Dostoevsky could not have put forth directly the horror of a father's defilement of a child, of course, and it was left heavily veiled by the oblique responsibility Totsky had taken upon himself, and possibly by the attentions of General Epanchin, the father of daughters, thirsting to defile a daughter. In these notes Dostoevsky does allude, indeed states, that Umetsky had lived with his daughter Ustinia; and it seems apparent that Dostoevsky's elaborate experimentations with the general's lascivious proclivities are an attempt to find that delicate line between concealment and revelation. He was not to find it.

The overriding importance of this plan must consist, of course, in the radical change that Dostoevsky effects in the Idiot's character. The change is not as extreme as some have thought. The Russian editor of these notes says: "Nothing remains of the former Idiot." This is not wholly true. Even in this plan something of his enigmatic quality remains: *"The Idiot's personality. A bizarre creature. His oddities. Gentle. At times he says not a word."* Most important, however, such a statement ignores the fact that Dostoevsky had been trying to nudge the Idiot toward some magnanimous, some great deed from the very first plan. The thirst for true love, sacrifice, humility—all the qualities the Idiot has now and which Myshkin is to have—was always part of his character, but up to now was always perverted by his will and pride. It would be more correct to say that nothing remains of that frustrating, perverting, causeless, and vengeful impulse to corrupt everything he touched, and nothing remains of the qualities that this impulse engendered, or which engendered it: pride, self-will, and outrage. Dostoevsky has the "beautiful" Idiot he sought, but he was not able to wrest him from the tormented and largely destructive creature he had characterized up to this point. The love of Dostoevsky's heart won out over his sense of what was realistically probable. If he was to have his beautiful Idiot, he would have to create him, for the world and its realities would never grant him a beautiful soul.

---

*List of Characters for
the Seventh Plan*

The General's Family

The general
The general's wife
The Idiot
The daughter Varia (and her fiancé)
The son Ganechka
Yasha
Kolia
The ward
The aunt

The Umetskys

Vladimir Umetsky
His wife
Olga Umetskaia
Ustinia Alekseevna, who has a son Sasha
Nastia, perhaps the sister of Ustinia

---

10 November

Further points. . . . . . .
It was long known that he would marry the ward.
Official announcement.

(Letter from the fiancé)

It is now 5 months since the mother died. Scene with the general. It begins with the children. The daughter's fiancé. The children's conversation, *about everything and about the son*, even about the poisoning. They pawn the spoons. Hard times. The Idiot has not come. The general's toast. The gloomy Yasha. The son arrives, he hears about the sister. They all urge him to leave, but he doesn't leave. (The children's suspicion that he is going to marry the ward.) ("Is that how you ought to behave at the Umetskys?") [The daughter is locked up in her room for having been impertinent to the ward. Yasha intends to protest. To the son: "If you cannot, I *must*." Rumors about the Idiot.]

The general appears, irritated, sarcasms and quarrels. The daughter, the fiancé, are against the son (after he spoke). "How did you dare put in an appearance?" *To Yasha:* "You were the cause of mother's death." Yasha rebels and contradicts. "Out of my house!" *Yasha's* flight. They look for him. Some degree of reconciliation with the son. The son goes away dissatisfied. The Idiot appears.

The general is overjoyed, he recounts to the Idiot about the son (the fact that he wants to propose). The children treat the Idiot like an informer. The general's proposal to the ward when they are left alone.

Early next morning the Idiot goes to see Nastia, stops at the Umetskys. Sees the brother. [Perhaps in the 2nd Part.]

At the general's, the children's conference. Olga Umetskaia. The reception of the ward. The Idiot returns. A children's magazine. The general is in excellent spirits, "Oh, you little imp!" (Yasha is ill.) The general announces his marriage to the children. He goes out.

The children. Quarrel with the ward. The Idiot with the ward. Again the son—falls into despair. She has plunged into debauchery. It is Umetskaia who did this. Slight reconciliation with the general. He found out about the marriage: "What a stupidity." Suddenly the aunt appears. "You want to get married, it's out of the question." "No, I don't want to."

"I want to go to Dmitri Ivanovich." The general is in a rage with the daughter. "I'm going to question you." "Yasha, hit out!" The Idiot is given a blow in the face. "Beat him, but you're not to hit me." The aunt departs, infuriated with the daughter and the ward.

N.B. The Idiot with the children, 1st conversation ("And we thought you were so boring") about Fyodor Ivanovich, about Mont-Blanc, about Switzerland, about the story of a teacher and a little boy, about Olga Umetskaia, about the existence of God, and finally about the ward and her engagement, about her future situation, he brings about a reconciliation between her and the children. He also talks of the general. He draws them into an alliance. (The son wants to marry a low woman. The children speak of this with horror.) Yasha's declaration. At this point Umetskaia, the aunt, the son, the grandmother appear, Yasha is beaten, and so on.

Essential: to set forth the personality of the Idiot in a masterly fashion.

On receiving him and talking with him, the general tells him a great deal about the past.

The children's conversations also deal with this topic.

Bring the novel to a close with an interesting idea for a sequel.

More significance in the novel.

The Idiot's personality.

Further points.

Nota bene.

How she gave way to depravity after she became a laundress—in the 2nd Part.

The son gives off the *odeur* of despair. The children have no great respect for him, they fear him. Scenes between the Idiot and *her* in the 2nd chapter and *before that a chapter about his former mistress in the country.*

In the 3rd Part there is one *room for the children* and another for his wife (women's occupations). Some come by the day, some live in.

Chief variations: greater frenzy in the son.

The general (while the school is in session) marries Umetskaia.

When they were persecuting Nastia (whom perhaps the son marries), the son cried out to the father that his wife was a whore and that he knew this for a fact.

The Idiot: "Ask forgiveness."

The Umetskys.

The children.

The Idiot (1st appearance).

The general (scandalous ways and a Russian soul).

The general to his daughter: "I don't want any disorderliness in the house."

I

The first *Part* takes place in the country. (Perhaps.) *Must be very concise.*

In the beginning the Idiot is with her, with the children, he receives, *scenes,* 2 chapters. She ran away.

They found themselves in the country. Tableaux of the Umetskys, the general.

Blows. The elder son attacked him. The general intervened.

Meanwhile: the general's despotism, scenes with the son, because of the *mother* (N.B.), Yasha, who regards himself as unloved. (Excursions, hide-and-seek games, the Umetskys' children and the general's children, *Umetskaia's* baby, *Olga Umetskaia*), the ward and her role in the house. The general sidles around Ustinia. The son with Ustinia. Yasha does not want to ask forgiveness.

The general does not release Nastia. Battle with the Umetskys.

The general's wife is jealous of Nastia. Reproaches. Nastia is in a fury.

"I am not going to give in. I won't ask forgiveness."

She runs away with the son. Ustinia arranges matters. "You, Ustinia, vile though you are, still, you can be of service."

(In general, she is under a hysterical tension continually.)

The general in opposition to his wife: unexpected death. Hypertrophy of the heart.

The funeral. "Today, for the first time, I am beginning to live!"

Then he led the way to the grave.

N.B. (The children *know* the Idiot and remember about him.)

N.B. After the Seducer left she lived at his house in the country. (Only Ustinia came to see her.) The Idiot came to console her. She was waiting, no letters! Anguish, childbirth, the Idiot took the baby. The letter comes, refusal, and 10,000 rubles. (Illness. "Well, now!" Then the Idiot offered her his hand.)

When his wife died, the general says, after seeing Yasha: "You, you killed her!"

Yasha wanted to hang himself. Then he flung himself on her grave.

N.B. Here glimpses of the general's affection for the children. Comical scenes.

They made friends with Umetsky. (Ustinia the consoler.) He sold the property to Umetsky.—He went to Petersburg with the children.

In Petersburg the general thinks about a post. (Creditors.) Everything has collapsed. Before the Idiot's arrival, the 2nd Part. (They pawn the spoons.)

II

When the general (2nd Part) had settled matters with the ward, he took sides with Umetskaia. The ward is jealous, furious with her, and with the daughter, and so forth. So that everything was prepared with Umetskaia when the ward refused.

1st Part. He flogs Yasha. Yasha is found innocent.

N.B. The Idiot thinks himself *hideous*. Once when he was consoling her and daydreaming with her—something very sweet made itself felt in both of them. The Idiot fled. Then when he came back the next day—she laughed at him.

They went out, he did not run away, and after they had arranged marrying, the next day she kissed his hand and went away (having partly explained herself, leaving him profoundly astonished).

The son to Umetskaia in the country: "How vile you are! You have a vile soul." Hence love (in actuality) and envy. (The son is 21.)

N.B. Umetskaia on the other hand persecutes Nastia, but she does not help her. And at the same time (in the 1st Part) she incites the old man against the son.

She was with the Idiot in the beginning, there was a rumor about him that he was occupying himself with the children.

On his arrival in Petersburg the children take the Idiot to be an informer.

N.B. The story of the beginning of the son's love; when they beat her and locked her up, and she together with Olga set fire to the house—pity seized him. He intervened and forbade them. He took her away and shut her up. He entered into relations with Ustinia. Ustinia had even seduced him at one point. (For this reason the son is horrified when the general wants to marry Ustinia.) But this relation was an ephemeral one, and when the son suddenly fell in love with Nastia (he is a wild, rabid character, "I don't ask for forgiveness," but he embraces the son), he suddenly offered her his hand. She says to him: "What a catastrophe I would bring down on you." Since the whole thing depended on her, she made up her mind. The mother agreed. Ustinia schemed, and she ran away the day before the wedding.

Ustinia is not her sister.

Characteristic trait: Before the wedding the general was in an excellent frame of mind, he took counsel with the family and was even reconciled with the son. (The magazine, and so on.) But everything was excessive. If he becomes reconciled, he wants friendship too. He narrates his whole life (a characterization of this person) and finally when he announces his marriage—a quarrel.

Before this the son was <illegible> unhappy, she had listened to the sister and run away. He would have liked to wipe out all memory of her with contempt, and he came to the family. *The Idiot.* But after the quarrels, he flew back to her. Though the general had been comforting him.

She is 23 years old, she remained because she was sorry for the children (but she had come for the sake of her daily bread), she was living openly with him near the country estate, she had come of age. (He was influential in the province.) Suddenly he went off and left her. She ran from him. The father overtook her, beat her, and locked her up. The son intervened.

Everything else remains as before.

That is, Nastia is 23.

Ustinia ~~Umetskaia~~ 31.

The ward at Suzdal.[1]

Vlad. Umetsky would have been delighted to pursue Nastia.

The son of the second marriage is 21.

The Idiot of the 1st marriage is 26 (is well-to-do), has been abroad.

---

[1] Suzdal: a small town in the province of Vladimir, on the Kamenka River, with a population of about 6,000 in Dostoevsky's time. It was mainly distinguished by its cathedral and by the Spaso-Efimevsky Monastery-Prison, where many heretics and dissenters were customarily incarcerated.

Directly on returning from abroad he goes to the country to the Umetskys. He is educated, an odd creature.

At first the general wanted to marry the child ward. But the aunt arrived to take the sister, "Well, do you want to or not?" She burst into tears: "No, no, I don't want to!"

She behaved with pride in every respect, though no one had expected this of her, solely in order to argue with the children. On saying goodbye to the children, she took them into her arms and shed tears, and they did too. They went off to Suzdal.

"No, I don't want to."

"Do you want to go away with me?"

"No, I don't want to."

"But what do you want then?"

"I want to go away with Ivan Nikolaevich" (the Idiot). And that is how she declared her love.

No family. At this point, while Ustinia is deceiving him, he becomes reconciled with the elder son, who had intervened on his behalf. Together they go to find Nastia (who is his wife moreover). Nastia is 20 ~~23~~. "What kind of a husband are you?"

In the beginning, Nastia, though she had married the son, wanted to kill her seducer. (For the sake of her daily bread, the little old man.) They all shame her (she has a rebellious, violent, crazy character).

N.B. (Or else Nastia has not yet married him; she ran away simply so as not to make him unhappy. But he pursues her all the more.)

In Petersburg Nastia is vacillating and tormenting herself: should she marry or not?—Because she herself is in love, she even sets the day for the wedding. But at the first quarrel she decides not to go ahead with it. "He will torment me, and I am not good enough for him, and too, I can't truckle to anyone," and she decides to follow Ustinia's advice. The latter acts as a go-between, and so on.

The son is in despair, but he wants to forgive even this. Nastia is touched. The general agrees. The wedding day is set. But Nastia wavers (her pride) still more. The son was jealous, the cup flowed over, and before the wedding Nastia drowned herself. (This is the character that was formerly the Idiot's: magnanimous, bitterness, pride, and envy.)

N.B. (The general did not marry Ustinia, though he behaved meanly. He drove her away.)

N.B. But Ustinia managed to get a note of hand for 10,000 from the general and locked it up.

The Idiot paid up. He is ill, the children. He has been taking an extraordinary interest in the son and in Nastia. He returned to his family. He gave the son permission to marry Nastia. He went to find her when she ran away. (The son is a Byronic character. Melancholy.) Suddenly the general (when everything had long since been ended with Ustinia) takes a knife and goes to cut Ustinia's throat. He did not succeed in killing her.

(Hence all this tenderness and his return to the family and to the son indicated a psychological trait: suddenly he killed.)

~~Nastia is 22. The father was already running after~~ her when she was only 20, when he could still—.

She said to the son: "Well, how could I ruin you, handsome and charming as you are."

But Umetsky's wife and Ustinia silenced the old man. Just before the wedding she suddenly fled.

Nastia had the right to run away, but the father beat and tortured her like a wild animal. *She set the house on fire,* they caught her red-handed. But when the son said: "I will marry her, and if you dare. . . . . . ."

(1st signature)

Or else: the ward is a member of the household.

The general marries her, was jealous of her.

But she was frightened, she ran off on her wedding day.

They find her.

Cursory outline. Points.

1) The unexpected death of the mother from hypertrophy of the heart. The family. *Central plot.* The general. The toast. Accentuated scene.

The general and the family. Not without some description. (According to Yasha's friend's opinion, he poisoned her.) Quarrels, tempests, horrors. Curses to the grave. He is a *yurodivyi.* The general himself (story). ("What don't they want of me?") Conversations and pacts. The elder son. Reconciliation with him. Finally the consent to run away. Yasha is 15 ("I don't want to give in"). Kolia. The Umetskys' children (savages). Olga Umetskaia. Reconciliation with the elder son. Three days of joy. Ferocious rupture. The elder son is driven out. Kolia's rebellion and flight. He runs after him. (The sister is made to give evidence.) Reconciliation. Marriage.

General dissatisfaction. Indignation. Speeches. The *yurodivyi* arranges matters. (He got married.) V's character. (Perhaps with the ward the eve of the wedding.) The sister is made to give evidence in the 2nd Part.

2nd Part

P.S. Perhaps he is a naïve youngster of 17, and at first she assumed the appearance of being his wife. (The magazine 2nd issue No. A 1st No. The general himself encourages.) He quarrels with the children, even comes to blows, and suddenly he and they all run away together. The general grew jealous of the elder son. Horrible scenes. The Umetskys too. ["Whip Kolia—I'll hang myself in a fit of passion.]

3) The whole herd flock to the *yurodivyi's*. (The elder son is 21.) (N.B.? The Umetskys, the password, the elder son, the *yurodivyi*.) Olga Umetskaia. The burning of the house. The *yurodivyi* knows where Umetsky's daughter was hidden.

The Idiot's personality. A bizarre creature. His oddities. Gentle. At times he says not a word.

For example. Somewhere in Petersburg he has a little boy.

He visits him. (He is always with the children.)

At times he suddenly begins to hold forth to them, all about the bliss in store.

There are other matters of which he knows nothing, he has doubts, he stands for an absolutely equal footing. The Idiot is 19, soon to be 20.

They called each other fools.

He went to ask a boy of 12 to forgive him.

He said to the Umetskys: "Give the children over to me." Umetsky wants to get money from him.

A son rejected ever since childhood, the Idiot is wrapped up in his passion for children. Everywhere he has children about him. The Idiot and the woman in childbed.

Once he explained everything to the general. He is 26. How he arrived—they all laughed at him, the children were especially struck by his anecdote of how he helped the woman in childbed.

Chief point: *the nature of his attitude to the children. He is in very frail health.*

N.B. Incident in which the Idiot's full character is demonstrated. This is what happened.

The Idiot was in the province of Saratov. When Nastia's seducer abandoned her, he took her in, she gave birth, and he took over the child, et cetera. In her anguish and rage at having been deserted, she inveighed against *him* and jeered at him, but afterward she threw herself at his feet, and in the end she fell in love with him, he offered his hand, and she *ran away* ("I am furious, I won't ask pardon, I am defiled").

Absolutely has to be worked out: He assented and believed as she did, so that he ridiculed himself, as if he were as distorted as she made him out to be. She is stunned by his *simplicity and humility*.

"Teach me." "But you are ill now." "It's nothing, nothing." "Teach me." "Yes, yes." "That's what, I want to learn," and she relates, shaking with fever, how she will avenge herself!

"I am defiled, I am vile, I don't acknowledge any truth, <illegible> I am defiled, I am a lost creature."

Her entire education was got from the Idiot.

She arrived at the Umetskys', there they seized her and beat her. The son intervened, *took her away to Petersburg* (he is to blame for this), and fell in love with her. She jeered at him and deserted him. A laundress. Then *she does indeed* fall in love with the son and resolves to lead a whore's life. To the Idiot she says: "I look on you as on God, *but I love him.*" Rushes to the son in deep shame, storms, tears, and the Idiot's consolations; "There, there, it's all right!" And suddenly she runs off to drown herself, and so forth. Bright falcon. A passionate girl.

N.B. At first the Idiot's Christianity obsessed her through and through.

But then the son. N.B. *She* is astounded at herself. "How can I dream of the possibility that this inexperienced creature could ever be my husband." While she was leading a whore's life—she heard about the heroine and was jealous of the son <illegible> spies on him.

Chief point: The general gave his last 12 rubles to Umetsky to invest. Debts and an estate of 12,000.

Umetsky is carrying on a piece of chicanery in Petersburg. He is glad of having sold his daughter to the rich son.

Change of plan.—Ganechka is 20. He is the child of the second wife. The children all have but little means. The general has long since dissipated their capital.

The Idiot is the child of the first marriage; aged 26. He is rich. Has just come into money.

Umetsky wants to marry Ustinia Aleksandrovna off to the general, she is the widow of a lieutenant, she is hot-blooded, well educated, corrupt, distantly related to Umetsky's wife. Lives with Captain Pavlenko, is kept by Trotsky.[2] Pavlenko and Ustinia thrash Trotsky.

Ustinia wants to marry for the sake of position, thinking that the general has money and a pension, she is 27 years old, it is high time for her to get settled in life.

She (Ustinia) is the one who, at the mother's prayers and at Nastia's desire, whom they had beaten, took Nastia to Petersburg. But Nastia instead of becoming a whore went out as a laundress. She just did not want to marry the son. Her character: "I don't want to ask pardon of anyone." Nastia is in her 20th year. Her father was pursuing her. (N.B. Ustinia—when she was Umetsky's ward and lived with him. They got the lieutenant drunk and when she was pregnant they married her off to him. Her son Sasha is 14, she is bringing him up herself. He is friendly with the others.)

The general is madly in love with Ustinia.

But the son has found Nastia. He torments her. Spies on her. She ultimately accepts Ustinia's proposal and takes up with some man or other, to score off the son. But the latter only suffers the more and wants to kill her. "What, you my husband." He is 20.

Umetsky spies on Nastia and would like to do her harm. But Ustinia has some notes of hand of his in her possession, and he is under her thumb.

The father doesn't allow the son. Nor does the son ask his permission. Ustinia is dissolute and passionate. The son has attracted her. Battle between the general and the son.

(N.B. Suddenly Pavlenko enters, creates an uproar. Ustinia says: "These are my guests." The general keeps silent. Insults, to the daughter. Yasha. General scene. The blow in the face.)

Ustinia is [not] Umetsky's daughter by the 1st wife—she lived with her father. The remaining children are by the 2nd wife.

~~Umetsky is an old friend of the general's—they married at the same time and cast out their wives at the same time. Umetsky's 1st wife hanged herself.~~

~~When the son found out that the father was to marry the older sister, he was beside himself.~~

~~N.B. Though the father [the general] knew that the son had proposed and that there was a story, nevertheless he knew that Nastia~~

---

2 Trotsky: presumably this will be the Totsky in the published version of *The Idiot*—the protector of Nastasia Filipovna.

~~had run away and he did not want her. When he was still living with
Ustinia[3] the son found out that he was about to marry the sister. This
produced battles and storms.~~

No relatives. N.B. The general gets married. Umetskaia discovers
he has nothing. Laughs at him and leaves him. Her dissolute behavior. The general goes after her. He is passionately in love. He
agrees to put up with her depravity.

In this period he becomes aware of the need for a family. Kills
his wife.

2nd Part: The children's rebellion. *3 months later. The father's
adventures.*

The Idiot in action. The little boy, the loose women, and so forth.
Ends with the rupture because of Umetskaia. The Idiot is everyone's
leader.

? N.P.

The children. Revolt. Yasha.

Explanation with the children as to why he broke off. Honor.
Awaits the son so as to be reconciled.

The son. The project of a marriage with the ward. With the
daughter. ("You are angry, but I've broken it off.")

The Idiot with Umetskaia. Explanations between both of them.
The Idiot keeps silent. Explanation with the ward before going to
bed.

The next day with the ward, the magazine (before this the Idiot
was with her. With the little boy. Scene concerning the son. About
the Umetskys and their children.)

(The Idiot and the children.) "Mine" <illegible> the ward. (N.B.
The main scene.)

The arrival of Umetskaia and Umetsky. The general's fury because she loves the son. "This cannot be." Interrogation of the son.
Initial bursts of rage with the daughter and with Yasha.

The aunt's unexpected arrival. Judgment. "I don't want to." Slaps
the Idiot. He drives out the son, and so forth. ~~Yasha runs away.~~

---

[3] Dostoevsky first wrote "Umetskaia" and then crossed it out.

The Eighth Plan

(*Written in the first half of December, 1867. One date
in the manuscript is December 11.*)

After the stunning insight into the character of the Idiot in plan seven,
and the brilliant sketch of the essential dramatic situation of the
defiled and self-defiling Nastia and the forgiving and compassionate
Idiot, this section reads like a step backward. As the deadline for
submitting the first part of the novel approached, Dostoevsky's brain
still teemed with alternative plans. The sudden emergence of the
Idiot of the final version in plan seven was apparently still only one
of many possibilities that Dostoevsky was entertaining, and even at
this late date he apparently was not giving to it the exclusive importance that we, with the benefit of hindsight, are tempted to give to it.

What Dostoevsky takes from the seventh plan, curiously, is not
the new sketch of the Christian, forgiving, compassionate Idiot, but
the rivalry of the father and son over the proud and provocative
woman. This was sketched faintly in plan seven in the general's and
the son's rivalry over the sensuous Ustinia. The Idiot's role is secondary in this section, and most of the notes have to do with the rivalry
of the son and father over the hand of Ustinia. Ustinia is only vaguely
distinguished from Umetskaia, and sometimes their names are juxta-
posed in virtual identity. Nastia appears only a few times, and she
too is now identified with Ustinia. As before, Ustinia-Umetskaia has
been mistreated by her father and has retaliated by burning down
her father's barn. Ustinia-Umetskaia has been seduced by a rich
landowner (Trotsky); she gives birth to a child (which her father
almost kills), and the Idiot tries to help her. She apparently slaps
Trotsky in public, and the son defends her. Out of gratitude, perhaps, she permits the son to seduce her, but after the seduction she
taunts him with the fact that she is going to be a general's wife.

Up to now Vladimir Umetsky has been more of a dramatic premise
than a living character, a kind of archetypal evil father against whom

the daughters revolt. Dostoevsky attempts to bring him more into the plot by involving him with the general. The precise relationship between the general and Umetsky is not known, except that at some point they had been in the army together. The general remembers him: "I knew him, in the regiment he used to like flogging. He was an informer. For 30 years he would remember an offense. On the other hand, he ran things very well. Out of nothing! Out of nothing! He built a fortune." There are shady speculations between them. The general sees an issue from his hopeless economic situation in Umetsky's help: "The general—dismissed, a most infamous situation, but Umetsky will save me." It may be that Umetsky influences the general in his sensuous habits, for there is the hint that Umetsky encourages and arranges the love affair between the general and Nastia: "Umetsky himself while in his cups incites the general to pursue Nastia to Petersburg."

Ustinia encourages the attentions of the general, presumably for social rank and for money, although given the economic situation of the general, this is a dubious point. After seducing the son she taunts him with the fact that she will be a general's wife, and the son spits in her face. One of the consequences of the rivalry between father and son is the death of the mother, who is apparently brokenhearted by the father's perfidy. This situation, it will be remembered, has its parallel in a previous plan in which the Idiot's wife dies because of the Idiot's love for the heroine. The general becomes cruel and coarse in his passion. He desecrates the memory of his wife by drinking champagne on her grave, and immediately after rushes out with horses in pursuit of Ustinia and his son. Dostoevsky has more than once in his various plans returned to the theme of father and son competing for the same woman, and its disastrous consequences. He will, of course, treat the same theme in *The Brothers Karamazov*. The Umetsky affair had influenced him greatly, and he tried mightily, with minimal success, to work it directly into his novel. Now, on the eve of the publication of the first part, he returned to it again, with the same lack of success.

Dostoevsky liked to remind his readers that everything he wrote about really happened, and he often pointed to some newspaper account of an actual happening that was as extraordinary as his own fantastic creative world. The Umetsky affair had all the real-life elements of Dostoevsky's febrile imagination. It was, in a sense, made to order. Yet, if life confirmed what Dostoevsky imagined, he was almost never able to use directly what life offered. When one surveys the multiple efforts he made to use the theme of the maltreated child, the cruel and ugly environment of childhood and its effect upon the soul of the adult, the horrifying prospect of a father's betrayal of his God-like trust, one is struck even more how little finally found its way into the finished novel. The Umetsky affair became more of a restriction than an opportunity. Dostoevsky's imagination was finally more real and deep than any of the confirming instances. And it was finally his own vision of the logic of reality that he followed.

With the deadline for submitting the first five chapters of the first part upon him, Dostoevsky is still experimenting; almost nothing is yet fixed. It is no wonder, then, that he finishes this section with these words: "Set up a detailed plan and tonight *begin*."

List of Characters for
the Eighth Plan

The General's Family

The general
The general's mother
The Idiot
The daughter (Varia)
The son Ganechka
Yasha
Kolia
The ward
The aunt
The nephew

The Umetskys

Vladimir Umetsky
Olga Umetskaia
A daughter who lives with Bogdanovich

Ustinia Umetskaia
Nastia
The elder son
A son, a schoolboy

11/30 *November*

1) First Part.

(The Idiot's tutors are Petersburg relatives. It is they who sent him to Switzerland.)

The Idiot and Umetskaia, *the business has begun,* concise story.

The Idiot had been living in the country with the Umetskys—(why?), no one can guess. The thing is, he was already living with the Umetskys, in peace, in fresh country air. Even before his step-mother ~~mother~~ could not bear him (though until age 10 he had lived in her house) because he was a stepchild and wealthy and an *Idiot.* Then because of moving for professional reasons from one place to another, they established him at the Umetskys (in the country. Grew up with the elder son and the daughters. Then they sent him to Switzerland when he was 19. 4 years in Switzerland). He came straight back to the Umetskys (the father was serving somewhere in Simbirsk)[1] and took a salaried post with them in the country (for the children), but they took the children away. The children lived *under the care of* the daughter as long as she lived with Bogdanov. When he left they were taken away. The Idiot concerned himself with the deserted Umetskaia's situation. (But he met Olga, the first cousin, alone in the house.)

Scenes at Umetskaia's house. More vividness needed. All her *furia.* Ridicules him, crawls at his feet. He had received 10,000. She is in Petersburg. "Marry me, I am indeed a rich man." "I'll choke him with it." Or else wouldn't it be better to hand her over to the father because of her shame. She gave birth <illegible>—(Mishenka). She

---

[1] Simbirsk: then a small city on the Volga in the province of that name, south of Kazan; now called Ulyanovsk, the birthplace of V. I. Lenin (Ulyanov). In Dostoevsky's time dissidents of various sorts were transported to remote river valleys; by the end of the century the town contained both a Roman Catholic and a Lutheran church.

kissed his hand and went away with Olga Umetskaia (about the decapitated heads). *She* relates Olga's biography to the Idiot.

The Idiot stays behind because of his illness. Olga is with him. *In the country.*

Vlad. Umetsky drinks, weeps, talks about his obligations, his starving children, his son, a well-developed schoolboy of 15, who had arrived with the elder son.

His gloating sadism toward his wife, his daughter, his children, and especially his schoolboy son. The latter, whom he whips, is a spindly, frail youth. Quarrels with the elder son. Ustinia Umetskaia <illegible>. Suddenly *she* appears.

At that he attacked. Like a tiger. Gnashed his teeth at everyone, even Ustinia. He whips her on the pretext: "I am punishing you for your depravity, give me your money." (She is fully of age, but he cares for no laws.)

On the other hand, the general's family. The mother, Gania, the daughter, Kolia, Yasha, Nina? The ward—a little jealous. The general himself. [Quarrel about the Idiot: "Is this all your doing?"]

The mother is ill. The general—dismissed, a most infamous situation, but Umetsky will save me. ["We are beggars."] The mother begs him not to listen to Umetsky. Scenes with his wife, "I am the head, and I want to remain so." Jealousy of the ward developed in the household. About the Idiot. The *aunt* arrived, upset everyone, and went away.

The children in the 1st Part. The daughter. N.B. (Show her character.)

In the 2nd place Kolia and Yasha with the schoolboy of the Umetsky family. Yasha is rather depressed, quarrels with the ward, the mother is on his side, the general is against him.

2) Reading poetry. *The aunt:* "I'd have whipped you." With the schoolboy. Kolia (to Ustinia), and so forth.

Suddenly a rumor: the general is leaving for a minute. But Gania, having collected the children and handed 15 rubles to the peasants, smuggles Umetskaia, who has been beaten, out of the barn at night.

The general's wife is terribly ill and shattered, takes her in. Until then they had not received Ustinia ~~Umetskaia~~ but Ganechka had been *up to tricks* with her. Captain Pavlenko. A duel.

The general arrived, intervened. *Fight with Vlad. Umetsky.* Ustinia, whom the general's wife did not receive. They beat him off her.

Umetskaia, ridicule, and so on. She liked the son. (She is a beauty.)

This manuscript page corresponds to pp. 150–51, beginning with the date "11/30 November" and ending with "the general is against him." There is a break in the middle of the page corresponding to a break in the content, a fairly frequent habit of Dostoevsky. The first half concerns the Idiot's background, and the second Vladimir Umetsky. The violence of both parts is contained within rather geometric neatness of handwriting and spacing.

The general takes her too much to heart, at first he is on the son's side. The children, the schoolboys. He talked about the Idiot.

Umetskaia began a love affair with the son, the general's jealousy, fury. Savage scene with the son in the mother's presence. The latter guesses. Umetskaia with Olga <*sic*> sets fire to the house. The son snatches her out of it. She flings her arms round him and kisses him. Scene amid the fire. (Umetskaia, having seen that the general is already so shaken because of her, slanders the son.) He drove the son out. He left in indignation. Yasha defended him and was rude to Umetskaia. "Ask forgiveness." The mother is opposed. She dies (hypertrophy of the heart).

In the night Umetskaia fled.

The funeral. To Yasha: "You killed mother." Toast. "Dance!" *Yasha:* "Hang him, hunt him down." He led him to the grave.

Papasha: "Unharness the horses! Let's go on, let's go on." He had forgotten something. They got him into the *tarantas*[2] shuddering with fever.

After they had set the fire, she ran away, saying to Olga: "Jump into the fire, but the bright falcon is mine."

She ran away and met Gania. Tremblingly, she threw her arms round him.

"You, only you." The general watches, astounded.

The toothless old man comes (but the day before he had grabbed her in a kiss and had been kissing her repeatedly for three days: "You shall be a general's wife." Yasha watched and listened).

3rd Part. Finale. The son snatched at her dress (she was streetwalking), the duel. She: "I am going to marry the general."

The latter beside himself: "I will get married!"

N.B. Thus she seduced the son. The latter wrenched himself away in despair. "I am going to marry the general." She gave Trotsky a slap in the face, in public. The son again defended her, and it was

---

2 *Tarantas:* a traveling carriage without springs—the usual mode of progress in rural Russia—drawn by three horses (a *troika*). The middle horse wore a high arch with a bell over his head; each of the side horses, always turned outward, wore a collar of small bells. The precise design varied somewhat between a phaeton and a cart. When Dostoevsky left Semipalatinsk in Western Siberia to return to Tver in European Russia (a distance of 2,700 miles), he and his wife and stepson traveled some six weeks in the summer of 1859 in a *tarantas* he purchased in order to make the journey.

at that point that he was seduced by her. Then he spat on her. But she said: "I am going to be a general's wife."

The Idiot, the institution.

1

2nd Part. 2 months later.

The general is frantically in love—he sought her out.

The proposal, and ridicule. In a quarrel with the son.

But soon he discovered the son's innocence, yet he accepted.

All of a sudden she slandered Ganechka. She runs after him.

The general is furious.

2

Two months later—everything neglected and gone to pot. Debts and so on. A single idea in the general's head. His melancholy love, he wanders over the city. Enters the son's house. Reconciliation, slander. He takes him home, joy in the household. "I have another idea: I want to get married." The Idiot.

3

The next day the Idiot is with Umetskaia, the little boy. About the Umetskys. *He* and Vl. Umetsky. The magazine. The betrothal (official). The Idiot's conversations. In the evening, the aunt. Judgment. On the daughter. The ward, and so forth. Yasha—he rebels on his sister's behalf.

The Idiot, on Yasha's account.

With the elder son—a duel.

The general is unwell.

Main point. N.B. The general seems calmer, but Umetskaia weighs on his heart—there will be an explosion.

3) *Should she or not remain in the country. (Scenes with the Idiot?)* The daughter *went out.* The nephew began to talk.

The general (conversations with the nephew). "A preposterous thing. Unfortunately, it does happen. Rarely, but still it happens."

The nephew half smiled <illegible>. "Why are you smiling?" the general asked brusquely. "Well. . . . . . Nothing. I like your determination now and then."—"Rarely, but it does happen, very rarely, but it happens. . . . . . ." "It's just that <illegible>—I am amazed on such occasions by your calm, your high principles."

(Gania returns enchanted by her beauty.)

N.B. The nephew. ~~the son~~ The character of the former Idiot. *Tirade about the King of the Jews.* Varia is with him. She had dreamed of saving him. He has a certain tenderness for her.

The nephew is the one who told that story. They had sent him out to earn his bread. (On the question of vile intentions: "It would be hardly possible to bring a conviction in court, for if thoughts cannot be judged, still less can they be sentenced.")

They first brought the children (the general's indignation and his remarks about the children).

"But now, I really don't know what has gotten into him. During the day he was all right, but then he suddenly turned into a tiger." "I'm not afraid of anything, she is my daughter." ("Give me money.")

N.B. (Vl. Umetsky had begun by saying that he had killed the baby.)

"No, he is lying."

"But I nearly did kill him." And she related in this connection how she gave birth to Kolka, with the Idiot's help.

False cynicism.

The general's wife admonished her.

The cynicism of her words astonished the aunt, *"A fine bird, that one!"*

N.B. On the ward's account: the general's wife is very affectionate to her.

Notes for the 1st Part: N.B. Outline *her* personality. False cynicism, fury, gentleness.

N.B. *Main point.* First the chapter about Umetskaia. (Fits of regular Jewish stinginess.) Fits of tigerish rage (delineate the characters).

About the Idiot, only stories.

The general talks about Vl. Umetsky. "I know him, in the regiment he used to like flogging. He was an informer. For 30 years he would remember an offense. On the other hand, he ran things very well. Out of nothing! Out of nothing! He built up a fortune."

Quarrels with the son. He is visibly jealous of Umetskaia.

Umetskaia laughs at him.

The general: "Dance" (to his daughter).

Sic. (Still earlier: scene with the children.)

Main point.—On the 1st day of his arrival he went to Umetskaia. He saw the daughter, a beauty. The general's wife was put out.

(Gania about her beauty.) The children. ~~Chatter.~~ "Dance!" She is taut with strain.

4) Gaiety. Poems. Little imp. The general's wife burst out laughing. "Well, of all things!" And suddenly Gania runs in, crying, "What has happened with Umetsky."

? *The general's wife.* After the scene.

N.B. (He left with the Idiot.)

As they left the general began to howl, and his wife died.

"*If* the Idiot has come, he must absolutely be slapped without fail."

The general's wife hands the children over to him. (Excuses. He reproaches him for his idiotism.) The Idiot is ill.—Chat with the Umetsky children.

At the beginning of the 1st Part the mother was angry with Yasha and he took refuge (behind the ward). Later—he takes his mother's part.

Perhaps (after the quarrels *with the son*), which are not explicit but which are evident to everyone, and after the son's departure— which again provokes scenes.

After the storm the general takes advantage of their being alone: "Wait a bit—you'll be the wife of a general—don't you want to be?"

N.B.? But even before that she had said, *"Here comes that old one-legged fellow."*

On leaving, the son says to the Idiot: "Wasn't he once jealous of Ninochka because of me?"

N.B.—When the Idiot sent Umetskaia to Petersburg, the general said to him: "That's a good thing for you to have done, very good!" Fewer stories. Yes! Fewer stories.

Another time even earlier he had said to the Idiot: "My business is in bad shape."

"I am master in this house!"

Afterward: "Don't beat him!" He persuaded the general's wife, he treated her tenderly. But in the morning, while taking tea, she suddenly died.

When the mother was lying in the coffin, the children gathered round. The Idiot said: "Shouldn't the father be called in?"—"If you love him, then call him in."—"Nonsense!" And then—.

Afterward the general kept silence. Drank champagne. Then suddenly he said to the Idiot: "Swear to me, swear to me on your word of honor that *she* did not go after *him* and that there was no understanding between them."

Then suddenly he calls for horses (he had raged at Varia). Varia says: "I've seen and heard quite enough." He had raged at the children after the funeral. Only when the mother was already lying in the coffin: "This" (to Yasha) "is your doing!" Yasha had not changed himself as yet.

"Horses!"

They get ready to go away. He is silent. *2 tarantases. "Get the coachman."* For 24 hours they were packing up their things. At dawn the *tarantas* was brought round. "Let's go, to the grave, say a farewell." And suddenly he fell down.

They brought him home. "Don't go away, let's stay here!"

"Horses!" They all departed.

The Idiot's personality.

(He drinks champagne with Umetsky and Ustinia. Umetsky's choristers.)

The little boys, *Vasia and Kolia.* Their story (they had been sent to the country for having stolen).

(Umetsky: "Sing a sad song for me.")

("I" <illegible>.)

Umetsky (half drunk) relates how he saw a man taking charge of a party of prisoners for the price of a ruble and a red blouse—infanticide drinks up one's last penny, one woman was dancing, uproar, din, boozing. . . . . . "That's what I like. A sad song for me."

But while all this was going on as they were drinking, she talks with the nephew—about the King of the Jews.

The nephew explains how he was brought up at the uncle's, he relates how he used to sell portraits in the flea market, "I am a poet," a little *drunk.*

She turns pale.

The Idiot *is there too.*

"But there, your father is shouting something."

"Horses!"

The general.

She.

The children.

The Idiot's personality.

And lots of other persons.

N.B. The general in highly outspoken conversations with the children. See 5 <Sic.>

5) Make *her* personality display more nobility. (Deeply injured.) (Account for the general's love.)

How she described her lover's voluptuousness.

The Idiot to the nephew: "Moreover, you will never be a rich man."

"Why?"

"Because you have a heart."

"Hm. I would just like to have the prospects for capital that you have, 75,000 rubles, for me no such 75,000 are in sight."

N.B. He is either a tremendous criminal or—.

"God grant."

"That remark shows that I am a nonentity, a milksop."

N.B. Even earlier, *just on his arrival,* just before the catastrophe, the general had declared to his wife that he was not pleased with *the nephew's* hanging round their daughter. Nor was the general's wife pleased either, but she said out of a spirit of contrariness, "Why not?" But then, when the catastrophe occurred, she suddenly burst out: "It's because you are laying plans to get married that you made sure my nephew should not propose to Varia." "Mercy, Nina, why, they aren't related at all." "Well, almost not related. . . . . . ." "That's not so, they are related. . . . . . ."

Suddenly to Varia (until then she had not uttered a word) to her: "Love him, perhaps you will lead him onto the right path. That's what he needs."

(Then in the 2nd Part Varia says that she is unhappy with him.)

However, they set to work. . . . . . .

The Idiot on leaving the country with the general is troubled at leaving the Umetskys' children.

Umetsky himself while in his cups incites the general to pursue Nastia to Petersburg.

The 10,000 and the seducer's letter had been received before Umetskaia's arrival. The Idiot comes of his own accord.

The children, because Vl. Umetsky had thrashed the schoolboy (because he did not do any work), say of him so persistently that he is eternally disgraced that he decides to set the house on fire. Then, after his father had whipped him—the Idiot took him in. But later he died. Give this little boy a personality.

N.B. Up to the time of the blow in the face, everyone laughs at the Idiot, and he is terribly despised. He invariably keeps silent.

Set up a detailed plan and tonight *begin.*

Notes on Part II of the Novel

(Notes written from March, 1868, to July, 1868, the period during which Dostoevsky submitted the second part of the finished version.)

The first part of *The Idiot* had already been published (all sixteen chapters) in the January and February issues of *The Russian Messenger* and Dostoevsky had not yet written a single line for the second part. Indeed, all the evidence indicates that he did not know how to proceed, and that he had no over-all conception of the subsequent development of the novel. In March of 1868 he set to work on the second part, and on the form of the whole. The notes of this section—according to the few dates we have in the text itself—were written between March and the middle of July. On April 21, Dostoevsky complains that the work is going badly. He manages to get only two chapters off for the April issue, three more for the May issue, three for the June number, and the last two for the July number. He had written a brilliant first part, but the first part was complete in itself. The dynamism of the novel had to be sought again.

According to his letters, Dostoevsky was satisfied with the first part of the final version. Well he might be, since it moves in orderly crescendos to one of his great scenes, perhaps the greatest of his novels. After the frenetic money-burning scene, Nastasia Filipovna goes off with Rogozhin, and the Prince follows after her. There is no indication in the text itself what is to follow. And the truth was that Dostoevsky himself did not know. He is not even sure of how much time elapses between the end of the action of the first part and the beginning of the second part. In the notes, he gives variously three weeks, five weeks, five days, one and one-half months, three months, and six months. One might mention in passing that Dostoevsky habitually refers to the second part of the novel as the "third" part, conceiving of the first part (in the finished version) as composed of two parts. Dostoevsky is not sure whether Nastasia Filipovna will marry Rogozhin or the Prince; whether the marriage to the Prince, if it happens, is to be secret or open; whether Nastasia Filipovna will kill herself, be killed, or die naturally; whether Aglaia will marry Gania or not; whether Nastasia Filipovna and Aglaia will hate each other or be reconciled to each other; whether Rogozhin will be a murderer or whether he will be redeemed by the Prince's teachings. Dostoevsky's mind teems with possibilities, but the tyranny of art and the tyranny of publishing require a choice.

The many variations he considers for Nastasia Filipovna fit more or less into the following two broad patterns: the day after the orgy with Rogozhin, she runs away from him and marries the Prince; or, she marries Rogozhin, who eventually kills her. The first possibility had already been anticipated in those early plans in which the Idiot marries a "fallen" woman with a child. Dostoevsky is attracted to this possibility and considers several variations. He cannot make up his mind whether the marriage is to be secret or not: "N.B. Is he secretly married to her or not, that is the question?" In some of the variants she is not married to the Prince, but is in a quandary about whether to become a princess. In any event the marriage never "takes" and in almost all the versions Nastasia Filipovna abandons the Prince (sometimes on the wedding day), rushes off to a brothel, and dies either by her own hand or in a natural way.

As in the novel, Aglaia is Nastasia Filipovna's antagonist for the Prince's hand. Her role in these notes is reduced almost exclusively to the explosive and inevitable confrontation with Nastasia Filipovna. In this scene she is pitiless: "Aglaia visits Nastasia Filipovna, says that it is vile of her to play the role of a Mary Magdalene, that she would do better to perish on a Japanese dagger in a brothel, out of sight and hearing. Laughs at the vileness of her soul. Offers her arsenic, calls her 'thou.' At one point Nastasia Filipovna gets her revenge on Aglaia by urging both Rogozhin and Gania to seduce her, and indeed at one point there is a reference to Aglaia going off with Rogozhin." The results of the confrontation are various. In some of the notes Nastasia Filipovna demands that the Prince marry her, but more often she rushes away from the meeting to vice and death. Aglaia almost always rushes off to a meeting with Gania, where he tries to prove his love for her (often by burning his finger); in one set of notes she marries Gania, out of spite and frustration at being rejected by the Prince. More often she does not.

Dostoevsky also entertains the possibility that Nastasia Filipovna and Aglaia become reconciled, or if not reconciled, that Aglaia passionately forgives Nastasia Filipovna and works with the Prince to save her. Dostoevsky tells us: "The salvation of Aglaia, reconciliation with N. F. Confession, and so forth." Also, "She is seized with a passion for N. F. and begs her forgiveness." Following immediately, Dostoevsky says: "It is he who brought them together and *transformed them*." The beneficent and regenerative influence of Myshkin not only upon Nastasia Filipovna and Aglaia but also on Rogozhin and others is widely entertained in these notes. Thus, we get: "He rehabilitates N. F. and exerts an ascendancy over Rogozhin." And, "N.B. N. F. is naïvely and unconsciously happy, she perceives a new world in which she is being remade, as the Prince talks with her in that light."

In an extensive outline of Nastasia Filipovna's fate, Dostoevsky saw the "rehabilitation" taking this form:

> As for N. F. things go thus throughout the whole novel:
> —At the beginning she is astounded at having become a princess —a laundress.
> —Thereafter—a haughty and proud princess.
> —Aglaia stages a public insult to her (scene).
> 4th part conclusion
> —Unheard of depravity.
> —The Prince's confession to Aglaia.
> —Puzzling disappearance, *they track her down* in a brothel.
> —She wants to kill herself.
> —Rehabilitation. Aglaia and the Prince with her, trying to save her.
> —She dies or else kills herself.

One will notice that the regeneration in the outline is not permanent, for Nastasia Filipovna dies or kills herself. Despite the attractions of bringing his characters to spiritual rebirth, Dostoevsky was always the realist: "N. F. is engaged. Scenes with the Prince, her total rehabilitation, and her total downfall."

In some of the notes Rogozhin is brought to a finer moral state by the influence of the children who surround the Prince. The children are fairly prominent in these notes and were obviously meant to play a prominent role in the novel. In the final version, of course, their presence and influence are confined to the Prince's account of his Swiss meeting with the defiled but pure peasant girl, Marie. The Prince's moral influence in the novel is slight, and Dostoevsky entertains this possibility also in the notes: "N.B. The Prince has had only *the slightest effect* on their lives. But everything he might have done and undertaken perishes with him." Still the Prince accomplishes something: "But wherever he even made an appearance—everywhere he left a permanent trace."

The Prince is poised between Nastasia Filipovna and Aglaia; Nastasia Filipovna is poised between the Prince and Rogozhin; and Aglaia should be poised between the Prince and Gania. But Gania's role is never satisfactorily worked out either in the notes or in the novel. Dostoevsky knows this and is vexed by it. He asks himself: "And Gania? His role?" And, "The main problem now—Gania?" Near the end of this section he asks himself again: "What to do with Gania?" and a paragraph later answers his own question in this way: "Aglaia N. F. *marries Gania out of spite*—and drives him away. Gania is madly *in love with Aglaia,* to the last straw, ready to kill anyone at all—that's his role." But this was not to be his role. It is too passionate, too unreflective; it was a role already usurped by Rogozhin, and it was a role at odds with the other Ganias we get in the notes: primarily a petty intriguer, self-interestedly pursuing a love of mixed cupidity and vengeance.

Gania is not all of a piece in the notes, and he is even less so in the novel. In the first part of the novel his place is prominent, his stature is large. Torn between cupidity and love, he reaches almost heroic proportions when in pride he turns away from the hundred thousand rubles Nastasia Filipovna offers him. But in the middle of the novel he has become, inconsistently, something of a research clerk for Myshkin, checking on the facts of the Pavlishchev case; and at the end of the novel he has become petty, intriguing, and spiteful. Dostoevsky intended to follow up his prominent place in the first part in the second part, because we find the following note in this section: *"Project: Ought one to begin with Gania?* Gania's intrigues, Varia, Ptitsyn, Rogozhin and his *crew,* Lebedev and the rest."* But he never followed through, and though Dostoevsky fussed about Gania's role throughout these notes, he was never able to give him the essential role that his first appearance seemed to promise.

In these notes Gania intrigues against the Prince for Aglaia, and against Aglaia for the Prince. With the help of his sister Varia—as in the novel—he hopes to win Aglaia, either for love or for vengeance. "But Gania *in actual truth* is just vacillating under various agitated emotions. He would like to avenge himself on Aglaia, but having seen her, especially after the scene with N. F. (to which he brought the Prince), he falls in love with Aglaia and burns his finger. Thereafter, he again shifts to the Prince's side. (Toward the end he kills himself.)" But Aglaia seems to read through his motives and is contemptuous of them as well as of his cleverness. "It seems to her that Gania is still in love with her; and this being so, she knows that Gania, jealous of her marrying the Prince, will take revenge on her. She schemes to find out what he is thinking. She needs an ally; she wants to see whether Gania can qualify as one." At one point Gania betrays his sister in order to impress Aglaia with his devotion and his sincerity. "*Through Varia* he dedicates himself to Aglaia. He betrays the Prince, but flirts with Aglaia to such a degree that just when he has decided to act (to avenge himself) in Varia's way—he discloses to Aglaia all Varia's snares and how she was deceiving her. He says: 'There's the reward for my sincerity!' and plunges into vice." Aglaia is not impressed and treats this disclosure by spitting at him in contempt.

Even great novels can have structural flaws; even great novelists can, under the pressure of deadlines, fail to see the solution to a vexing problem. One wonders, in short, why Dostoevsky did not develop

Gania's role as one of the poles of attraction for Aglaia, as a parallel to the kind of doubling that Nastasia Filipovna experiences. In such a structural development Gania's role would parallel Rogozhin's, as indeed Aglaia's in the novel parallels Nastasia Filipovna's. And just as Aglaia is a budding Nastasia—the impulses are all the same, but still softened by youth and innocence—Gania would be a budding Rogozhin. But in truth it must be said that Dostoevsky did not do full justice in notes or novel either to Aglaia or to Gania.

From the earliest plans of the novel Dostoevsky struggled with Gania, in the guise of the handsome youth, without success. Ipolit and Lebedev, both important characters, spring full-blown in these notes. Neither has been mentioned before, and the versions we get of both are in essential respects no different from what we meet in the final version. Dostoevsky seems to have a slightly higher opinion of Lebedev in the notes, for at one point he says of him: "Lebedev—a highly talented person. He is pious, he weeps, and prays, and deceives the Prince and ridicules him. Having deceived the Prince, he is naïvely and sincerely ashamed of this." But in another place the Prince notices that Lebedev's confessions are not wholly sincere, and Dostoevsky adds: "A very warped character, Lebedev's." As in the novel, he is faithless and hypocritical and cruel; but there is as yet no touch of his role as a reflector of the ills of the society.

Ipolit is one of the major characters in the novel; he dominates its middle sections. How does one account for so important a character coming so late into the conceptions of the author? It would seem to follow that Ipolit is brought into being by the central situation and does not bring it into being. The very opposite is true of Nastasia Filipovna (the heroine, Mignon), or the Idiot. They make the drama, and the drama is inconceivable without them, as the persistence of their situations in the various plans has made clear. In the most serious and sophisticated sense, Ipolit is an afterthought, an elaboration or refinement of the core situation. In many respects, but in a different mode, he repeats aspects of Nastasia Filipovna's role.

The Prince himself is what we find Myshkin to be in the final version: forgiving, Christian, loving, calming. Of him Dostoevsky says:

"N.B. His way of looking at the world: he forgives everything, sees reasons for everything, does not recognize that any sin is unforgivable." After all the searching, Dostoevsky has found his Prince among men. Like Christ, with whom he is identified repeatedly in the notes, he takes the outrages of the world upon himself, and like Christ he is needed by everyone:

> They need him at the Epanchins, Aglaia ~~Adelaide~~ (the general's wife). Gania needs him.
>
> Kolia—
>
> Rogozhin needs him. (He has already allied himself with the Prince and is presented as his pupil.)
>
> And especially N. F.
>
> Even Lebedev after leaving N. F. needs him, and the Prince's heart *is radiant*. (There you have a field of action ~~tableaux~~.)
>
> *Having comprehended, the Prince is very touched and, in his humility, frightened.*

Part 3

7 March

> The Prince was three weeks in Moscow.
>
> N. F. is behaving badly and tormenting Rogozhin so as to scare off the Prince.
>
> Aglaia receives the Prince with ridicule; Gania.
>
> The general is again hanging round N. F.
>
> The Prince understands N. F.'s behavior and wants to give Aglaia up.
>
> Frank discussions with Aglaia. Aglaia says all right and to avenge herself runs away with Gania—on the eve of the wedding.
>
> The Prince is engaged to Aglaia.
>
> *Finally* seeks out N. F.
>
> Account of Aglaia's incessant ridicule and hatred.
>
> He has institutions and schools.
>
> On the eve of the wedding Aglaia breaks everything off or else runs away with the count.
>
> The Prince and N. F., he marries N. F.

N.B. Is he secretly married to her or not, that is the question? Gania's lies and cunning intrigues against everyone (he helps the Prince against Aglaia, Aglaia against the Prince, relations with N. F. and Rogozhin).

Aglaia lets herself be trapped by Gania (the Prince, who is watching over her, gets her out of that).

The Prince is watching Gania and is aware of everything; he forgives Gania. Gania cannot endure this condescension and this alters his fate.

Rogozhin falls in love with Aglaia.

9 March

The Prince is married to N. F. ~~Aglaia~~

N. F. ~~Aglaia~~ could not endure the night at Rogozhin's. Three days of carousing. *She becomes a laundress.*

(Description of the carousing, brawling, etc. How she seduced Rogozhin. But she could not bear him, disgust, she runs away.)

The Prince enthralls her soul; to marry him. She accepts. But after accepting she runs away. (Or else she goes out of the house and runs away.)

Rogozhin looks for her. (N.B. Falls in love with Aglaia.)

The Prince has gone to Moscow. In Petersburg he has a kind of club.

Gania.

Part 3

N.B.

On his return from Moscow Aglaia receives him with scorn. He seeks out N. F. Gania is already in service to Aglaia and keeps her on good behavior.

Frank discussions between Aglaia and the Prince. The Prince talks of N. F. and tells of how she could not endure the carousing and of his proposal and of her flight. He says that he is hunting for N. F.

Aglaia visits N. F., says that it is vile of her to play the role of a Mary Magdalene, that she would do better to perish on a Japanese dagger in a brothel, out of sight and hearing. Laughs at the vileness of her soul. Offers her arsenic, calls her "thou."

N. F. declares that she is already a princess (mutual derision).

N. F. behaves to the Prince as if she were a princess. Abandons herself to debauchery. (Can the Prince bear this? At the very end she wants to poison herself.)

Though her dignity is restored, this does not go so far as to affect her actions.

The Prince forgives everything.

To Gania and Rogozhin and Aglaia.

Scheming on his part.

The children. The old man. The general.

Varia, Gania, and the rest.

10 March

N. F.

She is living in seclusion. She has run away from Rogozhin.

She senses at heart that she loves the Prince.

But considers herself unworthy of him.

She wants to become a laundress, with her own love, runs away *to a brothel.*

N.B. At this point Aglaia visits her, tells her she should take refuge in a brothel.

She spits on everyone and marries the Prince.

(Aglaia tells her she is marrying the Prince because he is a rich Idiot.)

But from certain intonations in her voice and from certain odd behavior, N. F. guesses that she loves the Prince.

N. F. is jealous of Aglaia. Jealousy impels her to marry the Prince.

Having married him, she plunges into debauchery. The general again.

Rogozhin, whose head she has turned once and for all. . . . . . .

She incites Gania and Rogozhin into seducing Aglaia. The latter falls into their trap (the Prince saves her). Then.

N. F.'s jealousy and rage.

Her death in a brothel (description).

The Prince secretly organizes a children's club.

N.B. Invent the roles in the plots for Gania, Ipolit, and the rest. For Varia.

10 March

The chief trait in the Prince's character:

—Downtroddenness.

—Timorousness.

—Self-abasement.

—Humility.

He is fully aware that he is an *Idiot*.

N.B. At every moment (inwardly) he asks himself the question: "Am I right or are they right?"

Ultimately he is always ready to accuse himself.

N.B. But when his heart and conscience tell him: "No, it's like that," then he acts against everyone's opinion.

He has a spontaneous love for children, but he seeks a counselor and has none.

N.B. His way of looking at the world: he forgives everything, sees reasons for everything, does not recognize that any sin is unforgivable, and excuses everything.

N.B. He hides the inmost state of his soul from everyone. And as he keeps himself apart, he is considered a melancholic and a hypochondriac.

As he listens to everyone without arguing, but subsequently does as he thinks best, he is considered to be very self-assured and proud.

He thinks himself inferior to and worse than others. He sees clearly into the thoughts of those around him. He perceives perfectly that they think him an Idiot and is convinced of this.

He finds grown men in children and makes them his companions. ("Am I an Idiot or not?")

Aglaia convinces him (even before) that he is an idiot.

(She does this on purpose; she expects to be contradicted and derided, but meets only with his acquiescence. He suddenly tells her about N. F. [The Prince explains all this to Aglaia in the 5th chapter.]

Gania deceives him—this is why the Prince is confidingly frank with him.

And when he led Gania to confess his deception, the Prince declares that he realized it long ago.

Someone wants to interfere in his affairs (the general?). But the Prince listens to advice and acts to the contrary.

(Ptitsyn's role?)

Gania. The burnt finger, the scene with Aglaia.

11 March

The relations between Gania and Aglaia.

As soon as he had recovered from his fainting spell, Gania immediately thought: "What will Aglaia say?"

He returns the 100,000 rubles to impress Aglaia. (He tries without success to convince people that he wanted to marry N. F. out of despair at having been rejected by Aglaia.)

He makes himself indispensable to Aglaia. *The sister—out of revenge.*

He makes himself indispensable to N. F., also to the Prince.

Toward Aglaia he began to play the role of a man devoted to the Prince.

He himself does not know whether he loves Aglaia or hates her? It seems to him that he hates her. He wants to marry her out of vanity.

Seeing Aglaia's love for the Prince, he hates the Prince.

He takes Aglaia to N. F.'s house. He gets her to fall into the trap by not revealing the fact that N. F. is already a princess.

He rouses N. F.'s jealousy of Aglaia. N. F. wants to go into a brothel and she detests Aglaia.

The interview. After Aglaia's triumph, suddenly N. F. shuts her up by announcing that she is a princess.

Thereafter Gania and Aglaia. The burnt finger. Strange scene. Both want revenge.

N.B. N.B. Finis, Aglaia gives way to N. F., and Gania strangles Aglaia.

N.B. Love out of vanity.

11 March

He is insulted by N. F. and Aglaia. The pride and dignity of humility. *Fully agrees* with them as to their accusations and considers himself worse than they are.

N.B.—*The socialist* attacks him and ridicules him because of his wanting as a private person to bring about the happiness of humanity by means of his own fortune.

He agrees; he is not a socialist.

His love for the Russian people begins to be a passion.

Aglaia is eventually impressed with his humility. She loves him with a feeling superior to infatuation and jealousy. She is seized with a passion for N. F. and begs her forgiveness.

It is he who brought them together and *transformed them.*

The Idiot does not consider himself capable of a sublime action, but he aspires to one. In saving N. F. and devoting himself to her, it is not to console himself by such a noble deed but rather because he is moved by a feeling of extraordinary Christian love.

N.B.

Project: Ought one to begin with Gania? Gania's intrigues, Varia, Ptitsyn, Rogozhin and his *crew*, Lebedev and the rest.

As soon as he came to himself, the idea,

The scene at the station—

What follows in the narrative—

N.B. (How the Prince seems to Gania. Scenes. In a word, all the attention is focused on Gania. Psychology.)

N.B. As N. F.'s wedding is a *coup de theatre*, it is not necessary to have N. F. appear before the scene with Aglaia. An all the more fantastic scene at Sofia Fyodorovna's—gropingly.

Projects.

N.B. Should the novel end with a confession? Publish it openly.—

N.B. *As for the relations with the children, arrange matters this way:* At the beginning, when the subject matter is especially concerned with Aglaia, Gania, N. F., the intrigues, and so on, why not mention casually and *almost enigmatically* the Prince's relations with the children, with Kolia, etc., etc. Do not mention the club, but rather introduce it abruptly, intimating that there are vague rumors as to its existence, and present the Prince like a tsar in its midst, in the 5th or 6th Part of the novel?

N.B. Would it be better to keep the Prince's personality an enigma *throughout the novel,* from time to time emphasizing the details (fantastically, questioningly, arousing curiosity) and suddenly at the end to reveal his personality, yet on the other hand—

N.B. Let all the other personages *from the very beginning* be defined and elucidated to the reader (as Gania, for example?).

12 March

> *Three* kinds of love in the novel:
> 1) Passionate and spontaneous love—Rogozhin.
> 2) Love out of vanity—Gania.
> 3) Christian love—the Prince.

Notes and Reminders.

When Gania in triumphing over Aglaia, who is caught in the trap, alludes to the wedding, that is, to her marrying him, Aglaia retorts: "All the same, it would be indecent to marry you."

"I don't dare be honest," says N. F.

(Lebedev and the Prince) (Lebedev's family)

Lebedev is a philosopher. He continually deceives the Prince. His characteristic. Lebedev's children.

The Prince says of sinful persons: "All sick people have to be taken care of."

Cannibal.

At N. F.'s house. The Apocalypse, prayers, about Christ.

1) "Where is she?—What's going on here? Let's go away, let's go away."

When Rogozhin shows him N. F.'s corpse.

She was screaming.

He kisses the corpse.

"I won't denounce myself simply because I've come to see her. How else then could I approach her?"

There's an undeniable smell from the corpse. He kisses her foot.

"Do you need some water? How she used to scream—right away, right away."

"To be alienated from our people is a sin"—

The bear and the wagon.[1]

The Prince says he has rarely seen real nobility.

The Prince: "It seems to me that every man has visions, but what he sees another man cannot even imagine."

Words and expressions. The definition of aristocracy. About Christopher Columbus.

Aglaia says: "If to keep your word means to kill yourself, then get married."

If D—v said, then Urus[2]—don't say the chairman didn't stop him—and put him to shame.

"I agree with you—how pleasant it is to debate with you, in this case I agree with you."

---

[1] The bear and the wagon: the conjunction of these two ideas suggests Lebedev and his astrological activities as a thaumaturge, a lecturer on the Apocalypse, a foreteller of the future, as he is in the final version of the novel. The Great Bear (Ursa Major) is a constellation of seven stars headed by Arcturus, a star mentioned in Job 9: 9 and 38: 32.

[2] Urus: the punctuation here, as elsewhere in the notebooks, is unreliable, and therefore there may be at least two possible interpretations of it. Urus Khan was a leader of the Golden Horde in the 1370's, and the reference therefore may be to the Mongol occupation of Russia. Alternatively, Prince Aleksandr Ivanovich Urusov (1843–1900), a liberal lawyer subsequently involved in the Nechaev trial of 1871, may be meant. See Dostoevsky's correspondence (*Pisma*, II, 499–500).

"I'll come to you."

A warped man.

The star *Wormwood*.[3]

He ate sixty monks, people were stronger in those times than in ours, he ate and ate and confessed and for this he was burned.

Keller: "If you knew, Madame, how hard it is in our epoch to get hold of any money. Everywhere the one answer: 'Bring us gold and diamonds, and we'll give you some money,' that is, precisely what I haven't got. Once I asked one of them: 'But what do you give for emeralds?' And he replied, 'We lend on emeralds, too.' 'Well, that's splendid.' I put on my hat and left, to the devil with him."

"Give me some wine, this tastes like *slops*."

The noble count sitting opposite

Of Keller's sort.

"In the article (on the Prince) I paid attention *only* to the style. (That was the first time I had appeared in print.)"

The Prince will say something about Christ.

"Yes, you are right, filthily and revoltingly [you syrupy thing] if . . . . but they will understand."

Beauty will save the world—two little types of beauty.

Then die well; one can die well even when spitting one's last, vanity, the baby, your sufferings, mountains—

When it becomes necessary—why not speak out?—Since you wanted to shoot yourself, why, shoot yourself.

Sick thoughts—still, there is nothing more intelligent in the world.

Humility is a very great force.

"You think I haven't the strength to shoot myself."

"But today is your birthday—I am disturbing you." Ipolit, "The sun, which is lavish to everyone, but not to me."

To the hospital, spittle, how stupid I am.

Then Ipolit says to the Prince regarding the latter's natural trust-fulness: "You are a noble man, Prince, with such trustfulness—"

The Prince thought: "Really? I didn't know I was like that."

The gossipmonger: about Kolia and the baby.

"If Kolia doesn't come, I'll kill him."

An aristocrat is a man who hasn't the least idea of what it means to work for his living.

---

[3] The star *Wormwood* (Absinthe): see Revelation 8: 11. "And the name of the star is called Wormwood: and the third part of the waters became wormwood; and many men died of the waters, because they were made bitter."

All our reforms amount to is the multiplication of bureaucrats.

"You make too much of a furor about your dying. One can die more nobly."

"Well, shoot yourself. As if you frighten us."

"But I don't allow you to, no, I don't allow it."

"Talk to me a little about Christ, Prince."

"Since I have only 2 weeks more, telling *the truth* or lying is absolutely the same to me."

Ipolit says of Rogozhin: "Strange, that man lives his life with all his strength, as intensely as anyone can, but it seems he is capable of understanding even my situation."

Why is it necessary in the construction of the world that there should be people condemned to die?

But is it possible to love for *two weeks?*

A good deed—within a recognized limitation, since any deed needing time or one demanding the dedication of my whole life is equally forbidden me [Comicality] lying to myself as regards love. Console the Prince with trees and with love. As for hope of some other life, what's the use of their having held all that out to me then taking it away?

I still have to die, for this is the one thing I can begin and end. I could also kill other men, the idea came into my head because of the false status of executioners and of society.

(A ludicrous pretense: why I haven't waited two weeks.)

At sunrise I shall fire.

The other world.

The depiction of that world, illustrations.

Whom shall I meet? I'd like to stay lying down.

To understand this means to ask a great deal of man.

There is a pride in helplessness.

There is a terrible voluptuousness in opposing oneself to an immense power, no matter how insignificant you are.

Or else:

Since I am insignificant, I want to oppose immense power.

There is a voluptuousness in subjugating oneself to immense power.

In the Prince's speech: "Here's to the sun, here's to life."

"You are terribly unhappy, I don't agree with you, but I have no right to say so to you."

"You slandered yourself—you could not love—(news of the little boy)." "It would be too egotistical to give up loving for the sake of some idea that there is no time, or out of bitterness."

Ipolit: "I should like to be condemned. What sort of power would judge me so as to torture me?"

"I would rather they condemned me."

(Christ. Perhaps I don't understand Christ in the least, or anything else.)

Bitterness: it's not even worth while to be embittered. Well, imagine to yourselves that I am not even embittered.

It would not be worth while to be afraid of a phantom.

Curious if I began to make money or fall in love now.

But to imagine that I could love someone—and to know all the time that I could do absolutely nothing for her.

Well, you'd have done better to have killed yourself right there. It's nothing, go along home.

If you make sure it is the truth, don't give yourself up.

Wants to kill himself in his room and says all of a sudden he has no desire to live.

You give that too much importance.

I know you are grinding your teeth because you can't kill us.

The Prince: "No, he won't kill himself now, having missed out on it, for it would make no impression on these people, so now he won't kill himself."

Lebedev asks suddenly: "Prince, what do you think: is there a God?"

"You ask that so lightly?"

"If you knew how I torment myself with this question, but I always put off deciding, I have too much to do, and I pray in any case."

"Well, if there were no occasion, wouldn't you pray?"

12 March

Detailed plan of the 3rd Part.

Three months later.

Morning. Gania. Ptitsyn. The sister is in the other apartment, where there are no roomers. They are expecting someone and something. Enigmatic conversation. (Explanatory chapter. Scene at the station.)

Or else:

1st chapter: explanatory; scene at the station. But the only major personage is Gania. Description of how Gania returned home, what was in his heart.

2nd chapter. Three months later. Waiting for morning. Enigmatic conversation. Aglaia and Adelaide come. Aglaia's conversation with Gania and Varia. A candid talk with Gania. Aglaia has heard that Gania and the Prince are on friendly terms, and that Gania can inform her about N. F. He has sought her out. Aglaia suspects that N. F. has a material influence on him. Gania assents to this. Gania tells her many things about the Prince during these three months. As to himself he is reserved. Absolutely indispensable explanation in a half-word. News that today the Prince is giving a luncheon. To show the cabinet of rare objects he has bought. Costing lots of money. The money the Prince has received is more than was expected. He arrived yesterday. N. F.—out of her mind (Aglaia was informed by Varia that she could come and therefore she did).

3rd chapter. Aglaia and Adelaide have returned, family explanations. The general and the mother. At three o'clock in the Prince's house. (Did they find out that she had been visiting Varia?)

4th chapter. Luncheon at the Prince's: Count Af. Ivan., Rogozhin, the old man, the teacher, Ptitsyn, Gania, Varia, the general, Kolia, Ipolit, Nina Aleksandrovna. The young writer. A lively morning. General Ivan Fyodorovich arrives, a bizarre social gathering.

Rogozhin. He arouses curiosity.

The old Belokonskaia is present at the luncheon.

5th chapter. Some plain speaking with the 3 young girls, especially with Aglaia; the main thing in this respect is that he has not proposed. On leaving, Aglaia makes an appointment with Gania at vespers.

6th chapter. A fantastic intrigue at Sofia Fyodorovna's—her flight.

Kolia and the Prince as spies.

7th chapter. Aglaia and Gania at N. F.'s. Scene, go into a brothel. Arsenic.

8th chapter. "I am a princess," the Prince comes in. Aglaia runs away. Chapter with Gania at the *Estaminet*. The burnt finger. "Take her home."

N.B. (About Rogozhin.)—(The Prince absolutely must be a witness.)

In the 4th Part. N. F.'s life. The humiliated Prince, Aglaia and Gania. Elucidation between the Prince and Gania. N. F.'s flight.

5th Part. The club. Eccentricities. The salvation of Aglaia, reconciliation with N. F. Confession, and so forth.

The ruin of Rogozhin, and so forth.

3rd Part. Gania to Aglaia:

In the 1st chapter—"I'm amazed at your insight." In reality, N. F. perhaps plays the chief role. In reality perhaps the Prince and N. F. are on good terms, nevertheless I learned positively that after a three-day orgy at Rogozhin's N. F. returned (to the teacher) and that for two weeks the Prince took an active part in things. But then the Prince almost completely stopped seeing her. *N. F. needed to be left alone.* But on condition that the Prince hover over her like a protecting spirit. I know this for a fact. Perhaps they did meet. I know too that N. F. has a strange temperament. I admit that for some time I thought her out of her head. Now I don't, but—however. In any case, a morbid frame of mind. That orgy at Rogozhin's upset her; her nature is not like that. Ptitsyn spoke with extraordinary truth about the Japanese. Now for the most part she is remorseful, she broods, she weeps, beside herself at the thought that she has someow brought ruin on the Prince. That she is unworthy of the Prince, but that he loves her so much that he is ready to sacrifice his whole life for her. This would be an impossible state of affairs if there were no love on her part but rather jealousy. She asked about you. She often clasps her head in her hands and cries, "What have I done? What have I done?" Sometimes she blames herself for everything and laughs sardonically at the memory of the scene at Ksenin's (100,000): "I was behaving like Totsky's martyred victim, now I am the lowest creature alive," she says. And so on.

Aglaia gazes penetratingly at Gania to discern what is in his mind.

Aglaia listens to this with hatred (but without exposing her thoughts). Gania is stubbornly incurious. "Why is Aglaia questioning him?" But he speaks with a deep though not obtrusive respect for N. F.

Aglaia does not deign to reply. But she recalls the 100,000 rubles and that perhaps she was the guiltier in having accused Gania. Gania's coolness.

When Aglaia left Gania and begged Gania to leave her.

The sharp though extremely polite and delicate reply of the Prince drives her frantic.

So that her visit to N. F.—is a hysterical and despairing scene.

In a word: In the entire three-month engagement period Aglaia has seen more clearly than others and discerned that everything depends on N. F.

Rogozhin's personality in the 3rd Part is mysterious.

Lebedev? (The boxer?)

Major point:

1) Aglaia declares to her parents point-blank that they have compromised her and that she knows for a fact that the Prince is taken up with N. F.

2) At the moment in actuality there are only vague rumors about the Prince's heroism and good deeds, *about the children* (so that everything comes to light in the end).

However:

3) There are sporadic flashes of meaning before the end.

(N.B. But what if at the beginning things develop faster. . . . . . .)

The Prince blames himself for everything. (Why did he marry.)— Aglaia is in love with the Prince throughout the whole novel.

As for N. F. things go thus throughout the whole novel:

—At the beginning she is astounded at having become a princess—a laundress.

—Thereafter—a haughty and proud princess.

—Aglaia stages a public insult to her (scene).

4th Part (conclusion).

—Unheard of depravity.

—The Prince's confession to Aglaia.

—Puzzling disappearance, *they track her down* in a brothel.

—She wants to kill herself.

—Rehabilitation. Aglaia and the Prince with her, trying to save her.

—She dies or else she kills herself.

N.B. Rogozhin.

Aglaia marries the Prince—or else the Prince dies.

The Prince is timid in *expressing* all his ideas, his convictions and intentions. Chastity and humility. *But firm in action.*

His principal social conviction is that the economic doctrine of *the uselessness of individual good deeds—*is an absurdity. *And that on the contrary everything is based on individual action.*

The course of events? N.B. N.B. N.B.? The course of events.

Gania wants to avenge himself on Aglaia and in doing so informs Rogozhin that Aglaia is going to be at N. F.'s.

Rogozhin warns the Prince (which Gania does not suspect).

N.B. —Rogozhin arrives with his crew, but the Prince hides at the teacher's.

Then the interview.

Rogozhin shows up to rescue her, then the Prince arrives.

Aglaia is put to shame. N. F. is jealous of the Prince.

Scene in the *Estaminet*. Gania feels that he loves Aglaia, not hates her.

13 March

N.B. *More of a role* for the general, bringing out his passion.

N.B. As his passion swells, Gania's character takes on colossal seriousness.

During the luncheon at the Prince's the general's wife makes friends with Rogozhin.

N.B. At lunch before Rogozhin's arrival, about Rogozhin, that the feeling between him and the Prince is mutual; the word "take!" uttered at the station is cherished in both their hearts, and that the Prince has had an extraordinary influence on Rogozhin because of his noble bearing. At moments Rogozhin gets rowdy, as if on *a drinking bout.*

In the 3rd and 4th Parts, abstruse and veiled words *about the children's club and secret scenes. Rumors and scenes.* N.B. Invent?

13 March

N. F. is not a princess, but is only struggling: to be or not to be?

How does the main scene with Aglaia turn out?

The scene has taken place. Sarcasms. Her offer to go into a brothel. Arsenic. This scene has settled N. F.'s vacillations (not a laundress, she merely moves to the teacher's) and she declares she is going to marry the Prince.

The whole of the 4th Part: she is engaged to him, but on the eve of the wedding she rushes off to the brothel.

The Prince does not marry Aglaia and is not engaged to her. But he sees her love and is amazed. On his arrival from Moscow he speaks openly with Aglaia. Talks of N. F. Aglaia assents to everything, but the outcome of this talk is a vindictive scene with N. F.

In the 4th Part N. F. is engaged to the Prince. Aglaia's plots. A scandalous scene staged by N. F. (the role of the general's wife?). N. F.'s triumphant flight.

N.B.—The brothels. Scenes.

Scenes between Aglaia and Gania in the 3rd and 4th Parts.

Gania's terrible disposition, gloomy, passionate.

Begin the 3rd Part with the scene at the station. *To lose what belongs to you* is out of the question.

Finally:

14 March

N.B.—*Not a princess.*

The gist of the plan is thus:

After the orgy at Rogozhin's—she is stunned; at the teacher's; is struggling; love for the Prince; horror at the thought of surrendering herself to the Prince and becoming his wife.

The Prince's tragic situation (in the 3rd Part), he has positively determined on marrying her, but is confiding this to no one (except to Rogozhin, it seems). He hides it from Aglaia, but in the 3rd Part he decides to make a clean breast of things. (He is prodded by Aglaia into doing so, for of himself he would not been capable of opening the subject, out of delicacy.) (N.B. It is not known where the 100,000 rubles are.) (N.B. They are lying at the teacher's.)

N. F.'s dreams of going out to work.

Aglaia and Gania, Aglaia asks all sorts of questions of Gania. They question each other as to their respective motivations. Aglaia and Gania are not frank with each other.

After the scene with Aglaia, who had foreseen everything.—Scene between Aglaia and N. F. (the brothel, arsenic, and so forth).

In a fury N. F. accepts the Prince's proposal.

(In the morning Aglaia summons the Prince and in her sisters' presence she *insists* that he does not dare propose to her. Sarcasms. The Prince's respectful and extremely decorous reply.)

(But about N. F.—not a word, either on Aglaia's part or the Prince's.)

The Prince agrees to the proposal after the scene between Aglaia and N. F., at which he is a witness (the tragic figure of Rogozhin).

Throughout the 4th Part N. F. is engaged to the Prince. The scandalous scene pivots on Aglaia's being put to shame.

The moment she is engaged N. F. plunges into wild depravity.

Rushes into a brothel.

Marries Rogozhin.

She suffers terror, blows, jealousy, reproaches, and desperate love.

Rogozhin cuts her throat. Zhdanov fluid;[4] the 100,000 rubles are discovered. Carousing as before.

But Aglaia had secretly become N. F.'s friend just before the latter's death.

The Prince learns of their friendship.

The Prince marries Aglaia. He would have liked, he dies.

N.B. (Gania and his role. His mad love for Aglaia.)

---

[4] Zhdanov fluid: presumably an antiseptic.

N.B. N.B. N.B.

The role of the general's wife in the 3rd Part, protecting Aglaia. Or else:

In the 3rd Part the role of the general's wife is merely *enigmatic*. She protects Aglaia and wishes intensely that she would marry the Prince, even quarrels on that account.

But in the 4th Part.—Her scene with the Prince, in which she tells him as to N. F.: "Marry her!"

In the 3rd Part the general's wife quarrels with Aglaia because the latter does not consent, but suspects something.

15 March

The general's wife behaves like an *enfant terrible,* and in the 3rd Part she clashes with Aglaia, reproaches her suddenly: "This is all nonsense on your part, in reality you love the Prince, I know that."

This drives Aglaia into a frenzy.

But at that Adelaide tells her mother when they are alone: "You've spoiled everything. There was no need at all for you to tell her that *straight out* (to her face)."

Wouldn't it be better to put the scene of the plain talks between the Prince and N. F. right after his return from Moscow, where N. F. in utter *despair* and distress is ready to give up, but the Prince begs her to put off her decision (until evening).—

In this preliminary scene with the Prince, N. F. insists on his marrying Aglaia, but at the same time she is jealous of her.

In a word: anguish and fever.

15 March

Brief outline of the chapters in the 3rd Part.

1st chapter. At Gania and Varia's. Ptitsyn. Awaiting Aglaia. Varia is on intimate terms with her brother, she even annoys him with her heatedness and impatience. She is Aglaia's enemy more than N. F. is. But Gania is much more serious than in the first 2 Parts. He doesn't let on about anything, remains silent. He is keeping his own counsel— however, Varia observes that he is nervously awaiting Aglaia's arrival. Why Aglaia could come. (Information about Aglaia.)

The reply to this:

2nd chapter. At the station. Gania has returned. . . . . . . End the chapter with Gania's relations to the Prince, which have been known and oddly defined ever since.

3rd chapter. Aglaia and Gania. Result, N. F. Mutual emotions. (Information about N. F.)

4th chapter. At the Prince's. The luncheon. Tableaux. Rogozhin, etc.

5th chapter. The Prince, Aglaia and her two sisters. Plain speaking. Most unexpectedly Aglaia suddenly perceives that the Prince is happy at her having refused him. Everything confirmed about N. F.

6th chapter. Scene at the general's. The general's wife and Aglaia. A paroxysm of fury. To vespers.

7th chapter. The Prince and N. F. Sarcasms. Passion, despair. She urges him to marry Aglaia and simultaneously is jealous of her.

8th chapter. Scene with Aglaia. The Prince is a witness. Rogozhin by accident.

9th chapter. Conclusion.

N.B. Kolia. Rogozhin. Sofia Fyodorovna, and so forth.

My job: to write more tersely. So that it should be polished, charming (concisely and to the point) and absorbing.

N.B. The mysterious relations between N. F. and Rogozhin in the 3rd and 4th Parts.

Cursory notes. Composition and elements.

Aleksei's son and Aleksei himself.

About those people with whom the aunt was living and about the aunt's last testament.

The skinflint.

The priest in whose house she was living.

The swindlers who tried to defraud him and whose schemes he frustrated. (A newborn babe. Some funny incidents Aglaia tells, laughing.)

He has a business manager. Ptitsyn is here too.

Ipolit.

(Only rumors about him, lots of rumors being circulated. At the *luncheon* at his house everything is decorous, elegant, as customary.)

But all of a sudden something extraordinary turns up.

(They say he is a skinflint. But suddenly it turns out that he is giving his entire fortune away. People come to present their claims to him and he evades them.)

(In a word, something happens through which he displays his remarkable intelligence, his wiliness, *his heart,* and his oddness.)

N.B. Of course people flock around him and badger him from all sides to get something out of him.

The result:

Only cloudy rumors about all the Prince's clever dodges.

But impossible without the scene at lunch.

16 March

The episode about Pavlishchev's son.

Ipolit is invited to lunch at the Prince's. During the Prince's absence in Moscow, Ipolit has got himself hotly involved with the business about Pavlishchev's son.

Pavlishchev's son declares to the Prince that he himself is Pavlishchev's son by a former serf girl.

The profligate Pavlishchev had married her off as if to B—, also a manorial serf, after giving them their freedom and providing a dowry.

But as they went on living at his house, he maintained his concern when the boy was born, looked after him, had him educated. The high school.

But after the 6th form of the high school, the son turned surly, imagined he was Pavlishchev's own son and began to demand money of him.

Now he was importuning the Prince: "Look here now, Pavlishchev used to take care of you, but now you are well to do. My mother cannot use her legs. Hand over everything Pavlishchev squandered on you to me, as his son."

When the Prince came back from Moscow, at lunch Ipolit began on this affair. The general's wife insisted that he go right on, so that she could defend the Prince.

The Prince responded that he had given the son 250 rubles. In reply to the latter's demand for everything, the Prince's steward and Gania triumphantly asserted that *he* was not Pavlishchev's son, the documents, Pavlishchev's letters, but Gania announced that the mother of Pavlishchev's son was here at hand.

The general's wife backed them up for the most part, so as to exculpate the Prince.

Aglaia's sarcasms.

The general's wife retorts: "Why, you'd be glad to marry the Prince." Aglaia flares up: "Impossible for you to say that."

Then in the next room Aglaia tells the Prince in the presence of her 2 3 sisters that she has been compromised. She has had a letter from the Prince's son, people have warned her that a rumor was spreading that the Prince was courting her, that her mother took delight in repeating this gossip. That she insists that the Prince state that he has never dreamed of laying claim to her hand, since to hope for this was an absurdity. (And that if she had come to lunch, it was only so as not to substantiate gossip by declining and absenting herself.)

The Prince does so state.

Aglaia is beside herself. The general's wife as well. Pouncing on an awkward expression by the Prince, Aglaia says, "How could you think I love you when you are marrying a public woman."

The Prince says: "Yes, I am going to marry, not a public woman, but N. F."

The general's wife says: "How do you dare invite me here with my daughters like this, my good man?[5] They'll say I knowingly brought my daughters here! You wooden-headed *batiushka,* you perfect Idiot!"

16 March

N.B. Indispensable to characterize the Prince's personality as fully as possible (*by his facial expression* and his idiosyncrasies) in the 3rd Part—especially when his situation changes because of his inheritance and because of his three-month sojourn in Russia.

N.B. Aglaia often laughs outright at him for being a skinflint, for refusing to give money for useful purposes and giving God knows to whom.

N.B. The Prince is weary. He is ill. (Inwardly he is totally preoccupied with the problem of N. F. He is terribly abstracted.—He is like an idiot.—But with Aglaia he is charming and often inspired in his remarks. *At the luncheon* he is aware of everything; that is evident; but he keeps silent, as if detached from it all. During the night he had had a seizure. Aglaia is suddenly almost sorry for him.

Two problems confront him at the beginning of the 3rd Part: N. F., and the necessity of breaking off with Aglaia—.

(Does he love Aglaia?)

---

[5] My good man: the Russian word here, as further in the speech, is *batiushka,* meaning literally, "little father." The term is used in addressing priests, but it also has other usages, as in a nobleman's speaking to a peasant, especially an old man; it might carry either benevolence or condescension. Madame Epanchin's use of it in ridiculing Myshkin is therefore a play on words with a sarcastic allusion to the Prince's moralizing.

16 March

N.B. Show the Prince's situation in full and all his queerness, also the full situation of Aglaia, in the first chapter during the conversation with Varia's brother and in the chapter with Aglaia.

Fundamental N.B.

Gania's silence toward Varia and toward everyone. Mysteriousness.

Varia sees that Gania is standing up for the Prince and she is uneasy: is it really possible, but she is convinced that he is pretending and that he wants to avenge himself, and she approves. She believes in him, and so as not to annoy him does not question him, and Gania maintains silence.

16 March

N.B.

Aglaia's motives

She says to Gania: "I've heard that you are his friend."

Her motives: 1) She does not believe that Gania is his friend, on the contrary, she is convinced that Gania wants revenge. But on whom? on everyone? on the Prince? on N. F. or on herself?

2) It seems to her that Gania is still in love with her; and this being so, she knows that Gania, jealous of her marrying the Prince, will take revenge on her. She schemes to find out what he is thinking. She needs an ally; she wants to see whether Gania can qualify as one.

3) After the scene with N. F., Aglaia tells him all about this, confesses everything, and offers him her love.

4) Does Rogozhin warn her? Or Kolia?

5) The Prince is aware of everything.

6) But Gania *in actual truth* is just vacillating under various agitated emotions. He would like to avenge himself on Aglaia, but having seen her, especially after the scene with N. F. (to which he brought the Prince), he falls in love with Aglaia and burns his finger. Thereafter he again shifts to the Prince's side. (Toward the end he kills himself.)

7) Toward the end he confesses to the Prince that he has been deceiving him. The Prince replies that he knew this.

Fundamental and definite notation.

16 March

After the luncheon at the Prince's, a direct *transition* to N. F. as was indicated in the notes just above.

(N.B. Little concerning the Prince in the 3rd Part. He merely takes a tragic decision. He is spiritless, dulled, sunk in thought. At moments he somewhat revives.) Shift to N.F.:

1) The scene at the station (remembrance).

2) Without further words, N. F., convalescent and panic-stricken, goes into a brothel, comes to an understanding with the madam, and promises to return in the evening. Immediately on leaving she falls to shuddering, longs to throw herself into the water.

3) But Rogozhin prevents her (he is keeping watch over her via sentries) (strong-armed fellows and so forth). N.B. Here it comes to light that Rogozhin is constantly in touch with her and this becomes evident during a feverish conversation.

"Is he here? Has he come? But Aglaia?" She is jealous of Aglaia. He has to marry her.

She goes back home. Throws herself in despair on her bed. Rogozhin goes out and encounters the Prince—and on the other side of the street Gania and Aglaia are approaching.

(About the earlier interview between Gania and Aglaia.)

Aglaia enters alone, having sent Gania away.

After the scene. N. F. laughs hysterically, she jeers at the Prince for having put in an appearance after the event because *he is afraid of marrying her.*

Aglaia is enraged above all because the Prince heard everything; she gives her promise to Gania in the *Estaminet.*

The essence
of the 4th Part

(Perhaps the scene between Aglaia and N.F., and the *Estaminet,*— this having found no place in the 3rd Part.)

And—

N. F. is engaged: the entire Part is given over to this. N. F.'s increasingly frantic state.—Her sarcasms about the Prince, the club.

The kind of people suddenly surrounding her.

Scandalous scene staged by Aglaia; N. F. overwhelmed.

Now tenderness, and so on. Finally the wedding. Passionate and tender scene with the Prince. (The New Testament story of the woman caught in adultery[6] being pardoned in the church.) She runs away from the wedding. To Moscow, and so forth.

N.B.   N.B.   N.B.

Let the 5th Part begin with the club and the rumors about the coming wedding of N. F. and Rogozhin, with the orgy, and so on.

Gania

He tells Aglaia about N. F. in the 1st scene.

"She loves the Prince. She is appalled that she doesn't run away, she listens to the Prince's urging her to marry him. She implores him to marry Aglaia. She wants to run away and sees with horror that she cannot. At the same time, she is jealous, she questions me as well as the Prince about you, she is going out of her mind."

In the morning Aglaia leaves Gania's, crushed, but yet persuaded that the Prince loves her. She does not want to believe that the Prince does not love her. A brief, rapid scene at home with her mother and sisters.

Write more concisely; only the facts; without rationalizing—and without describing feelings?

Gania also explains how Aglaia wanted to come.

Varia arranged this interview as she wanted it; that's evident.

Though Gania took this news with equanimity, it is apparent that he is upset.

17 March

3rd Part. Chapter 1

Gania's tone with Aglaia is frank without his saying everything. Before Aglaia's arrival he was upset, which Varia notices but keeps to herself and does not mention (so that Gania is quite mysterious).

Write only the facts.

Simply say that Gania brought the Prince 100,000 rubles; they have been friends ever since, *so they say.*

---

[6] The woman caught in adultery: a reference to the story told in John 8: 3–9, in which Jesus said, "He that is without sin among you, let him first cast a stone at her."

Gania's shabby lodgings bear witness to the fact that he has no money.

Write in the sense of "people say."

Ptitsyn, Varia, Gania—are waiting.

3 rooms.

Nina Aleksandrovna is ill and has not appeared. The general is in debtors' prison, so they say. Nor is Kolia there, he is at the Prince's.

N.B. Recount the facts, *lightly,* without special detailing.

Gania's outward appearance

N.B. N.B. Aglaia laughs at his oddities, but in passing, the Prince is spiritless and depressed.

"He had a seizure in the night" (Gania's sympathetic remark); about Pavlishchev.

The club and the children.

1st chapter. Sincerity and warmth when Gania spoke of the Prince. Varia exchanged a glance with Ptitsyn. As if she did not believe in his sincerity and warmth.

2. Explain Varia's partisanship of her brother.

3. About the general's wife and Aglaia.

Varia with Ptitsyn and her brother; about the general's wife and Aglaia.

Gania: "In my opinion Aglaia is in love with the Prince, and the general and his wife are delighted"; about the house.

Varia again casts an oblique glance at Gania.

Varia and Nina Aleksandrovna are invited to lunch. At first a discussion as to whether he should move to the Prince's house.

Varia says: "No, such a thing is not to be thought of."

Gania, coldly: "Whatever you say."

And point out here that it was not for the sake of money that Gania was with the Prince, and that Gania urgently wanted to stress this.

Varia to her brother about Aglaia: "Probably he drove her to the last ditch and this couldn't be avoided any longer."

Ptitsyn: "What is his object in liking or hating the Prince—that's what is interesting."

Varia and her brother exchange a quick glance and they all remain silent.

Gania about the Prince—more winningly.

[Then in the *Estaminet* Gania says to Aglaia: "My sister hates you."]

Here too: 2 words about the relations between Ptitsyn and Varia. These relations have not changed, but Varia puts off her decision until the family affairs are settled. Ptitsyn knows this and has played a major part in the affairs and projects of the sister and brother, though he barely knows what these are. Perhaps he also thinks he has guessed everything and is not in the least wrong.

Gania fusses, takes out his watch and looks at it: "If only she isn't late. I've lots of work at the office, and then the Prince has invited me. But <illegible> Varia, get ready to welcome father—he is being released."

"Where shall we put him?"

"Where he was before, in the hall."

"That's almost impossible. This apartment is possible only without him."

"But listen, brother: excuse my asking, wasn't it you who asked the Prince's help on father's behalf?"

"Of course," said Gania scornfully. "He *himself* certainly wanted to help and charged me with handling it. Here is the money to be paid over. But for God's sake, don't blab this to anyone. He wants secrecy, that is, not a word to father. Do him this favor.—Let him believe somebody else has saved him. I will send Daria Aleksandrovna alone. So then he will imagine some lady has fallen in love with him and ransomed him for love's sake."

"Of course."

"But he is going *to hand out* more promissory notes."

"No doubt. I've talked the Prince around, I've done all I could; there was a place for him, too."

"Don't speak so loud, mamma mustn't hear."

She is weeping for him.

Gania: "Yes, if you like, well, I'm sorry for him too, but this is the best thing that could have happened to him <illegible> it's already half past ten." [About the headmaster.]

19 March

Indispensable note

1) The effect of *Russia* on the Prince. How and in what way he has changed. *In the description.*

2) First thing in the morning Aglaia has a talk with Gania, in which she refers to the Prince with a kind of hostility:

"I don't much care for those simple and innocent people who are so cautious and so calculating in the measures they take and are so self-assured. When he arrived penniless and he accepted the 25 rubles from father, he was looking for some small job, he did not let on a word to us, he wore so humble an air, accepted that little job in the office, and yet he was carrying that letter about the legacy in his pocket!"

Gania (defending the Prince): "Oh, you've no need to take it like that. I myself was in Ivan Fyodorovich's office during their first conversation: four times the Prince began to speak of that letter, precisely that letter, he even took it out of his pocket; but each time something happened to prevent him from saying anything further about it. In my opinion, there was nothing calculating on his part, it's simply that the Prince, who understands absolutely nothing about business . . . . or about Russia, if you like, took no great stock in that letter. . . . . . . On the other hand, if you like, such prudence as that even deserves respect, it would have been imprudent to count on the legacy. How could he announce such extraordinary news without having taken steps to verify it beforehand?"

Aglaia:—"Yes, that's how we interpreted it at our house, but in any case he is quite a *prudent* man." And Aglaia smiled to herself.

N.B.

The general's wife, getting worked up, says: "As for me, I will tell you frankly: *you yourself are in love with him*" (N.B. that is why you are attacking him).

She expresses herself in such a way that what she says must be wholly *unexpected* to the reader, that is, the reader must not have suspected that Aglaia is in love with the Prince.

The general's wife to Aglaia:

"Don't worry, I've watched him closely, he loves you."

The general's wife is terribly anxious for the Prince to marry Aglaia.

Yet when he almost refused, and Aglaia back home blamed it on her mother—the latter was bitterly sorry that she had not seen matters clearly, out of her love for her daughter, and therefore she says obstinately: *"He loves you."*

(In the 4th Part the plain talk between the general's wife and the Prince.) 3 months *earlier* the general's wife had been astounded at hearing that the Prince wanted to marry N. F.

Show more clearly how all this *was made right.*

20 March

Conversation between Gania and Aglaia about Pavlishchev.—N.B.) About Aglaia's relations with Rogozhin.—N.B. About the general's passion.

20 March

N.B. The main scene is the frank discussion between Gania and Varia. (And perhaps a rupture on this account.)

N.B. A plain talk between the Prince and the general's wife.

N.B. The 3rd and 4th Parts *comprise* only the present third Part, that is, conclude it thus, so that after the scene with Aglaia N. F. wants to marry the Prince, but Aglaia expresses herself to Gania at the *Estaminet.*

N.B. The 5th and 6th Parts comprise only the 5th, that is, N. F. is engaged, explanations on the part of N. F. and the general's wife and Rogozhin. The children's club, N. F.'s flight.

Scene with the Prince at the church, forgiveness.

No need for the club, but just various episodes.

6th and 7th Parts. Rogozhin is searching. N. F.'s wedding to the Prince.—Secret interviews. Rogozhin cut her throat.

In the 3rd and 4th Parts (in the 2nd, that is), Gania's open talks with the Prince after his declaring to Aglaia that he had deceived him.

In the 4th Part N. F. runs away with Rogozhin on her wedding day. In the 5th and 6th Parts the Prince, having got engaged, is busy with other matters and does not pursue N. F.

(Invent many episodes.)

The general's wife, Gania, Aglaia, even the children—scandalous scenes.

The forgiveness at the church, the wedding, she vanishes.

The chapter about the luncheon at the Prince's.

He talks about the aristocracy.

21 March

The synthesis of the novel. The solution of the difficulty.

? How make the hero's personality charming to the reader?

If Don-Quixote and Pickwick[7] as philanthropists are charming to the reader, it is because they are comical.

The hero of this novel, the Prince, is not comical but does have another charming quality: he is innerect![8]

The children's club has already begun to form in the 3rd and 4th Parts.

It develops at the end of the novel.

All the problems *concerning the personality of the Prince* (in which the children play an active role) as well as *general* problems are solved and in all this there is a great deal that is touching and naïve, for in his very extremity, in his most *tragic,* most *personal,* moments, the Prince is concerned with solving general problems. N.B. *Prepare many incidents and stories.*

When *at the end of the 4th Part* N. F. again deserts the Prince and runs away with Rogozhin on her wedding day, the Prince is wholly absorbed with the club.

Mistrust of adults (of their projects, their counsels, their requests and their practical proposals)—*in the 3rd and 4th Parts.* F

In the 3rd and 4th Parts Aglaia and N. F. are already beginning to jeer at all this. N.B. The general's wife becomes a member of the club.

Beginning with the 5th Part all the Prince's personal affairs proceed concurrently with those of the club.

The extraordinary part the children play in the attitudes of the Prince, N. F., and Aglaia.

N.B. Influenced by the children, Rogozhin confesses that he has committed an outright crime.

General Ivolgin,
The general's wife,
Gania—
Aglaia—

---

[7] Don-Quixote and Pickwick: this reference is more amply set forth in the often quoted letter Dostoevsky wrote his niece Sonia on 1/13 January 1868 (*Pisma,* II, 71), while he was writing the first chapters of the final version. The letter (numbered 294) expresses his difficulty with the conception of his leading protagonist, Myshkin, and compares him with Cervantes' and Dickens' portrayals of a good man who is also ridiculous.

[8] Innocent: the Russian word here is *nevinyi,* meaning precisely "innocent," "guiltless," possibly "virginal." It is enclosed in a rectangle in the manuscript and is followed by an exclamation mark, emphasizing the importance of this new perception on Dostoevsky's part.

The death of the Prince.

At first Aglaia takes the attitude that the Prince is a fraud (on purpose) and tries to show him up as such. But from the very beginning she is wholeheartedly devoted to the Prince because he is *innocent*.

The same thing with N. F. She pities the Prince because he is *innocent*, and therefore she runs away with Rogozhin on her wedding day.

But then she understands the depth of the Prince's innocence—

The Prince does not get into debates with adults and subsequently he even avoids adults, but with the children he behaves with full frankness and sincerity—a completely new life.

N.B. *Three* young men come to his house for lunch.

30 March

~~April~~

The Prince—

"I've committed a great crime" (with reference to marriage).

He counts on Aglaia's influencing N. F. (regarding her moral state). It is with this object that he is courting Aglaia.

Finally he formulates a direct request of Aglaia regarding N. F. (scene).

Aglaia (having ridiculed the Prince, in a burst of rage, begins to give in to him).

Fundamental—the scene between Aglaia and N. F. In hiding, the Prince watches.

Scene between Aglaia and Gania.

N. F. is beside herself and demands that the Prince marry her.

Runs away with Rogozhin.

N.B. The scene at the Prince's house with some of the children. Ipolit. The general. Madame Epanchin.

1 April

Aglaia therefore could come to Ganechka because she had heard that he had changed, that he *had completely gone over to the Prince, kept close to the Prince:* she suspects the Prince and in the Prince's interest has come to scrutinize Gania.

The general had informed himself about the legacy and verified it. Gave a loan of 100,000. Is going to give more.

"I did not know myself; I love her, therefore," said the Prince of N. F.

He has an ever stronger and stronger tenderness for Aglaia.

Humility is the most terrible force that can ever exist in the world!
The Idiot sees all afflictions.
Impotence to help.
The chain⁹ and hope.
To do a little.
A serene death.
Aglaia is unhappy.
Her need of the Prince.

8 April

N. F. is at the teacher's house (Daria Aleksandrovna is often with her).

Rogozhin implores her to marry him. She refuses repeatedly. After each refusal Rogozhin's despair and carousing.

Finally she tells him: "I'll marry you when the Prince marries Aglaia."

Rogozhin is her slave (and at the end he cuts her throat).

Aglaia is jealous of N. F. (and *openly* ridicules the Prince).

Learns of N. F.'s resolve. Concludes that N. F. is in love.

The scene of the interview between Aglaia and N. F. The insult. N. F. is beside herself. "If that's how things are, I'll marry the Prince."

The Prince agrees. They are engaged. He is ridiculous. How he turns laughter aside.

She runs away on her wedding day and goes off with Rogozhin.

The Prince and his activity. Aglaia *convertie*. Rogozhin cuts N. F.'s throat.

N.B. The Prince has had only *the slightest effect* on their lives. But everything he might have done and undertaken perishes with him.

Russia had had its effect on him little by little. His intuitions. (x)!

But wherever he even made an appearance—everywhere he left a permanent trace.

Hence the infinity of events in the novel (the more wretched persons of all classes), along with the development of the main theme.

(N.B. N.B. N.B.) This is precisely the theme that has to be worked out.

---

⁹ The chain: here, and in a passage that soon follows, the allusion is perhaps to the chain forged to the shackles worn by a convict, which linked him to another preceding him and to a third following him.

He teaches the children in stories.

? Wouldn't it be better to present the Prince as a perpetual sphinx?
Several blunders and comical traits in the Prince.

The imperial guards officer insults him; the Prince with the most
(*sincerely*) innocent air in the world goes to him, questions him, and
disarms him.

N.B.—The Prince's courage in an important affair and how Aglaia
is all the more impressed.

9 April

The Prince and all the stories. Aglaia is in love; at first she plays
pranks, then she submits, and *suddenly she learns of N. F.*

N.B.—"I love you." . . . . . . "Yes, I love you." (She grows angry.)

Aglaia is afraid of N. F.

Rumors about N. F.

The Prince found her and hid her away.

Rogozhin hunts for her.

Aglaia and N. F.

N. F. marries Rogozhin (end of the 2nd Part).

N.B. The Prince talks to the children about Christopher Columbus and says a man has to be really great if he is to hold out despite
his intelligence for what goes against common sense.

(It is a good thing, his talking with the children, for they have not
yet lived and do not understand their own worth, and therefore each
of them can imagine that he himself in his own right can become a
Columbus.)

The sequence.

At first not a word about N. F.

Aglaia alone is to be developed.

Stories about the Prince.

Lebedev (vaguely).

Then he rejects Aglaia.

(At lunch.)

He goes to N. F.'s; his scene with N. F.

Aglaia's arrival.

The last idea.   N.B. To be developed.

Nastasia Filipovna is sick

and overwhelmed by his mysterious solicitude for her. N.B. (Her
indispensable scene with him is not a tender one but is strong and
gracious. Kolia and Petrusha Lebedev. The sister-in-law.)

N.B. Gania and Lebedev. Lebedev's perfidy.
(Rogozhin knows. Gloomy and resigned.)
N.B.—Not a word about the marriage of the Prince and N. F.
Her interview with Rogozhin. ("Perhaps I shall marry.")
The Prince is regarded as Aglaia's fiancé.
The insult.
"If I want to, I'll marry." Pride to the point of insanity.
She runs away with Rogozhin.

Dénouement

She is a sick woman, confusion.
Rogozhin informs the Prince that they have found her in Moscow.
But she is already in Petersburg.
And suddenly he receives an invitation from N. F. to a secret interview.
No one in the general's household *intends* her for the Prince.
On the contrary, the count is regarded as her fiancé (secret desire).
[Secret desire for Adelaide.]
It is only Aglaia's mockery that makes her mother suspect.
Secret love for N. F. (not a word about love) (complete solitude) (but a secret).
(A full description, all her grace, her wit.)
Her continual insistence (to him) that he marry Aglaia.
She has already summoned Rogozhin.
Suddenly the insult.
Thereafter,
She is encouraged, frightened.
Rebellion—(because of the Prince).
She is frightened (because of Rogozhin)
and so forth.
N.B. *A new thing.*
The first section.
The new Prince.
Aglaia—.
The story, mysteriousness, Lebedev.
The luncheon; the Prince refuses.
2nd Section.
Secret love.

This manuscript page corresponds to pp. 194–95, beginning with the words "The last idea" and ending with the words "She is a sick woman, confusion." The page is sparsely filled and contains, for the most part, various specimens of Dostoevsky's calligraphic skill.

Dénouement.

She is encouraged. Golden dreams. Suddenly feverish scenes. Interview with Rogozhin.

He refuses Aglaia. Fear. (Scene with Aglaia, and the insult.) [Terrible chastity.]

N.B. Her golden dreams: psychologist. Strangeness; her absolute wish that the Prince marry Aglaia.

Yet at the same time her jealousy.

(N. F.'s extreme anguish.)

And then the insult from Aglaia.

In Moscow—5 days.

The last word.

3rd and 4th Parts.

He arrives from Moscow.

The fact is, the Prince is very perplexed as to how to break off, and he wants a frank talk with N. F.

Catastrophe.

And Gania?

His role?

No catastrophe at all.

3rd and 4th Parts: he simply gives up Aglaia and the whole business.

5th and 6th: Restoration. She dares to dream a golden hope. Rumors about how the Prince is behaving. (Scene with Aglaia?)

The children's club.

She ran away with Rogozhin.

A frank talk with Rogozhin. ("Will you give me peace?")

She married him and became Rogozhin's slave.

He cut her throat because of her jealousy.

About Aglaia's marriage to the Prince.—

N.B. Throughout all the Parts develop the story of N. F.'s *rehabilitation* and of Aglaia's love and *the story*.

N.B. The Prince's feeling for Aglaia.

N.B. "I love you: Idiot!"

N.B. The episode with the imperial guards officer. [The Aide-de-camp.]

Serious conversations about Russia, about life, but never about love.

On her wedding day she runs away from Rogozhin to the Prince.

N. F. finds out that Aglaia is marrying the imperial guards officer and she verifies this.

N.B. N.F. is naïvely and unconsciously happy, she perceives a new world in which she is being remade, as the Prince talks with her in that light.

She is proud—(splendid!)

(*Retours.*)

At the Epanchins they learn finally that he is remaking N. F., resurrecting her soul (Aglaia *understood* this), but suddenly N. F. runs away.

10 April

One scene between Aglaia and N. F. is indispensable, after which comes N. F.'s rebellion. The Prince announces himself as her fiancé; and at that she runs away with Rogozhin.

The chief thing: *stories.*

The factual beginning. The Prince returns, receives the notes, and sets off accordingly.

(Gania's role.) (Incessant vacillating and shilly-shallying.)

At first she lies hidden, then Rogozhin finds out, and everyone finds out.

Rupture with the imperial guards officer, N. F. hesitates, then runs away with Rogozhin.

N.B. Prince Christ.[10]

About Gania: he is extremely irritated; doesn't the Prince suspect him—yet at the same time he is deceiving him. His passion for Aglaia.

Gania's sister urges him on to revenge; he is undecided.—

N.B.? N.B.?—(He regrets the 100,000.) He has stolen money from the Prince and flees abroad. Finale.

Conversation with Ptitsyn about the King of the Jews.

N. F. is immensely encouraged because the Prince does not say a word about marriage. (She ran away on her wedding day to Lebedev, to his sister-in-law's house in Petersburg. Lebedev had introduced her to the Prince [3 weeks earlier].

To be elucidated.

(Gania announces this to Aglaia.)

N. F. insists on the Prince's marrying Aglaia. She questions him as to when. She is feverishly trying to find out things at Lebedev's house. Paroxysms.

---

[10] Prince Christ: the Russian text is printed thus, without any punctuation except the period—thus: "Kniaz Khristos."

10 April

The factual program of the 3rd Part

1) The Prince's return from a 5-day journey to Moscow (too fast in 5 days).

The general says: "How did you manage it?"

N.B.—"But I was handling your affairs."

2) The letters.

3) Lebedev.

4) A frank talk with Gania (touchy and irritable). Gania about Aglaia.

5) Visit at the general's house. Aglaia. The episode with the imperial guards officer. Invitation to the house-warming.

N.B. (The episode with the imperial guards officer continues.)

6) The evening party at N. F.'s house. Lebedev. Timofei Stepanovich discourses on humbleness.

7) Kolia, Petia Lebedev. The story of Pavlishchev. Ipolit. Lebedev's children.

8) The episode with the general and Gania.

9) Gania's spying. *The Prince speaks openly to him?* Gania tells him: "I wanted to deceive you." ("I know.")

N.B. "Aglaia will be at my house." The Prince is heavyhearted.

Gania is furious because the Prince did not confide in him about N. F.

10) *An absolutely outrageous girl.*

11) The children's journal.

12) Ferdyshchenko and the borrowers.

(Correlate.)

13) *Fundamental frank discussion with Rogozhin.* (She ran away on the wedding day.) N.B. In my view, this seems far too much for the third Part.

Baffling mysteries and terrible tangles.

N.B. The problem of how to present N. F.

N.B. The Prince is like a Sphinx.

Like a Sphinx. He reveals himself without any explanations on the author's part, except perhaps in the first chapter.

What if Gania has already recounted at the very beginning what he knows about N. F. (to Aglaia).

(The Roman empress bathing before a slave.)

then Lebedev's report (*earlier in the morning*) to the Prince, then the reader is sufficiently enlightened so that the role of a Sphinx can be maintained.

N.B. N.B. N.B.

(Is Aglaia's visit too precipitate?)

Gania does not tell the Prince everything: he lets it fall that Aglaia *has let it fall* that she wants to see Gania but he doesn't say clearly that this is for the next day.

As to this he hints that Aglaia is going to ask about N. F. and says he is waiting to see whether the Prince will speak? But the Prince does not speak; peevish remarks about the father. Gania leaves, saddened. Wanders about. Wants to see Kolia. He insults Kolia because the latter tells him nothing. Goes to Ipolit's house. His craving to find out about N. F. (Kolia was the first to talk to him about N. F.) Ipolit dispatches him to Lebedev. (But Lebedev laughs at Gania and, this for the first time, takes him to the General's house. Gania thinks of getting Lebedev drunk. Lebedev does get drunk, but reveals nothing.)

Lebedev: out of servility
          the Apocalypse
          Prayers
          and infamous,
          Scene between Lebedev and General Ivolgin.

Lebedev investigates the intimate facts concerning Pavlishchev's son and learns that Aglaia *will be* at Gania's.

He reports this to the Prince. The Prince is astounded (he warns the Prince against Gania).

(Lebedev found this out from Kolia and got in touch with Aglaia herself.)

But he did not tell everything, he was drunk, yet kept things back.

Like this: Gania has often offered to help her, but she, thinking that Gania was on intimate terms with the Prince and that he was still in love with her chose Gania before capriciously rejecting the Prince. (N.B. Gania too is like a Sphinx.)

The Prince asks: why therefore does she go to Gania but not to him, Lebedev. The latter replies: "She believes that she knows more than I do, drunkard as I am."

(Meanwhile Lebedev is deceiving him likewise, for he has direct dealings with Aglaia and has already tipped her off.)

The Prince to Lebedev:

"So you have been deceiving me."

"Yes, I have been deceiving you, for I'm a vile wretch."

(And this several times.)

Prince Christ.[11]

The factual situation

1) After the Prince's initial arrival in the first chapter, before the letters—a certain *tale* about the Prince (his appearance and so forth. The letters from General Ivolgin, Lebedev, *the general's wife, Aglaia,* Pavlishchev's son, Ferdyshchenko—the proposal for a journal. N. F.'s feverish and incomprehensible note, etc.) is brought by Kolia.

(About Pyotr Lebedev, the journal, and so forth, about Ipolit, about Pavlishchev.) About Aglaia and the debtors' prison (Kolia is tactful). About Aglaia. N. F. The journal.

2) The Prince seeks out Lebedev. Next he stops at the Ferdyshchenkos (something to be added).—Lebedev's family. (He had never been at Lebedev's before.)

3) Goes home. Reads Lebedev's journal. (In another package.) Gania. Again about Gania (and even how he behaves at home. About his sister, his mother; he is irritated with the general). N.B. Perhaps about Aglaia.

In the 4th Part of the story (the *Interieur* of the relations between the Prince and the general's household).

5th Part. In the general's household. Aglaia. The scene with the imperial guards officer. N.B.

(Again about the Prince and his relations with the general's household. *His sphinx-like state.* He invites people to his housewarming. Aglaia asks him about the letter. He says, it is like this . . . . that he would like to talk with her. He is embarrassed. (He would like *to refuse Aglaia* and at the same time to tell her about N. F., and this was his intention in asking her for an interview. Aglaia thinks this is the explanation.) [More graciously, more ardor, as with Princess Katia, *work this out!*] Stinging remarks. Adelaide. Pavlishchev's son. An astonishing victory over the Aide-de-camp. (It was Aglaia who set them at each other by her mocking the Prince in a loud and strident

---

11 After the words "Prince Christ," the following calligraphically inscribed names are written large: "The humble Abbot Zosima, Vasili the Great, Gregory the Theologian, John Chrysostom, the Gospel of John the Theologian."

202 Summary of Parts

voice and humiliating him, and she was terribly happy at the Prince's victory. The scene in the *Interieur* of the general's household, after the Prince's departure, between the general's wife and Aglaia, and so forth.

Kolia at the princesses' house, and so forth.

Princess Belokonskaia. An ancient beldam.

6th Part. In the street. Inquiries of the little girl, and so on.

The *rendez-vous* with Lebedev's children. (In the morning there had been a letter from Lebedev's son asking for an interview. He goes over to Ipolit's. Conversations.—Quite like those future talks at the club.) *Aleksei's son.* The Prince expressly charged Kolia and Ipolit with keeping the accounts for the high school.

7th and 8th chapters.

At 8 o'clock. At Nastasia Filipovna's, the evening party.

This is when the Prince talks to the children about Aleksei's son. Lebedev, the Teacher.

> About foreigners, and the Russian people, and so on.
> Prayers, and so on. (Some sort of episode.)
> At Rogozhin's.

It is evident that they already have an agreement.

Rogozhin is not well. (Very little about N. F.) (At the moment of the wedding.) The Prince corroborates and swears to him that he will not marry without his knowledge, and will not say a word about this.

N.B. At Rogozhin's—everything is changed. He is even taking lessons. He warns the Prince about Lebedev, who is betraying him, and so forth. Opportunely, he asks about an explanation in the textbook. The Prince sits down and explains it to him.

4th Part.

9th chapter. At Ganechka's. Aglaia's anticipation. Varia talks with Ptitsyn about the 100,000.

10) Aglaia. Though Ganechka *has deceived Aglaia,* she has likewise deceived him, but after Aglaia's departure Ganechka flares up.

11) Aglaia returns upset because of gossip about N. F. Scene with her sisters and with the general's wife.

12. The luncheon at the Prince's. Episodes. (Pavlishchev, etc.)

13. And the plain talk with Aglaia. ("Don't you dare ask me.") Lebedev, the anonymous letter to Aglaia. "Make a sign." She shows the letter to the Prince, and complains, and demands explanations.

14. Her refusal of the Aide-de-camp and his near disgrace before the conversation with the Prince. The Prince agrees, tremendous joy.

(About N. F. Aglaia begins about N. F. The Prince is taken aback and confesses.)

Scandal at the Epanchins because of the refusal.

15. In the evening N. F.'s interview with Rogozhin. Horror. Paroxysm. All of a sudden Aglaia appears. The Prince is present. Scene (Lebedev helps). N. F. declares that she is going to marry the Prince, "but not you." Spits on Gania.

Fundamental point. N.B. Adelaide is secretly helping the Prince. She informs him about Aglaia (she wants them to marry). She argues with the Prince when he declares he does not love Aglaia.

General conversation.

"Well, the Prince is marrying a whore."[12]

"The clown."

N.B. In the 5th Part Gania succeeds in winning Aglaia's confidence.

6th Part. N. F. is engaged. (Scenes with the Prince, her total rehabilitation, and her total downfall. Aglaia's machinations. A concocted story in order to vilify N. F. Collapses. Gania falls madly in love. N. F. runs away with Rogozhin on her wedding day. [Insert various episodes and the dénouements—the general's theft—of the story for the sake of more interest.]

7th and 8th Parts.

6 months later.

The Prince is downright ill, a *yurodivyi.* Women and children surround him. (N. F. is with Rogozhin.) ~~They had squandered everything in Moscow.~~ Both are now in Petersburg. Rogozhin is enslaved, jealous, a skinflint, and casts everything out the window.

(All the 7th Part is taken up by him and N. F.) Rumors of Aglaia's wedding to the Prince. (Rogozhin is jealous. Cut her throat.)

N.B. (The Prince loves Adelaide.)

10 April

N.B. Write more charmingly and all will go well.

The main problem: the Idiot's character. Develop it. Here lies the idea of the novel. How Russia is reflected. Everything that would have come to maturity in the Prince is extinguished in the tomb. And

---

12 Whore: the Russian text here merely indicates the word by "b . . ." (*bliad*). It does occur spelled out on p. 41. In general, Dostoevsky's language is notably chaste.

therefore little by little showing *the Prince in a field of action* will be
sufficient.

But!

For that *the plot of the novel* is an essential.

So as to make the Idiot's character more fascinating (more charming), he has to be imagined in a field of action.

He rehabilitates N. F. and exerts an ascendancy over Rogozhin. He
induces humanity in Aglaia, he drives the general's wife to distraction with her attachment to the Prince, her adoration of him.

A stronger influence on Rogozhin and on his reforming (Gania
tries to ally himself with Rogozhin).

Adelaide—mute love.

Influence on the children.

On Gania, to desperation ("I've taken *what belongs to me.*")

N.B. (Varia and Ptitsyn *have withdrawn.*)

[16 April. Varia has a marked influence on Aglaia.]

Even Lebedev and the general.

The general in Ferdyshchenko's company.

His theft with Ferdyshchenko.

And this is why:

1) In general, the stories and plots (that is, the stories running
throughout the whole novel) must be rigorously conceived and
executed, parallel to the whole novel, and therefore:

2) Think this through, also the *essential* story about the Aide-de-
camp, and particularly the possibility of parallel stories.

The parallelism of the subsequent stories.

1) Lebedev, after his having deceived the Prince, and with the
general.

2) Ferdyshchenko and Ivolgin.

3) The children, Ipolit's death, and so forth.

4) Gania, Varia, and Ptitsyn—and so forth.

Lebedev.

Lebedev regarding the Prince:

"What he has hidden from wise men and sages, he has revealed to
the young."

Lebedev—a highly talented person.

He is pious, he weeps, and prays, and deceives the Prince and ridicules him.

Having deceived the Prince, he is naïvely and sincerely ashamed of
this.

He makes friends with Ivolgin. They drink together.

The general talks like a freethinker. Lebedev about faith and about the Apocalypse. Lebedev's profound remarks. (A half-baked philosopher. Drunkenness.) Tears. Reciprocal confession of the two drunkards. The general's lies. "But look here, you're lying." They lie to each other. The general does not believe. About tobacco, prayers, DuBarry,[13] the end of the world, he eggs the general into stealing, Ferdyshchenko. Informs on the general to the Prince. The general's death [from grief]. Kolia. The general's wife Nina. Kolia's sorrow.

The general lies on his death bed in deep despair, agony, and anguish. Lebedev follows the coffin and weeps.—

The vital point.

The episode with the imperial guards officer. Problem.

~~One of the Prince's chief worries on his return from Moscow: how to break off with Aglaia.~~

~~However, he does not say a word about proposing, neither in this or that sense, but it was evident.~~

Prince Christ.

The plot.

1) The general dies without having been exposed and without having had the strength to confess, he merely smiles bitterly. Nina knows.

2) Lebedev in the 3rd Section.[14] Suspicion.

3) Gania does not steal but behaves as if he were taking his own 100,000 from the Prince, and he intimates this to him. ("I behaved stupidly.")

4) The Prince and Ptitsyn—a chance conversation.

5) Lebedev makes certain observations to the Prince about N. F.: "No one has ever spoken to her as you have; they all have talked about their petty loves, whereas you (about confusion) [he was mocking] this elevates her in her own eyes; she likes having a learned conversation."

(And here he relates a similar story about a certain woman.)

The Prince says to him: "I like you, Lebedev, you're a greathearted man."

---

[13] DuBarry: the mistress of Louis XV, Madame DuBarry was arrested by the Revolutionary Tribunal and guillotined in 1793. In 1873 Dostoevsky wrote of the sensations of one about to be executed: "DuBarry cried to the executioner: '*Encore un moment, monsieur le bourreau, encore un moment!*'" See *The Diary of a Writer* (New York: George Braziller, 1954), p. 41.

[14] The Third Section: the department of the Tsar's Chancellery which controlled the political police.

Lebedev, pathetically:—"A man who has lived and suffered through a very great deal . . . . . . here, it's all here" (indicating his heart), "but . . . . . . a vile, vile man, who has brought about his own ruin precisely because he is a vile man."

The vital point.

Lebedev to the Prince: "Yes, but weak, weak, too weak . . . . it all comes from weakness, from being a remarkable rogue."

The Prince.—"You seem to be boasting of it, as if that were something gratifying."

Lebedev: "But you know, that's just it" (psychologically).

Lebedev in mourning the general: "He was a great man. . . . . . . Nevertheless, he was lying, even on his death bed."

(A very warped character, Lebedev's.)

Lebedev does love his little boy.

?—Petia Lebedev? Give him more of a lightsome role (Petia's character).

There are so many books in Lebedev's house that the Prince is astonished. (He owns his own cottage though his means are limited.)

Throughout the entire novel the development of the Prince's feelings for Aglaia.

During his conversation with Rogozhin, the latter questions the Prince about his inheritance; the Prince declares that he has not as yet received the money.

Rogozhin talks of *"Nastasia"* and of several episodes in his love affair. Rogozhin's frenzy. His full confidence in the Prince.

Gania makes a complete confession.

"I shall not marry, Gania, I told you so."

"Aglaia is coming."

(He is in a fever.)

Gania is in a fever.

"Don't speak if you don't want to."

"I am insulting you, but you!"

"Gania, Gania, that's enough!"

"I've been deceiving you."

"I know that, Gania."—"You know that?"

(And then when Aglaia came, he made up his mind again to deceive him.)

"If I could find out where N. F. is. But I haven't."

"I lied again: I know where N. F. is."

N.B. In general, he is in a highly feverish state: to Aglaia he reveals everything, everything, and burns his finger—(that he was with N. F. and didn't take her).

Bear principally in mind—

That in the Prince's absence from Moscow it was said everywhere that N. F. was with him.

The general talks about her. Gania talks about her. The general's wife and the whole household. The general's wife receives the Prince with a certain suspicion, but she then changes her mind, takes courage, and says that from the first she has always considered him an honorable man, and so on. Kolia talks about her. (Aglaia had already received Lebedev's letter, Aglaia alone is fully informed, and she chooses Gania.)—and so on.

(Gania is insulted in the highest degree because the Prince has not told him anything) (but the Prince does tell).

N.B. With Gania. (During their morning interview show absolutely clearly their relations in depth so as to make Gania's love for the Prince psychologically comprehensible.)

The Sudokhodov incident has been arranged by Aglaia, Ferdyshchenko is there too. Sudokhodov lives with Ferdyshchenko, Smirovsky is with them too.

Later the Prince stops by his house, having got rid of Smirovsky.

At first he receives him *defiantly*. Then things calm down. Ferdyshchenko says they have founded a society for raising money. They laugh. The Prince sits down and tells an anecdote. Sudokhodov shows him out.

("You consider me a crook?"—"What's that to you.")

. . . . "Yes, I don't consider that honorable." Smirovsky laughs, but goes away pensively.

The main thing is that Sudokhodov was *honestly* demanding money.

14 April

The Prince was in Moscow exactly a month and a half. Never a word or a hint.

The scene at the Epanchins. The Aide-de-camp. Aglaia is beside herself and drives him to distraction as well.

The Prince appears, saddened. His reception. *His description of Moscow.* The General. *Things.* He makes a profound impression on them all.

Within a week N. F. was sent away. Kolia, Lebedev, and the sisters.

A letter to Kolia from Moscow.

The Prince's interview with Lebedev.

With Rogozhin, who returned from Moscow 5 days earlier.

N.B. Then N. F. ran away to Moscow the next day. Rogozhin found her there. Again orgies. The wedding. She ran away on her wedding day. Probably to Petersburg (they had no time to turn round—)— Doesn't know what's at Lebedev's.

Episodes. Gania. The general, and so on.

N.B. To be arranged.

An idea.

1) The Prince is engaged to Aglaia—(3 months later) and the marriage is broken off.

1½ months later. 2) Neither sight nor sound of N. F.

She was hiding from Rogozhin.

The Prince seeks her.

The general's wife, "A good report of you."

15 April

My stock of ideas[15]

For 6 months neither sight nor sound of the Prince.

A letter to Aglaia via Kolia, which she has shown to no one. In the Prince's presence at the villa (and in her fiancé's presence) Aglaia suddenly says *in a loud voice* ("That letter you sent me") (stern face; "Your image came to me").

The general's wife lost her temper.

The Prince's account of Russia ("You remind me greatly of your first visit.")

(Gania)?

The general's wife visits the Prince.

The main idea of the first section of the second Part.

The Prince returns bewildered by the immensity of his new impressions of Russia, his anxieties, ideas, his state of mind, and *what there is to do.*

He sets all this forth at the Epanchins' villa, *in an account of the past 6 months.* (He is questioned by Aglaia's fiancé, a very serious man, *Prince Shcherb.*)

But after arriving in Petersburg—

---

[15] My stock of ideas: the Russian syntax is puzzling. Literally, the words say "Ideas and fund" (*Mysli i fond*).

They need him at the Epanchins (Aglaia) [Adelaide] (the general's wife). Gania needs him.

Kolia—

Rogozhin needs him. (He has already allied himself with the Prince and is presented as his pupil.)

And especially N. F.

Even Lebedev after leaving N. F. needs him, and the Prince's heart *is radiant*. (There you have a field of action [tableaux]).

Having comprehended, the Prince is very touched and, in his humility, frightened.

1st half of the 2nd Part in 1 day.

2nd half—in several days.

(Scene between Lebedev and General Ivolgin while they are drinking, in the 4th Part.)

The plan of the novel. See the reverse of this page.

The Prince's discourse to Aglaia at the villa; comparison between East and West.

He goes first to Gania's, Gania is cold and rude, then at night Gania comes to him saying: "I was waiting for you."

15 April

My stock of ideas

Wouldn't it be possible?

Kolia goes to the Epanchins, doesn't find Lebedev, goes to the Epanchins' villa—Lebedev is not there either—to Rogozhin's—to Lebedev's house (the next day?). Gania—waits for him at his house all evening. Gania's confession.

In the morning the general's wife, Kolia; the general is bought off —in the evening at N. F.'s. (There was an appointment.)

N.B. *The chief thing is that they all need him.*—

Gania is waiting (description of the scene with Gania) (Gania's circumstances).

N.B.—At Rogozhin's (description of the scene at the station) Ekaterinov.

(15 April: problem: *what is the sequence?*)

The Prince arrives full of *something new* and somewhat troubled. (More simply, for instance, with Rogozhin. The Prince is obliged to explain at length.)—But joy <illegible> is flooding him. It is this joy that he expresses to Aglaia, suggesting that she help N. F., and even before that to Kolia (briefly).

This manuscript page corresponds to pp. 208–9, beginning with the date "15 April" and ending with the words "The plan of the novel. See the reverse of this page." The page is an example of Dostoevsky's habit of underscoring, by various devices, important ideas and intentions. About one-third of the way down the page he notes in large writing, by a break in the page and by various underlinings, "The main idea of the first section of the second Part."

The general's wife (at the villa). "I've been hearing good things about you."

"Aren't you getting married?" "This happens."

Aglaia's fiancé has already had time to bluster to the Prince and let fly his jibes at him, when suddenly Prince Shcherb., Adelaide's fiancé, appears, and treats the Prince as an acquaintance. Tells of his meeting with the Prince and of the latter's heroism.

15 April

The plan of the novel

?(Everyone is a traitor. Rogozhin out of passion. Gania out of <word omitted>. (Lebedev—).

Love is just beginning to form in Aglaia.

(Rogozhin schemes and wins over Lebedev and Aglaia.)

The Prince calls on Aglaia to help ameliorate the general misery.

The scene with the two rivals, in which Aglaia behaves unexpectedly *and uncontrollably.*

N. F., beside herself after the insult, says to the Prince: "If you were making me all over anew, you said I was without sin," etc., etc. (N.B. In such a way that all the rehabilitating can be left out, since it is apparent.)

"Then marry me!"

The Prince: "Yes."

(5th and 6th Parts), 3rd. ~~2nd~~

1st half. The fiancé and the fiancée. (The Prince is insane—according to general rumor, that is), and except for a few people they all desert him.

N. F. says to Rogozhin: "Will you give me peace?"

She runs away. The Prince's disgrace.

2nd half, that is, the 6th Part.

Or else:

the 6th, 7th, and 8th Parts—the dénouement.

16 April

The arrangement of the materials.

How to make it seem more natural? The more natural thing is that:

1) Lebedev—

Catches up with Lebedev and Kolia (N. F. behaves in a more characteristic but a more equivocal manner) ("Tomorrow, tomorrow, no, today!") or something of the kind (Kolia: "I'll be there.")

"To the general's—at 11" ("Come at one ~~two~~ o'clock). [He understood perfectly.]

(In the meantime he goes to Gania's and Rogozhin's.) Gania is in a feverish state.

Again to the general's. (At the villa.)

At 6 o'clock he returns to Petersburg. By chance he meets Rogozhin at the Pavlovsk railroad station. Goes to Rogozhin's.

At 7 o'clock *goes to Lebedev's*, at 7 thirty to N. F.'s. At Lebedev's, the general, released from prison, makes Lebedev's acquaintance. ("But why are you lying, General?")

At N. F.'s house at eleven o'clock in the evening, at N. F.'s at the villa. Rogozhin is hunting for him.

At 11 Gania was there, and so was Kolia (the crazy Prince).

In the morning in Petersburg—the encounter with everyone, with Aglaia, the general's wife, and so forth.

In the morning the general's wife—.

Aglaia simply asks the Prince—the Prince reveals everything to her. "She thinks you are going to marry me." (The scene between Aglaia and Gania.)

Was the interview with N. F. arranged?

Either the interview with N. F. was an accidental one, or else N. F. (in her frenzy) wrote Aglaia a note, out of jealousy, having seen her with the Prince.

All at once she came to her house and brought the note.

N.B. After the general's wife arrives, the narrative can then be unfolded more quickly, inserting only some scenes here and there. Lebedev. The general, and so forth. Finally—one scene between the Prince and Aglaia, and the scene of the interview.

The main problem now—Gania?

The layout. At Lebedev's house, a certain curiosity.

The scene at the villa, and so forth.

16 April

Particular notations.

My stock of ideas.

N. F. at the villa, also at Pavlovsk; the Prince frowns darkly on learning that she is likewise at Pavlovsk; but N. F. intended this, and Aglaia is aware of this.

(And the general's wife is aware of it.)

N.B. *The visit of the general's wife!*

Lebedev says in the morning that he lives in the Petersburg district and there is a little garden. In reply to the Prince's observation that for the sake of air and solitude a villa in the country would be better, Lebedev says that the fiancée owns a villa at Pavlovsk, but that it is impossible to come to Pavlovsk with . . . . [in the Sailors' Quarter].

"Is she very anxious to come to Pavlovsk?" asks the Prince.

"Yes, very" (. . . . . . . that is, for Aglaia Epanchin).

The Prince says there is no need (there was no tenant at the villa).

After he was at Pavlovsk, the Prince returns home with the Aide-de-camp.

Then he goes to Rogozhin's.

At Lebedev's he learns that he has already been at the villa since yesterday. This shocks the Prince. He is embarrassed. At the villa. Again at Pavlovsk. The Prince wants not to be noticed, but the Aide-de-camp with Lebedev, Lebedev speaks of various matters on the way.

Gania waits from eleven o'clock until 12—

(the Prince's gentle joy at being useful)

In the morning the general's wife:

"You made no mistake yesterday in saying that you were going to Petersburg and not to her." (The daughters do not know.)

With Aglaia (three days later)—Gania asks for financial aid.

The interview and the scene of the two rivals.

Aglaia's love is revealed.

In the 5th Part the scandal about the Prince must be on a tremendous scale.

The public insult (Ch—'s wife.) The Prince's explanation.

The Aide-de-camp, almost a duel. *The scene at the church.* She says in her interview with Rogozhin: "Will you give me peace?" (Lebedev's betrayal.)

Gania's passion. The Prince's wedding, a crowd gather to watch. The bride does not arrive.

The disgrace.

The scene with Gania. Gania says: "Do you know, I had given everything up until you came."

At Rogozhin's the Prince incessantly looks at his watch, and Rogozhin notices this.

In the 3rd and 4th, merely sketch Gania's part.

In the 5th and 6th (Gania plots with Aglaia and the latter finally pulls a long nose at him and drives her fiancé away)—

In both the 5th and 6th—the Prince's wedding.

N.B. Here among others the roles of Lebedev, the general ~~and Gania~~ (my friend's son), the general's wife, Rogozhin (all the plots). Lebedev and Gania are traitors. [They signal each other and make ready.]

In the 7th and 8th: Depiction of the ill and wandering Prince.

N. F. has fled from Rogozhin. The latter is seeking to kill her. (N.B. Immediately after the wedding he carried her off to Moscow.) The Prince reconciles them. The Prince's role. Aglaia's role. Aglaia breaks off with her fiancé. "I love you." (To the Prince.) The general's death (in the epilogue). (The Prince is present at his death.) N. F.'s throat is cut.

Gania's flight. Lebedev has discovered Rogozhin and the murder. (Aglaia has also been watching.)

They take the Idiot abroad.

Aglaia is with them, all—"At last we are going ~~to Switzerland~~ abroad!"

Gania.

He is in a feverish state all this time.

Ptitsyn marries Varia. Gania lives alone perhaps, or else with them.

On Gania's first appearance, indicate clearly that, while he loves Varia with a strong brotherly affection, still he differs from her in all his convictions. (In her, vindictiveness derives from pride.) (Varia has a strong influence on Aglaia.) Ptitsyn says but little; he expresses himself later.

This is one of Gania's tableaux (in the 1st or 2nd).

2) *Tableau.* Feverish confession to the Prince. (On the first occasion he receives the Prince sourly, on the 2nd, he comes round.)

3rd *Tableau.* After the confession: his envy of the Prince and his craving for revenge. (N.B. No occupation. Quarrels, and plunges into society. *Through Varia*—he dedicates himself to Aglaia. He betrays the Prince, but flirts with Aglaia to such a degree that just when he has decided to act (to avenge himself) in Varia's way—he discloses to Aglaia all Varia's snares and how she was deceiving her. He says: "There's the reward for my sincerity!" and plunges into vice.

Because of all this, Aglaia finally spits on him. ~~They have a villa in Pavlovsk.~~

The 4th scene with Gania; he goes to the Prince's house and there he talks to Ptitsyn about the King of the Jews.

The father's death—

Gania takes the 100,000 and escapes abroad.

Daria Alekseevna. N. F. runs to Daria Alekseevna's villa in the Sailors' Quarter. Immediately after Kolia brings a letter from the general's wife.

(Rogozhin tells the Prince: "I know how you have lifted me and my spirit—up to yourself.")

Gania at Pavlovsk.

Gania is ill. "I love Aglaia."—He meets the Prince, he knows the truth about N. F., but maintains silence. The Prince's arrival interests Gania in the light of its effect on Aglaia (at first it was the fiancé who interested him).—He unbosoms himself to the Prince at Pavlovsk.—

(The Prince at Gania's, Ptitsyn, and the King of the Jews.)

Gania. Ill, almost an idiot. A Herostratus,[16] ashamed of everything. His dreams.—He is watching over Aglaia. At the villa. The Prince gives forth in a tirade about the King of the Jews. Gania does not give way, does not betray himself. The Prince's arrival upsets him and makes him anxious about Aglaia. He is watching. Varia's morning encounter with Aglaia in the park and Gania; Aglaia tells him: "I can appreciate how it was you refused. Perhaps I am quite wrong." (Gania is ill. Varia has contracted a marriage [only] because of her devotion to him, because he is ill.)

And so Gania *is ill.* His role = a slave's role.

(N.B. This is a role that can be made very genuine, beautiful, and gentle.)

17 April

Eureka[17] with Gania

The interview, silence.

Dreams. The Prince of the Jews. The Prince has called. (*Note:* after the general's wife, three days later. The Prince has been at Pavlovsk. He visited Gania. King of the Jews.)

---

16 A Herostratus: in B.C. 356 an Ephesian named Herostratus set fire to the temple of Artemis at Ephesus so as to immortalize himself, as he confessed. On the night he did this, Alexander the Great is said to have been born. Dostoevsky refers to "a wild Herostratus" in an article he published in *Vremia* in August 1861 (Vol. 4, p. 93), in a context suggesting a crazed and destructive kind of self-assertion. This article is reprinted in F. M. Dostoevsky, "Knizhnost i gramatnost: statia pervaia," *Polnoe sobranie khudozhestvennykh proizvedenii* (Moscow-Leningrad, 1926–30), Vol. 13, pp. 96–111.

17 *Eureka:* the word is written in Greek characters and means "found" or "discovered."

Then the silent encounter of Gania and Aglaia. Flame <illegible>.

Then, before the encounter, when the Prince is anxious, Gania comes, embraces him, and tells him that Varia and Aglaia and all of them are deceiving him.

Aglaia receives a note from N. F.

Here will be the scene at N. F.'s and the meeting with Gania.

17 16 17
April

News of the Prince—the visit.

[At 5 o'clock, he is in the city, at Rogozhin's.]

Kolia (in the little garden), Lebedev (he has come back, has come in).

To the general's, directly to the villa. Finally he confesses that he is uneasy and wants to return to Pavlovsk.

[To Lebedev's, at the villa.]

At 5 o'clock in Petersburg. Goes to Rogozhin's.

At 7 o'clock goes to Lebedev's.—(in the city) [at the villa], at N. F.'s house. N. F.'s intelligence. The Apocalypse—enthusiasm. They analyze Lebedev. He conceals—[the news of N. F., that she is nervous and irritable, she weeps, screams, and sobs.]

Rogozhin: "But here is Lebedev."

["I have the right."]

On leaving N. F.'s house, Rogozhin—yes, yes—I believe so. Perhaps about Rogozhin—Here he is, here—he won't do it.

(Kolia's reflections.) Gania at home.

2nd half.

The general's wife.

Gania's *interieur*. Scenes, Gania's coolness. Ptitsyn—

N. F. Pavlovsk—at Pavlovsk—N. F. rebels.

"I have the right." He calmed her.

Three days—King of the Jews.

Rogozhin, after learning about Lebedev. Orgies with the general—Very brief preface (one page).

The outward appearance

Rogozhin: "Stop by my mother's," *in a feverish manner,* "let her bless you."

The old woman blesses him.

"What's the matter?"

"But what are you to me."

["You are an innocent!"]

"Is it possible I could ever (stop loving) you?"

"I believe! I believe!"

And then: "He is taking me abroad"—"I don't want to"—"Will you give me peace."

Aglaia and N. F. At first Aglaia was all of a tremble, then suddenly she called her "thou."

17 April

She had already gone twice to Pavlovsk.

Varia at Pavlovsk. Varia all too rightly guessed that Aglaia was enthralled with the Prince.

"The Poor Knight," Aglaia talks of him to the Prince. Perhaps some kind of self-sacrificing martyr whom one could love with a pure love, adoration of pure beauty, adoration of the ideal, perhaps even . . . . But they were reading the Bible, who after all can he be:

Lumen Coeli, Sancta Rosa[18]

To whom can those words refer . . . . [he is filled with a pure love].

"Well, you've been talking nonsense."

"I love the poor knight."[19]

N. F. B. with his blood

"That's your poor knight for you. In the first place, he is rich, and in the second. . . . . . ."

Perhaps N. F. loves with an impure love.—

(Some candid talks with the Prince.) [And then: "He is like me" (the poor knight). And she calls the Prince, "Oh, you, my poor knight."]

"Sketch the poor knight for me, Adelaide."

But when he lifted his steel visor from his face. . . . . . .

---

18 *Lumen Coeli, Sancta Rosa:* a line from a medieval Latin hymn.

19 The poor knight: this refers to Pushkin's poem recited (in part) by Aglaia (Part II, chap. 7). Composed in 1829, it was not published during the poet's lifetime but appeared in an abridged and altered version in his "Scenes from the Age of Chivalry." Originally, the poem had no other title than its first line. The Annenkov edition of Pushkin's works referred to in *The Idiot* was issued in 1855–57 in seven volumes.

Adelaide. "How did you happen to come into an inheritance, Prince."

"Read me the poor knight. I don't know it."

"It's a lofty idea, that, the idea of a good and noble man consumed by an ideal."

The general<'s wife>: "Well, he's some kind of a fool. Read it, anyway, read it."

"How delightful it is. Who wrote it?"

"That's Pushkin, aren't you ashamed."

"But I did read Pushkin, lots, a long time ago. But living with you makes one stupid, I don't know how. Have you a copy of Pushkin?"

"There you sit like a regular ass."

"We do have some odd volumes."

"Forevermore those odd volumes! Let them send Fyodor or Mark the coachman out at once to buy a copy."

And then at the end, in tears:

"Yes, he was filled with a pure love."

"He was faithful to his sweet dream."

Reform and resurrect mankind!

N.B. *Varia's machinations. Varia and Gania.*

She backs her brother up; she means him to have Aglaia and reckons on Aglaia's strange, ardent nature. Ptitsyn shakes his head; she says: "Why are you shaking your head? You know whom she would like to marry, a beggar, NN, because he is being persecuted. She is dreaming of the poor knight."

She tells Aglaia a story about a hussar, to stir up a quarrel.

She talks to Gania about Aglaia.

She brings Gania and Aglaia together.

"And your poor knight, what a fine regard he has for women; he is keeping N. F."

Aglaia receives N. F. in silence. A bizarre outcome.

N. F. (bitch). "What's the matter with her, is she mad?" thinks Aglaia.

On seeing all this, Varia says: *"We have to pit N. F. against Aglaia —so that N. F. out of spite will make the Prince marry her. Then she'll see what a slave Gania is to her and Aglaia will fall into our hands out of spite."*

In a transport Gania explains all this (emphatically) to Aglaia *at the interview between the two rivals.*

But earlier he bursts out to the Prince in an exasperated effort to make him see what a desperate, rotten world he is living in.

After the conversation about the poor knight, a frank discussion with Aglaia about N. F.

Aglaia's ridicule—in place of A. N. B.,[20] N. F. B. "Mamma calls you the poor knight."

The Prince talks to her about N. F. At first she is touched—but the words, "You will soon marry," and so on—these set her wild.

She remains silent, but shows him N. F.'s letter.

After the letter, N. F. *goes to see her.*

(She herself leads the Prince to the house and says abruptly, "Introduce me, I want to see her.")

The Prince considers this, he is apprehensive, but he introduces her.

Aglaia is trembling, and the other girl is trembling.

At first Aglaia speaks quietly,

then "thou" and contempt. Revenge.

N. F. tells her: "You yourself are in love with the Prince," and having sent Aglaia packing, she laughs for joy—the bride to be.

Aglaia and Tania <Gania?> and the rest.

(N.B. But before all this she had said repeatedly to the Prince that he ought to marry Aglaia.)

The woman in black comes.

A heroine out of a novel by Grech.[21]

22 April

Revision

Throw out all the 5th Part, etc.

Scene. N. F. had really worked herself into a passion, but then she gave in, handed the Prince over to Aglaia, and ran off to Rogozhin.

Just as the Prince appeared in the 3rd Part, she ran to Rogozhin.

---

[20] A. N. B.: the initials given in Pushkin's poem were "A. M. D." standing for *Ave Mater Dei.* Dostoevsky evidently intended to substitute Aglaia's initials (*A*glaia *I*vanovna *E*panchina) and add Nastasia's (*N*astasia *F*ilipovna *B*arashkova), or so one supposes. The obvious disparity of "A. N. B." may be a lapse of memory on his part, or perhaps a calligraphic or typographical error of some sort.

[21] Grech: Nikolai Ivanovich Grech (1787–1867) was an active reactionary, an agent of the Third Section, and publisher of *Syn Otechestva* (*Son of the Fatherland*); with F. V. Bulgarin (1789–1859) he was an editor of the official gazette, *Severnaia chela* (*The Northern Bee*).

But again she abandoned herself to dreams. In the scene with Aglaia, everything collapsed for her: let the Prince be happy.

Aglaia (is compromised). For the Prince, *a new romance, and a romance between Rogozhin and N. F.* Death from jealousy.

The Prince—(before he comes himself) sends a 2nd letter to Aglaia —telling her everything.

The two of them have it out face to face.

N.B.—In this scene Aglaia says: "How can anyone marry that Idiot?"

"Yes, that Idiot, because that Idiot—."

23 April (*Shakespeare*)[22]

N. F. marries Rogozhin.

N. F. meddles so as to bring about Aglaia's marrying the Prince.

Aglaia is offended. She sees that the Prince is trying to calm N. F. Aglaia is jealous, and N. F. is jealous.

[Aglaia is married to the Prince.]

The interview.

Aglaia rouses Rogozhin's jealousy. The Prince's exhortations— Rogozhin slaughters N. F.

Aglaia expires. The Prince is at her side.

N. F. has married <Rogozhin> but has separated from him—so that the Prince should marry <Aglaia>, and then, she says, she will come back to live with <Rogozhin>.

Or else: she promises to marry <Rogozhin> when the Prince marries.

But inasmuch as this is quite difficult—she entices Velmonchek, writes a letter to Aglaia, to the general, to the general's wife—

A spiteful scene between Aglaia and N. F.

"*thou—*"

They separate in spite. [N. F. tells the Prince, "I'll prove to you that she loves you."]

Rogozhin is engaged

in Rogozhin's house.

At the villa with the mother.

Rogozhin says of her: "She is respectful, humble."

"Mamma, she has won, it's nothing to me."

---

[22] 23 April: Shakespeare's death date (1616). The spelling here is "Schakespeare."

"I'll kill her! Mamma, bless me."

("You gave her to me. You united us
but you didn't separate us.") "You watched over her."

N.B. (N.B. And at the same time Rogozhin was afraid of the other's arrival.)

N. F.'s wedding to Rogozhin is being prepared, the vow exchanged, the wedding day fixed.

(N.B. Earlier she had run away immediately after the orgy.) Rogozhin sought her out in Moscow, induced her consent to marry him. At the end of 2 months she ran away on her wedding day; the Prince was in the province; N. F. was terrified of losing her heart to the Prince. Again Rogozhin won her over, in Petersburg, reports of the Prince's imminent arrival alarm Rogozhin, and N. F. halts the preparations for the wedding. N. F. declares that so long as Aglaia is not married to the Prince, she herself will not marry Rogozhin. (She lives irregularly, at times with her mother, at other times in the smart world.) The fact is that, having learned in Petersburg on arriving there that Aglaia is engaged, she suddenly grows very agitated and is obsessed with the idea of *making the Prince happy with Aglaia.*

Lebedev declares to the Prince that he is secretly Rogozhin's enemy. The Prince strongly suspects that Lebedev is in Rogozhin's service and that he is charged with spying on the Prince while pretending to be Rogozhin's enemy and the devoted servant of the Prince.—

In talking to him about N. F., Aglaia tells him of various insults. N. F. talks to him about Aglaia. Signs. "She loves you."

The scandalous scene at the concert. N. F. has seduced Velmonchek. The Prince goes to visit Aglaia. Rogozhin loses his temper and creates a scene when Velmonchek dares to joke at his expense. N. F. drives Rogozhin away (then after the scene between the two she calls him back). Aglaia is furious with Velmonchek.

Velmonchek exerts an influence on the Prince. The latter listens to him.

At first Aglaia shows the Prince that she loves Velmonchek, but then she becomes disgusted with him.

Aglaia behaves to the Prince as if she loved Velmonchek. She is furious because the Prince is glad of this and congratulates her.—
In the scene it is revealed that Aglaia loves the Prince.—

24 April

After *the knife.* Rogozhin says to the Prince: "You know that my life is yours now; take it."

But the Prince says: "You are giving her your life for this reason? Come to your senses. . . . . . ."

Rogozhin—"my grim punishment."

Then in the 4th Part, in the scene between the two rivals: "Why, why, is he going to punish me?"

Or else she says to Rogozhin: "Why are you going to punish me, tell me, please."

28 <April?>

After Rogozhin's attempt at murder, the Prince is worried that Rogozhin will marry.

He takes counsel with Aglaia.

"I am going to marry her."

"He will kill you."

"No, he came to tell me: take her!"

"She's not in her right mind. Say a word to her."

"Yes, she is bold enough without that."

"That's because she considers herself lower than a slave before you."

"Raise her up to yourself."

The theory of practical Christianity.

In the 2nd Part N. F. receives the Prince by proving to him that Aglaia is in love with him.

For the 1st time Rogozhin takes the Prince to N. F.'s house in Pavlovsk.

(N.B. She is staying here *with Daria Alekseevna.*)

The scene suddenly takes place unexpectedly.

But before this scene N. F. had been at Rogozhin's: "You will bring me peace"—and then she fled from the Prince on her wedding day.

21 May

N.B. Having learned that the Prince is at Lebedev's and is ill, N. F. acts with extraordinary mysteriousness, does not come herself, but contrives an interview with the Prince (through Gania). The Prince comes openly on purpose to visit her (speaks of Rogozhin) (of everyone) (charmingly and graciously) (says that Aglaia is in love) and makes the arrangements for the wedding (give the scene more originality).

24 May

N.B. The complete account of the rehabilitation of N. F., who is engaged to the Prince.

(The Prince declares when he marries N. F. that it is far better to resurrect one woman than to perform the deeds of Alexander of Macedon.)

N.B. The school at the Prince's house takes form spontaneously from among the visitors. Begin it in Pavlovsk.

N.B. Kolia conveys a number of things to the Prince about Aglaia's feelings, and so forth.

The evening party at the Prince's house. Lebedev. The general. N. F. Gania, Kolia, Ipolit, and so forth.

24 May

After N. F.'s flight various complications ensue (*some incited by Aglaia*. The judgment of Solomon, and so forth.)

The death of N. F.—

6th chapter. The general talks of long-ago encounters with the Prince. The general's wife has taken sides with him and with Lebedev.

10 June

Velmonchek: eternal and continual mockery of an artful and supercilious sort; he is a fascinating character.

The relations between Aglaia and Velmonchek. She does not reject him point blank, so that he goes on hoping.

—She is even a little in love with him—

—Her ridicule of the Prince

—Refuses him but allows him to come

Velmonchek sees that the Prince does not understand that Aglaia loves him (but the Prince does understand this). Velmonchek explains this to the Prince.—He develops relations with Gania (contempt for him). Sees that Gania is a tragic character. Declares further their mutual indifference to him, which makes Gania wild. Advises him to ask for 100,000—Gania bristles but finally does so.

Don Juan. (Marries Lebedev's daughter out of perversity, after Aglaia refused him, out of braggadocio.)

? N.B. To marry N. F.

Rogozhin comes to buy him off. He turns him down and talks Rogozhin out of the idea.

(Sequel.)

Velmonchek wanted to pretend to Aglaia but got enraged at the Jews and blurts it all out to Aglaia.

(The uncle's death, *the Jews were hounding him*. Agreement with the uncle that he would not poison himself before the wedding.)

Secret calculation, he knows that she loves the Prince.

He proposes to Aglaia, Aglaia's coldness (he did not understand; love).

Explains himself to the Prince with cynical frankness.

—(Lebedev's daughter).

Scandalous scenes with Nastasia Filipovna, Rogozhin comes to buy —"You've given me an idea."

Wants to marry N. F. Simpleton—

Lebedev's daughter. The whole story. The wedding—

"I, I marry Lebedev's daughter,"

"He is offering 400,000—don't shoot yourself—"

"My uselessness,

$\left.\begin{array}{l} \\ \\ \\ \end{array}\right\}$ —he shoots himself—

but Lebedev's daughter?"

His uselessness, his aristocratic connections all go up in smoke—

Sinks lower and lower, vanity.

The bule <bulle> de savon has burst.

But—sincerity or ambition.

They—it's not so much that they are vapid but rather that they have no sense of nationality, they have only a feeble attachment to the soil, that's why they are so flighty.

Nevertheless this man is one of *the better sort*.

"But you yourself are Russian?"

"Yes, but there's little I like in Russia."

In particular

[X] N. F. writes to Aglaia that Velmonchek possesses nothing. Aglaia is angry with N. F. and lets the Prince see this. A strange love! Aglaia is angry with the Prince. The interview with N. F.

And Velmonchek is with Rogozhin.

Two problems:

? What to do with Gania.

? Aglaia ridicules the Prince incessantly.

Respects and *attracts* Evgeni Pavlovich.

After the uncle's poisoning: gossip in the household as to Evgeni Pavlovich's resources. Aglaia abruptly announces that Evgeni Pavlovich long since enumerated his resources to her and that he loves her.

N.B. They catch Velmonchek at night at Lebedev's. That very night *another* rumor: 1,700 rubles have disappeared.

They suspect Velmonchek, but it was the general who had stolen. (Sequel 2nd.)

Velmonchek cannot shoot himself before the thief is found. N.B. The general's conversation with *Lebedev,* after which the idea of stealing comes into the general's mind.

Velmonchek takes the theft upon himself, so as not to disgrace Lebedev's daughter—At this point he kills himself.

Scenes. Everyone at the Prince's house.

Velmonchek and the Prince.

Velmonchek, the Prince, Gania, Ptitsyn—

The general and Lebedev—

The Prince and N. F. (The Prince goes to explain the reason for Aglaia's insistence and about Velmonchek.)

Sum total:

Velmonchek—a brilliant character, flippant, skeptical, *a genuine aristocrat,* devoid of any *ideal* (not the kind of man we like, and this is what distinguishes him from the Prince). An odd mixture of cunning, subtlety, calculation, mockery, vanity) he kills himself out of vanity—He confesses to the Prince that at first he made fun of *him* and exaggerated his own good qualities so as to damage him in Aglaia's mind, that he loved, not Aglaia, but Aglaia's good opinion of him, but that he did not want her money.—He was sorry for Lebedev's daughter.—Aglaia took pity on him.—He declared that he had been terribly angry with the Prince because the latter stood first in Aglaia's opinion. *He tried to ally himself with Gania.*

(In part, the vanity of a *Lacenaire.*)[23] "The only thing left me is the life of a profligate, but I am too cultivated for that, and I cannot make myself over into a Gogolian landowner."

The fantasy of marrying Lebedev's daughter.

He marries her, the evening after the wedding—he shoots himself.

---

23 Lacenaire, Pierre-François (1800?–1836): poet-assassin who was guillotined for one of a long series of murders and was a notorious figure in France throughout the nineteenth century. As editor of *Vremia,* Dostoevsky published a translation of a long article about him (February 1861, pp. 1–50).

He shot himself after the wedding, he married so as to console Lebedev's daughter, at the Prince's urging,
(out of a special kind of swagger),
so as not to go to prison for debt.
The Prince gives 400,000 rubles, just out of pride.
The general brings 1,200 rubles to the captain's wife. Ipolit divulges this—they *all* know. But it is decided not to say anything to the general.
Velmonchek laughs incessantly at the Prince and makes fun of him. A skeptic and an unbeliever.
To him everything in the Prince is *truly* absurd, up to the last moment.
"If they put me in prison, they can buy me out again for 200,000."
N. F. herself does not want to see the Prince, she is afraid of Rogozhin, which Lebedev explains to the Prince, declaring that he himself is Rogozhin's secret enemy.
Pavlishchev's son.
Varia denounces Velmonchek and settles with Gania.
Aglaia drives Velmonchek (1st Part) into an intolerable position. He does not know: Is she his or not? And he decides to confess to her. "A mountain off my shoulders!"
But before his confession: he tests the Prince: he laughs at the Prince, exaggerating his virtue, tries to create a scandal in connection with N. F.
After the confession he says to the Prince: "I don't know whether or not I am capable of sinking to the lowest vileness."
N.B.—(He challenges the Prince to a duel.)
He accepts the 400,000 and this is what maddens Aglaia all the more, this is why he kills himself.
He incites Rogozhin against the Prince.
He muddles Gania's head.

11 June

The Prince genuinely marvels at Velmonchek and praises his qualities to Aglaia. Until the very end the Prince does not want to understand that Aglaia loves him (the Prince), he grasps this only in the scene with N. F.
Aglaia ~~N. F.~~ *marries Gania out of spite*—and drives him away. Gania is madly *in love with Aglaia,* to the last straw, ready to kill anyone at all—that's his role.

? N.B. (Perhaps:) When he confessed his situation to Aglaia, Vel-monchek declared out of braggadocio that he had never loved her. However, having confessed, he falls in love out of chagrin. He confesses to the Prince. Aglaia senses [understands] this.

The burning of the finger. "Well, go on, burn it." He detests Aglaia after this.

Aglaia wants to marry the Prince off to N. F. (from a perverse contrariness).

N. F.'s madness.

Don't forget that from the first day the Prince has been anxious about N. F.

The whole crowd encounter N. F. just when the Prince is being conducted (accidentally? Gania? Kolia?).

The Prince's humility. The Prince positively considers himself worse than anyone else therefore.—What amazes Aglaia, who former-ly never stopped accusing the Prince (and this exasperated her) of being haughty and of imagining God knows what about himself.

The death of Ipolit.

Ipolit to the Prince: "I wanted to destroy you all, but I was not even capable of doing that. The impotence! The impotence of the whole tribe!"

"One more moment like that and I shall rise from the dead."

N.B. Aglaia rushed to Gania, stirred up a scandal, declared that they were tormenting her, forcing her to marry the Prince.—They engaged her to Gania. Evgeni Pavlovich stood her in good stead (not Prince Shcherb.) and saved her. That's his role. He explains Aglaia to the Prince—by her shyness. "You are the guilty one in all this." "Yes, I'm guilty of the whole business."

N.B. N.B. Evgeni Pavlovich asks the Prince: "But what happened to you in the very beginning?" That is, in the 1st Part.

"I was completely bowled over. I had never seen any women . . . . I, I was quite bowled over. I didn't understand her, I remem-ber how sorry I was for her—"

N.B. He said to her at the church: "I was bowled over—I didn't know what had hit me. I was saying at that point, I remember I was saying—"

N.B. *The chief point.*

After the scene of the two rivals:

We admit that we are about to describe strange happenings—— Since it is difficult to explain them, let us confine ourselves to facts.

We recognize that nothing different could have happened to the Idiot.

Let us bring to an end the story of a person who has perhaps not been worthy of so much of the reader's attention—we agree as to that.

Reality above everything. It is true perhaps that we have a different conception of reality, a thousand thoughts, prophecy—a fantastic reality. It may be that in the Idiot man is visible in a truer light. Furthermore, we admit that we may be told: "That's all very well, you are right, but you haven't succeeded in presenting the thing, in justifying the facts, you are a bad artist." But as to that, of course, there's nothing to be done.

I saw Gorsky.[24]

They ~~merchants~~ are more intelligent than we are.

I saw a priest once.

He interpreted the Apocalypse—bought a field—

Pavlishchev's son.

The Prince set the murderer free. (Did he kill the whole family?) <illegible>

Lots of news; I can't understand a thing.

The famine year.

What's to be done?

[Married?—]

[No—it happens.]

About the situation.

Comparison of Russia with abroad. Man, development.

The wagons—(the silly boy) he wanted to kill (then he burst into tears).

At night—"But I see everything."

I let him go free, but he burned down the whole village. (The peasants held me responsible.) Oh, no, he won't repent.

The priest's appeal—

The death of Belaev <illegible>

The poor knight.

He kissed Adelaide.

In my opinion one should defend one's own class F. Ad.

---

[24] Gorsky: perhaps an eighteen-year-old tutor who murdered six persons of the merchant Zhemarin's family in Tambov, allegedly because of his poverty. Quite a different Gorsky (Pyotr) contributed stories of his life in the slums to *Vremia* and *Epokha,* the two monthly reviews Dostoevsky edited in the 1860's. This Gorsky was briefly the lover of "Marfa Brown," who for a short time evoked Dostoevsky's charitable interest.

The general's wife reads his letter. "What sort of a creature is this 'poor knight'? That's why she is always reading 'The Poor Knight.' " Aglaia, unembarrassed, rose and began to read "The Poor Knight" aloud.

Aglaia: "I'd like to know what you have come to do? When God knows how other people hesitate, why, you. . . . . . ."

"Yes, 'What Is To Be Done,' "[25] said Ionchek—(Velmonchek).

"The Russian nobility like that of the West are wrong to be so aloof; I saw the Prince sitting with Aleksei. He is a noble, but Aleksei is a servant."

"No, like you, we are not capable of this."

[Laughs deliberately and passes by the Prince.]

The chain—speaks of *the chain.*

In Pavlovsk at the villa

chapter—the general and Lebedev

in the tavern.

The Turkish war[26] and the baby, Crete.

But he had the 12 *sleeping virgins.*[27]

In the 2nd Part

The Prince about Holbein's picture[28]

about Lebedev and DuBarry (to Aglaia)

---

25 *What Is To Be Done:* This is perhaps the widely discussed novel by N. G. Chernyshevsky (1828–89), *What Is To Be Done?* It sets forth his ideas on utilitarian socialism and was written while he was incarcerated in the fortress of Sts. Peter and Paul (1862–63).

26 The Turkish war: presumably this is a reference to the Balkan and Cretan uprisings against Turkish oppression in the 1860's.

27 The 12 sleeping virgins: this refers to a long poem by V. A. Zhukovsky (1783–1852), "Dvenadtsat spiashchikh dev: starina povest v dvukh balladakh" ("The twelve sleeping virgins; an old tale in two ballads"). It consists of a dedication and two ballads, "Gromovoi" (1810) and "Vadim" (1817), and was inspired by a novel similarly entitled by Christian Spiess (1755–99), a popular author of stories of knights, robbers, and ghosts. The Gromovoi of the first ballad sells his soul to Asmodeus (the demon who laid an evil spell on Sarah, the daughter of Tobit, in the Apocrypha). By a trick, Asmodeus also captures the souls of Gromovoi's twelve virgin daughters and lays a deep sleep on them, from which they await their deliverance. In the second ballad they are ultimately freed by Vadim, whose longing to know what to seek in life, and where, drives him out into the world.

28 Holbein's picture: it is not clear here whether Dostoevsky means the *Madonna* or *Christ in the Tomb,* but presumably the latter.

About Faith. The temptation of Christ.
Compassion—the whole of Christianity.
The chain.
The highest servility (ST. Lous <Louis>—DuBarry).
Make the shackles clank.
To do a little—
Humility is the most terrible force that can exist in the world!

31 July

Florence[29]
Childhood.
Children and fathers, intrigue, the conspiracy of the children, entering the boarding school, and so forth.[30]
In reality N. F. wants to marry the Prince.
(The whole Part is about this, after her scene with Aglaia.)
Aglaia seemingly gives in.
The Prince's fear. (He withdraws from the world.)
Be more anecdotal. (The Prince's charm.)
The Prince: "She" (that is, N. F.) "gave me to understand that we had better not meet."
Tremendous scandal about Velmonchek because of N. F.
The Prince thinks Aglaia is laughing at him (the poor knight) and so forth, but he bears this without taking any notice of it.
No one in the household takes Aglaia's passion for the Prince seriously. (All of a sudden she begins pursuing Velmonchek.)
N.B. The Prince's interview and frank talk with Aglaia about N. F. (in a playful sort of way).
The interview between Aglaia and N. F.
After the frank discussion between N. F. and Aglaia, the Prince still does not realize fully Aglaia's love, though her mother speaks of it.

---

[29] Florence: at this point in his writing Dostoevsky was still in Vevey, which lacked the Russian journals and newspapers he regarded as indispensable for information about affairs in Russia. He knew that Florence had a remarkable library, the Vieusseux, which received Russian periodicals. Perpetually short of funds, he got as far as Milan toward the end of September 1868; but not until 27 November or thereabouts did he reach Florence, where he spent the winter, and where *The Idiot* was completed.

[30] Children and fathers: P. N. Sakulin, the Russian editor of the notebooks, thinks this passage may be an interpolation from some other project than *The Idiot.*

The time has come for Aglaia to relate herself to others, the persuasion and *rehabilitation* of N. F. (activity).

N. F.'s flight—with Rogozhin—

Aglaia's eccentricity.

Velmonchek: The multiplication of bureaucrats is all our reforms boil down to.

An aristocrat is a man who has not the least idea of what it means to work for a living.

Un million des faits.

"I'm stupid."

—Of the fools.

Lebedev—a *factotum* of Velmonchek.

The uncle of the family, Velmonchek—*Politk.*[31]

Lebedev betrays him. Lebedev's daughter.

He reports everything to Aglaia.

"I'll shoot myself."—

He expresses a judgment of the Prince to Aglaia.

"My affairs cannot be put right."

(Velmonchek to the Prince): "Today my uncle is going to shoot himself."

(The Prince to Velmoncheck): "400,000 will put things right for you, take them."

He shoots himself—out of vanity, and in dying takes revenge on the Prince—and on Aglaia—for their having allowed him to shoot himself.

At first he *questions* the Prince (Lebedev knows).

Then his tactic was to exaggerate the Prince's virtue—(Aglaia understood this. "Shoot yourself").

The uncle's poisoning himself shook his position in the world.

For a long time now he has been in the clutches of his creditors. This is the reason he is going into retirement.

The lowliness of his situation—and envy. He cannot bear the thought that to meet his creditors' claims he has to marry.

"I'll shoot myself."

He reckons that Aglaia will not let him shoot himself, or will appreciate his nobility. But they do let him shoot himself and do not esteem him.

---

[31] *Politk.*: probably this is Dostoevsky's abbreviation of *Politkatorzhanii,* a term in use up until the 1917 revolution to signify a person sentenced to prison labor for revolutionary activity.

(He recounts all this to the Prince, with laughter.)

(Lebedev's daughter meanwhile—).

—the 400,000 rubles.

(N.B. When he explains matters to Aglaia he says: "To tell your parents means my not coming to see you any more.")

After the offer of 400,000—he shoots himself—

(N. F. tries to seduce him.)

In Moscow N. F. went straight to the dogs.

She is ill,

joins Rogozhin.

"I'm a free woman" (she had run away on her wedding day).

In Petersburg at Lebedev's, as yet she has not refused Rogozhin. Rogozhin goes to see Lebedev.

"I've made friends with the Prince because I'm a free woman."

Rogozhin consents to everything, trembles, enthralled.

Intimno N. F. has heard that things are not going well with the Prince and Aglaia and that he has been constantly searching for her <N. F.> in Moscow; she comes back so as to get him married <to Aglaia>.

Early in the morning Rogozhin visits the Prince at the latter's hotel.

Rogozhin informs him that he has seen N. F. and that she tells him she will not marry him until the Prince marries Aglaia.

The Prince talks to the dying Ipolit against atheism: "I do not know any objections, for Christ (we)—"

The end of the novel.

Aglaia is the chief cause of Rogozhin's murdering N. F.

At this time Aglaia is living at Gania and Varia's house.

After the murder of N. F., Aglaia rushes to the Prince and stays at his house.

The Prince's last days and hours. He has become an eccentric, the children, they have all been deceiving him, and so forth.

Notes on Parts III and IV of the Novel

(Written between August, 1868, and January, 1869.)

The quantity of notes that follows for the period in which Dostoevsky worked on the third and fourth parts is small. One must remember that much of what has been grouped under the "second part" includes notes pertaining to the entire novel. Dostoevsky worked on the third part of the novel in August, September, and part of October, 1868. He worked on the fourth part of the novel in October, November, December, and half of January, 1869. In November the first four chapters were published; in December chapters five to seven; and the last two chapters reached the editor on January 25, 1869.

After the novel was finished, Dostoevsky wrote on February 6, 1869, to S. A. Ivanova: "I am dissatisfied with my novel. I did not express a tenth of what I wanted to express, although I refuse to give it up. I still love the idea even though I was not able to bring it off." And, to N. Strakhov on March 10, 1869, he wrote: "There's much in the novel that was written rapidly, much that is drawn out, much that didn't come off, but something did come off. I don't stand behind my novel, but I do stand behind my idea."

The notes are concerned primarily with the characters of Ipolit and Aglaia. Ipolit had sprung full-blown in the previous section, and his character as described here shows no variation, either from the previous notes or from his role in the novel. In the notes his character is somewhat abstract: he appears more as the speaker for a position than as a full and living person. Quite obviously, a great deal of amplification went on between these notes and the writing of the final version. The individualizing detail is missing, indicating perhaps that once Dostoevsky had seized the moral center, he had no trouble investing it with realistic detail.

Dostoevsky is sure of Ipolit's importance: "Ipolit—the main axis of the whole novel." And he puts forth more than once Ipolit's problem: "To die or not to die? (Ipolit's question)." And: "Write tersely and powerfully about Ipolit. Center the whole plot on him." Nor is there any ambiguity in Dostoevsky's judgment of his character:

> Thus he was an *indispensable* image to Aglaia, necessary and influential. He kindled jealousy in her to a *nec plus ultra* degree.
>
> He dominated Rogozhin (he dominated N. F.   N.B.?)
>
> He dominated Gania, incited him.
>
> He stirred up the Prince by saying that he must keep his word to N. F. That she is insane. And he dominates the Prince—all the more because of his sarcastic remarks that both girls love him.
>
> And then after *the scandal* and N. F.'s flight on her wedding day,—He wants to crush the Prince with the idea that he had no right to play with the hearts of both girls.
>
> Confession, the Prince's condemnation of him.
>
> The murder, death.

The notes make stark and clear the unpleasant, indeed vicious, side of Ipolit's character. More than one commentator has been taken in by Ipolit's vain posturings. The petty, intriguing, and cruel side of his character at the end of the novel is already implicit in his falsely heroic gestures when he reads his last confession. The notes confirm this: "*Ipolit—the vanity of a weak character.*"

In contrast to Ipolit's finished character, Aglaia remains undefined for Dostoevsky, and indeed in the novel itself there is much that is inconclusive about her. In the notes for the second part she is essentially the furious, passionate, and vengeful counterpart to Nastasia Filipovna. She treats Nastasia Filipovna with coarseness and cruelty and treats her suitor Gania with mockery and contempt. In the novel itself she is presented as a young Nastasia Filipovna; she is impulsive, passionate, contradictory, vengeful, but because of her youth she is also childlike and innocent. In the notes of this section Dostoevsky says of her: "Aglaia must be presented simultaneously as a child and a furious woman." It is true that in the previous section Dostoevsky had hinted at her good side, since she forgives Nastasia Filipovna and works with the Prince to transform her. But this good side is the result of the Prince's beneficent influence. In the novel, and here in almost the final notes, Dostoevsky touches on what he will do in the novel: he will show us the impulses of self-destruction in the child itself.

Aglaia here, as in the novel, is in love with the Prince and he with her, though he is simultaneously in love with Nastasia Filipovna. They become engaged, and Aglaia, again as in the novel, treats him with anxious contempt as her fiancé. Dostoevsky attempts to transform her into a generous and warm girl, self-sacrificially giving up the Prince to Nastasia Filipovna. Aglaia confesses to the Prince that she has been a spoiled little girl: "She wants to show the weakness and inadequacy of her love and thus soothe N. F. and the Prince—but on the contrary, *naïvely and unconsciously,* she only lays bare all the grandeur, depth, and richness of her feeling. After some tender words with N. F., though these are spoken with an effort and with a certain naïveté, they separate. N. F. is overwhelmed and the Prince perceives the despair in her face as she goes away to dress. Aglaia returns to Gania's and there the hysterical scene of *the burnt finger* takes place."

The Prince himself is as he has been since plan seven. He is humble, forgiving, compassionate. His capacity for forgiving is tested. Aglaia apparently murders Nastasia Filipovna, and the Prince at first does not forgive and then does. Ipolit, too, murders someone, and there is some indication that this too is used as a test of the Prince's forgiveness. Dostoevsky is still trying to do something with Gania and in a note has him become an emigrant.

The notes that were written during the writing of the fourth part of the novel begin on page 245 with the title "Conclusion." And they are, for the most part, only a sketch of the conclusion of the novel: of that lyrical and deathly still-life of Rogozhin and Myshkin in each other's arms by the side of the body of the woman they both love. The scene is close to the finished version, but by comparison it is only a pale sketch. Once again the details, so expressive and poetic of the idea, must have come easily to him. Truly, as he himself so often said, the idea came first, and once it was seized, truly seized and held in the soul, the world's forms were not hard to find.

8 September

Late in the evening they are all still up. "After all's said and done, I'm puzzled," says Evgeni Pavlovich (who is present).

Everyone is morally intoxicated.

To die or not to die? (Ipolit's question).

It is strange that, drunk as he was, morally speaking, still, a *double* thought persisted in the Prince's mind: *Evgeni Pavlovich's* having made a visit that night, in his situation, he certainly had some object of his own.

(N.B. Evgeni Pavlovich explained in a whisper that he was leaving at dawn.)

The Apocalypse and the Star Wormwood.

Ipolit is distraught: to live or not to live? Italy (absolutely Italy). A rose—love. *Gibberish, all that.* Or else to live like a skinflint. Ptitsyn laughs. "If I were in your place, Ganechka."

"Do you agree, Prince?"

"No, I don't agree. Each blade of grass, each step, Christ—." The inspired discourse of the Prince (*Don-Quixote* and the acorn).[1] "To the sun's health—."

They have all left. The Prince and Evgeni Pavlovich.

The Prince sits down on a bench and goes to sleep.

She awakens him.

Letters. Ipolit is ill, the evening party *at her house.*

15 September

Ipolit—the main axis of the whole novel.

He has a hold even on the Prince, but in essence he is aware that he can never dominate him.

Ipolit's relations with Aglaia; at first he is received with contempt (scene). But he cleverly shows her that the Prince can <omission> N. F. (but as if he did not suspect that Aglaia loved the Prince but on the contrary as if he believed she loved Gania).

Thus he was an *indispensable* image to Aglaia, necessary and influential. He kindled jealousy in her to a *nec plus ultra* degree.

---

[1] Don-Quixote and the acorn: the reference is to a passage in chapter 11 of *Don Quixote,* in which the knight describes his dream of a Golden Age, when men lived ignorant of "mine" and "thine" and all was peace, amity, and concord.

He dominated Rogozhin (he dominated N. F.   N.B.?)

He dominated Gania, incited him.

He stirred up the Prince by saying that he must keep his word to N. F. That she is insane. And he dominates the Prince—all the more because of his sarcastic remarks that both girls love him.

And then after *the scandal* and N. F.'s flight on her wedding day,— he wants to crush the Prince with the idea that he had no right to play with the hearts of both girls.

Confession, the Prince's condemnation of him.

The murder, death.

Little details about Ipolit.

An enemy to Kolia (he slanders the Prince), a despot to his little brother and his mother.

100 rubles.

Gania—

The little brother (a wounded child).

The Prince is bound up with the baby, the children. Meanwhile— the sequel with Aglaia and N. F.

The main point. N.B. The Prince has not once given way to Ipolit and because of his insight (which Ipolit himself has experienced and which sets him wild) and because of his gentleness to him, he reduces him to despair. The Prince overwhelms him by his trustfulness.

The scene of the murder. The judgment. Ipolit dies in despair (he has exhausted the general)

Gania,

Kolia—

Aglaia,

Rogozhin,

the little boy.

Aglaia *with the Prince at home.*

Scene of the two women rivals.

Ipolit agitates Lizaveta Prokofevna and the sisters by saying that Aglaia loves the Prince—

Major scene at their house.

A frank talk with the Prince on the part of Lizaveta Prokofevna and the whole family.

Aglaia and Gania—Aglaia declares spitefully that she is interested in Gania. She writes a letter to Nina Aleksandrovna asking for her hospitality.

The scene between the two rivals has been concocted by Ipolit.

Public flight to Nina Aleksandrovna's house.

Ipolit achieves a hold on the Prince by showing him that N. F. is not insane.

The Prince marries.

Ipolit torments N. F.

After several days of the married state. N. F. Foolishness.

Her flight on her wedding day.

The evening party at the Prince's house with the children.

Ipolit wants to cut his throat. Ipolit is judged.

In the 4th, conclusion.

In the 5th and 6th

The Prince and the children. Aglaia at his house. Secret love. A plain talk with Aglaia. ~~Proudly and haughtily, she breaks off with Gania.~~

Rogozhin—suspicion, murder.

Aglaia is still at Gania's house. *The Prince judges Aglaia.*

Out of pride she does not want to justify herself. Aglaia demonstrates that she is N. F.'s friend.

Idiotism. At that, Aglaia breaks off with Gania. *She goes off alone.*

Aglaia and the Prince

In their 1st interview Aglaia persuades the Prince that N. F. is in love with him. The letters as evidence.

In the evening the Prince is at N. F.'s house and convinces himself of the contrary. He reconciles N. F. with Rogozhin.

Aglaia dissuades him.

He is upset. Goes to Ipolit's. Ipolit counsels him. (Ipolit's pettiness and squabbling at home. The gossipmonger.) A chance happening with the little boy.

Write tersely and powerfully about Ipolit. Center the whole plot on him.

Toward the end Ipolit remarks that he is *not a counselor* and that the Prince has seen through him. Here his relations with Aglaia and N. F.

Evgeni Pavlovich—*a skeptic.*

Scandal at the Epanchins.—

Aglaia's refusal of the Prince, who had already proposed to her. Ridiculous.

The scene between the two rivals.

Aglaia (ashamed at having bared her love for the Prince) hides at Gania's.

The wedding to N. F.

Evening.

Ipolit kills.

The Prince's judgment.

The death of Ipolit.

In the 5th and 6th Parts.

Aglaia has now been reconciled even with her family. Triumphantly the Prince's bride.

All at once the death of N. F.

The Prince does not forgive Aglaia.

With the children.

In the Prince—*idiotism!*

In Aglaia—*modesty.*

Ipolit—*the vanity of a weak character.*

N. F.—derangement and beauty.

(A victim of fate.)

Rogozhin—jealousy.

Gania: weakness, propensity for good, intelligence, *shame,* he became an emigrant.

Evgeni Pavlovich: the last representative of the Russian gentleman-landowner.

Lizaveta Prokofevna—untamed honesty.

Kolia—the new generation.

It turns out that the captain's wife was pursuing the general on Ipolit's instigation. She dances to his piping. *They all dance to his piping.* His power over them all.

Toward the end the Prince: *his triumphantly serene state.* He has forgiven people.

Prophecy. Each one has been illuminated about himself. The times. Aglaia's forgiveness.

Aglaia lives with her mother—they travel.

The Prince and Aglaia

Lechers and fornicators alone will never enter into the Kingdom of Heaven.

About the Children, about Columbus.

The Prince regarding N.F.: "I don't love her."

Aglaia: "Listen, are we going to quarrel?"

"As it is impossible to love you, since you are very ugly, I shall make you my friend."

The young generation.

"I did this on purpose so as to test you. I don't know anything. What are we going to do?"

"Let's devote ourselves to education."

Incessantly in the 4th Part. "Go to see her."

Aglaia accuses the Prince, and accuses her family of having decoyed him like an Idiot because of his money, and says that she does not want to marry him out of pity.

Lizaveta Prokofevna: "She loves you. Come, that's better than quietism."

She threw herself to the ground, she was so shy.

"I'll thrash you."

"Talk about something else."

"About Renan—about Christ."

The Prince went to N. F.'s, and came to tell Aglaia that he would never go to her any more and that he is certain he would have made N. F. unhappy had he married her.

(N.B. In the first chapter with Aglaia, the Prince did *not* say that N. F. would be unhappy with him, but only that he did not love her.)

Aglaia's sarcasms.

Lizaveta Prokofevna says that she loves him. "Come, talk about something else."

About Renan—

"Do you know why I lied about this hand?" she suddenly asked him [Do you know why I told you before that I burned my hand?] with the most childlike confidence, her lips still tremulous with laughter— "because when you lie, if you've cleverly suggested something not at all ordinary, something bizarre, something that happens only by an impossible chance, or even never happens at all, then the lie seems far more convincing. I couldn't manage this simply because I didn't know how. . . . . . ."

She frowned abruptly, as if she again remembered.

"Do you rarely lie?"

The Prince went to Rogozhin's.

On returning he finds Evgeni Pavlovich at his house.

Then with Aglaia—the interview with N. F.

Pavlishchev's son, Ferdyshchenko—the conversation between the general and Lebedev.

The theft—

The fiancé and the fiancée with Aglaia—N. F.'s sudden triumph—

Gania—the scene of the interview at Gania's. Brings in Velmonchek, but she runs away.

28 July

The third Part begins directly with *the most indispensable*(!) admission that the Prince had considered all Aglaia's tricks as mockery.

About the Prince's being in love.

The enigma of the situation.

Ipolit's intrigues.

The scandal at the station with N. F. showing her jealousy of Aglaia. Rogozhin. [The scandal at the station because N. F. found out that Aglaia was with Gania. Aglaia involved in the scandal, storms at the Epanchins.]

Aglaia and Gania.

N. F.'s letters to Aglaia.

Stormy scenes between Aglaia and her family.

The interview of the rivals.

Her flight to Gania's house.

N.B. The Prince's love for Aglaia is suddenly destroyed, and he becomes N. F.'s husband.

Rogozhin secretly goes to Petersburg. He is afraid of showing himself to N. F. because she will die at the mere reminder of his name, he has found out where she is. He summons the Prince.

N. F. is being secretly nursed at the Prince's house. N. F. has but one desire, that he should marry Aglaia.

Troubles with Aglaia.

The idea of
4 October
~~November~~

The 3rd Part (sequel). Ipolit. Interview with Aglaia. N. F.'s letters. Rogozhin and the Prince.

N. F. to Rogozhin: "Can you forget that."

(N.B. The Prince is all the more attracted to Aglaia because she insists on the generous idea that he should marry N. F. This is the last *coup de grace* for him. He tells Aglaia this *in such a way* that she summons him to the house and says: *"I love* the Prince." They clear up matters between them. Fiancé and fiancée. The Prince is confused.

(N.B. Aglaia acts like this partly because of jealousy, because the Prince has not concealed from her the fact that N. F. filled him with a sense of profound pity.)

The Prince returns home after proposing to Aglaia and takes out N. F.'s portrait. *Then he leaves the house.*

After this the 4th Part, in which:

Aglaia insists on his love for N. F. and reproaches him. She laughs at him. Gania. Ipolit is in her good graces (by a story—Rogozhin's wedding). The Prince's wedding is set.

Aglaia is driven wild by Ipolit, Gania, and the Prince.

The scene of the 2 rivals; to Gania's house.

Give an account of these 3 weeks by varying the scenes.

Here Evgeni Pavlovich.

N.B. Thus in 3 weeks.

N.B. And this is the 1st half of the 4th Part.

The chief point. Aglaia, *having given her word* to the Prince [fiancé] is afraid they will laugh at her and the Prince; at times she makes jokes, pokes fun at the Prince, *rompe* <rompt> *avec lui.* She is ashamed of the Prince <omission> tells him: "But what if I don't even come to the church."

2nd half of the 4th Part.

N. F. is engaged to the Prince.—

Eccentricity. One colorful scene.

Goes to Rogozhin in despair.

(He murders.) Summons the Prince.

Rogozhin and the Prince beside the corpse. Finale.

Not bad.

The Prince and N. F.

(two lunatics. At Pavlovsk people crowd around to stare.)

The Prince's philosophy. "I am an idiot—I don't know—I was not right in not forgiving Aglaia, I was acting from the heart—"

They tell him: "You are the cause of everything."

He: "Yes, I am the cause of everything."

What has become of the Burdovsky crowd? The Lebedevs, 1st and 2nd.

(Did they take any part in the plot?)

Gania as banker.

[N.B. *The major point*]

Aglaia has managed to turn her marriage to the Prince into a sort of joke. (She *threatens* him with Gania, she loves Gania. The whole family are bewildered by this joking. Lizaveta Prokofevna: "Are you serious or not?" On the wedding day both sisters are together. Battle with N. F., suddenly runs to Gania. Aglaia *with the Prince.*

6 October

Lebedev's question: "Is there a God? No matter what—"
Rogozhin goes to Ipolit *in search of God.—*

15 October

~~15 November~~

N.B.—Aglaia *deliberately* creates a scene with N. F. in order to expose the Prince by ridiculing him and taking revenge on him <omission>. At home she blames everyone for having forced the Prince on her. She insists on marrying Gania.

15 October

N.B. The scene at the church exhibits the Prince in full. Gania engaged. Aglaia gave <illegible>. She ran away to the Prince.

15 October

N.B. Indispensable scene after N. F.'s flight on her wedding day. Scene with the children, in which he explains everything to them as if they were adults. Lebedev. A feast of faith.

15 October

N.B. For the whole time.
After the wedding.
The Prince goes home alone, a crowd of people come, *even unknown persons* (Keller, indignantly). The Prince takes them by the hand and invites them in; many do come in. "Are you concerned with learned matters?" Ipolit. Lecture on culture, on self-knowledge, on petrol, *on the manufacture of machinery,* which is bound to immerse everything and set people free (the article on the Exposition by

Chevalier in the September issue of *Russky Vestnik*)[2] from the struggle for existence, then Socialism will solve everything and the problem of marriage will be solved and man will come to Christ.

Many went away unaware of the scandal, others were moved and
enraptured, but the Prince remained with Ipolit, who dies that night.

In the morning the Prince set off after N. F.—

(Among the crowd come to stare at the Idiot—a murmuring: "He is
talking about machines, he is talking about machines.")

Among the main points.

1) The scene (in the church) on the wedding day, before Aglaia's
arrival, between the Prince and N. F., in private.

All the time he was undergoing the *scandal,* the Prince suffered
terribly *at N. F.'s having gone out of her senses,* and finally on the
morning of the wedding day he talks to her from the depths of his
heart. Torn between despair and hope, she embraces him, says she is
unworthy, bows down to him, and vows. The Prince *simply and clearly* (Othello) tells her why he loves her and that it is not merely from
compassion (as Rogozhin intimated to her and with which Ipolit
plagued her) but from love, and that therefore she should calm down.
Suddenly the Prince speaks his mind *as if on a pedestal.*

2) At this point Aglaia appears, calmly, *nobly, and simply sorrow-
ful;* she says that it is all her fault, that she does not deserve the
Prince's love, that she has been a spoiled little girl, a baby; *that this is
why she loves the Prince:* (here Othello)—a naïve and high-minded
speech in which N. F. senses all the immensity of her love, but Aglaia,
thinking—

< She wants to > show the weakness and inadequacy of her love and
thus soothe N. F. and the Prince—but on the contrary, *naïvely and unconsciously,* she only lays bare all the grandeur, depth, and richness
of her feeling. After some tender words with N. F., though these are
spoken with an effort and with a certain naïveté, they separate. N. F.
is overwhelmed and the Prince perceives the despair in her face as she
goes away to dress. Aglaia returns to Gania's, and there the hysterical
scene of *the burnt finger* takes place. Then comes a scene with Gania

---

[2] *Russky Vestnik (The Russian Messenger)*: in its September 1868 issue (pp. 164–
203) there was a review article by Gustave de Molinari on the thirteen-volume
report published shortly before in Paris on the World Exposition held at the
Champ de Mars in 1867; Michel Chevalier provided an introduction to this essay-
review of the report.

and Ipolit, who *drags himself* over to the Prince's house; the wedding; the evening party; the future world of Russia and humanity, and conversations about economics.

And then—

Conclusion

7 November

After the wedding—the children—

The Prince's anxiety for N. F.

In the morning he rushes off to Petersburg.

The whole day he looked for N. F. He went to Rogozhin's. The latter denied any knowledge of her whereabouts. Said N. F. had not been there.

All day he tramped over Petersburg—*visions.*

At twilight he encountered Rogozhin. "Come" (in a whisper), he led him in, made him sit down (beckons him toward the curtains). In the darkness, the half light, the corpse.

In her heart, drops of blood. She had said: "I will be your mistress, don't kill me." I was pacing up and down.—She went off to sleep; in her sleep she felt nothing.

("*What is going to happen? You won't go away?*")

They lay the mattress down. Rogozhin goes to sleep; a dream, "as if a kind of tree."

Don't tell anyone about this, *for anything in the world.*

(Both make up the bed.)

(Both out of their heads.)

(About this strange but tragic and fantastic thing.)

Rogozhin: "If only you don't have a seizure?" Caresses him.

Rogozhin: "As I crept up to strike (toward dawn) she was not asleep. One black eye was watching me. I struck her with all my strength."

Rogozhin about the corpse: "I chose the site of the heart, as her eye was watching me, then I drove down in with all my strength; in a second, with my 2 thumbs, I raised her head; a single drop of blood, an internal hemorrhage."

About the corpse: "But they'll take it away, my friend!"

"They'll take it away," cried the Prince.

"So don't breathe a word."

"For nothing in the world!" cried the Prince.

Yet in Rogozhin's question, "What is going to happen?" there was no trace of any fear of punishment, as if it had to do with something else. (N.B. That is, so as to keep her body there, no matter what.)

"The smell, it's hot in June, there is a smell though faint—some Zhdanov fluid. Downstairs in my mother's apartment there are some pots of flowers, shall we bring them here? But then they'll guess, they'll guess. Perhaps we could buy some. Surround her with flowers."

"How pitiful she will be, how pitiful, surrounded with flowers! Like a bride."

"Don't grieve, friend!" Rogozhin's word to the Prince. Rogozhin begins to stroke his cheeks, tenderly.

N.B.—Abruptly they lay down on the mattress; then Rogozhin stood up, sat down again, as if remembering something N. F. had said once, a long time ago, *something absolutely incongruous*—recalling this with intense concern.

He was remembering the officer she had turned against, she had slapped him—and he rocked with laughter.

"Do you remember—those boots of his—"

("We used to play cards together. Evenings were a sad time for her. I'd bring a deck of cards and every night we'd play.")

Rogozhin wants to decorate the room with silks.

"I still don't know. . . . . . I still don't know a thing . . . ." said Rogozhin again and again, sunk in thought, as if struggling in anguish, cogitating, as if unable to call something to mind.

All at once Rogozhin says: "Stop, someone is coming!" They listen —"Someone's coming!" . . . . He opens the door.—"Or aren't they. . . . . . . Someone's come."

"Someone's come."

"I'll shut the door."

? N.B. In the hall, an apparition.

Rogozhin found the Prince toward evening, in the very tavern in which the murder had taken place, in the darkness.

"Let's go away, it's not nearby, come on. You go on one side of the street, I'll take the other. Keep always behind me, come on."

"But look, I was so certain you wouldn't be afraid I had brought you here in order to murder you——"

Rogozhin confides to the Prince beside the corpse: "Without you, I couldn't have stayed here."

About killing himself: "Yes, I'm thinking, how can she stay here."

11 ~~8~~ November

The scene between the two rivals.

Unexpectedly the Prince comes because of Ipolit's hints, so as to warn N. F. (he arrived one minute before Aglaia).

N. F.'s proud and exalted speech, spoken simply and with great dignity.

"Kiss me."

"Thou."

Silly Rogozhin.

"You little thief."

~~N. F.~~ "But you're furious because he isn't yours—"

"I sent you word through those people you pointed out to me. Perhaps my letters went astray."

"Of course he's mine."

"Sour grapes—"

"I'll give you—"

"I'll take him myself and put you out of the running—"

(Aglaia must be presented simultaneously as a child and a furious woman.)

Aglaia: "I knew he would behave like that."

N. F. to the Prince: "You've brought your mistress to my house—"

Aglaia is terribly shocked by the Prince's behavior with N. F. "Then I began to think about him. His letter startled me, then he completely absorbed me, he never left my mind, I saw him in my sleep, I read his letter 1000 times over and over."

Name and Topic Index

Plans one through eight, later discarded, run from pages 1 to 158. Plans for the final and definitive version run from pages 159 to 247. The Idiot of the discarded plans is to be found under the entry "Idiot," and Prince Myshkin is to be found under the entry "Prince." Pages 1 to 74 refer to Dostoevsky's initial conception of the character; pages 75 to 158 reflect the shifts in this conception before he arrived at his final version.